The New American Empire

The New American Empire

A 21st Century Teach-In
on U.S. Foreign Policy

EDITED BY LLOYD C. GARDNER AND MARILYN B. YOUNG

THE NEW PRESS

NEW YORK
LONDON

Requests for permission to reproduce selections from this book should be mailed to:
Permissions Department, The New Press, 38 Greene Street, New York, NY 10013

Published in the United States by The New Press, New York, 2005
Distributed by W. W. Norton & Company, Inc., New York

LIBRARY OF CONGRESS CATALOGING-IN-PUBLICATION DATA

The new American empire : a 21st century teach-in on U.S. foreign policy /
edited by Lloyd Gardner and Marilyn Young.
p.   cm.
Includes bibliographical references and index.
ISBN 1-56584-933-7 (hc.) — ISBN 1-56584-905-1 (pbk.)
1. United States—Foreign relations—2001–   2. United States—Foreign relations—
21st century.   3. United States—Foreign relations—20th century.   4. Imperialism.
5. Imperialism—History.   6. World politics—1989–   7. World politics—1945–1989.
I. Gardner, Lloyd C., 1934–   II. Young, Marilyn Blatt.

E902.N47   2005
327.73'009'0511—dc22   2004052425

The New Press was established in 1990 as a not-for-profit alternative to the large,
commercial publishing houses currently dominating the book publishing industry.
The New Press operates in the public interest rather than for private gain, and is committed
to publishing, in innovative ways, works of educational, cultural, and community value
that are often deemed insufficiently profitable.

www.thenewpress.com

Composition by dix!

Printed in Canada

2   4   6   8   10   9   7   5   3   1

To our grandchildren

Contents

ACKNOWLEDGMENTS   ix

INTRODUCTION: *An American Empire?: The Problems of Frontiers and Peace in Twenty-First-Century Politics* by Charles S. Maier   xi

Context

1. *Present at the Culmination: An Empire of Righteousness?* by Lloyd C. Gardner   3

2. *Imperial Language* by Marilyn B. Young   32

3. *The Drums of War* by John Prados   50

Changed Relationships

4. *American Hegemony and European Autonomy, 1989–2003: One Framework for Understanding the War in Iraq* by Thomas McCormick   75

5. *Anti-Americanism and Anti-Europeanism* by Mary Nolan   113

Analogies

6. *Iraq Is Not Arabic for Nicaragua: Central America and the Rise of the New Right* by Greg Grandin   135

7. *Improving on the Civilizing Mission?:
   Assumptions of United States Exceptionalism in
   the Colonization of the Philippines* by Michael Adas   153

8. *Occupation: A Warning from History* by John W. Dower   182

9. *Japan and the United States in Re-Imperial Times*
   by Carol Gluck   198

The Future

10. *Onward, Liberal Soldiers?: The Crusading Logic of
    Bush's Grand Strategy and What Is Wrong with It*
    by Edward Rhodes   227

11. *A Most Interesting Empire* by Anders Stephanson   253

     Notes   277

     Contributors   301

     Index   305

Acknowledgments

This book grew out of various teach-ins and other public events in which the editors participated in the brief period just before the war began. It occurred to us as the war drums beat louder that the focus on Iraq was simply too narrow to do justice to the complex issues confronting the nation. The editors would like to thank all the authors for their timely response to our call for chapters examining the diverse elements of the New Empire. These days, when our empire is being celebrated both in historical terms (once again) as Manifest Destiny, and for its supposed future promise as the last, best hope of globalism, it is all the more essential that we look closely at the premises on which the imperial vision depends.

An American Empire?
The Problems of Frontiers and Peace in Twenty-First-Century World Politics

Charles S. Maier

Only a year and a week separated the events of September 11, 2001, when Americans felt so vulnerable, from a presidential declaration in which their leaders spoke so imperiously. The so-called Bush Doctrine reaffirms laudable support for democracy, religious tolerance, and economic development, but further claims the right to act preemptively against terrorist states who arm themselves with weapons of mass destruction. We have no cause to be surprised: the Bush Doctrine has emerged from a public discussion by policymakers and journalists that has increasingly transgressed an earlier American taboo: what Edmund Burke would have called one of the "decent draperies of life," or in this case, of political discourse. Increasingly, that is, Americans talk about themselves, and others talk about America, as an empire.

A decade ago, certainly two decades ago, the concept aroused righteous indignation. How could the United States be compared to Rome with its conquering legions, its subjugation of peoples, its universalist claims to law and order; or even to Britain, the former ruler of millions of subjects in India, the Middle East, and Africa? If an empire, post–World War II America was the empire that dared not speak its name. But these days, on the part of friends and critics alike, the bashfulness has ended. "The Roman and the British empires have had their day. Why should we begrudge the new American empire the right to protect its citizens from a jealous and hostile world?" writes a former British European Union official in the *Financial Times*. The historian Paul Kennedy cites the overwhelming preponderance of military power the United States possesses. In full agreement, the Bush administration has vowed to preserve that decisive margin against any rivals.

Except for a minority of tough-minded realists, Americans have tended to reject the idea that our own high-minded republic might be imperial (much less imperialist). Empire has traditionally been identified with conscious military expansion. Washington may have organized an alliance, but it did not seek to conquer territory nor, supposedly, to dominate other societies. President John F. Kennedy, certainly an activist in foreign policy, declared explicitly that the United States did not aim at any Pax Americana. But British imperial historians also long denied that there was anything intentional about the creation of the Victorian domains in Asia and Africa. Modern liberal internationalists prefer to think of empire as the reluctant acceptance of responsibility for peoples and lands who must be rescued from the primitive violence that threatens to engulf them if left on their own.

In fact, some historians of international relations, myself included, have resorted to the concept of a quasi–American empire for a long time. Still, we believed it was an empire with a difference, a coordination of economic exchange and security guarantees welcomed by its less powerful member states, who preserved their autonomy and played a role in collective policymaking. We used such terms as "empire by invitation" or "consensual" empire. What, after all, distinguishes an empire? It is a major actor in the international system based on the subordination of diverse national elites who, whether under compulsion or from shared convictions, accept the values of those who govern the dominant center or metropole. The inequality of power, resources, and influence is what distinguishes an empire from an alliance (although treaties of al-

liance often formalize or disguise an imperial structure). Distinct national groupings may be harshly controlled within an empire, or they
may enjoy autonomy. At least some of their political, economic, and cultural leaders hobnob with their imperial rulers and reject any idea of es-
caping imperial influence. Others may organize resistance, but they, too,
have often assimilated their colonizers' culture and even values. Empires
function by virtue of the prestige they radiate as well as by might, and
indeed collapse if they rely on force alone. Artistic styles, the language of
the rulers, and consumer preferences flow outward along with power
and investment capital, sometimes diffused consciously by cultural
diplomacy and student exchanges, sometimes just by popular taste for
the intriguing products of the metropole, whether Coca-Cola or Big
Macs. As supporters of the imperial power rightly maintain, empires
provide public goods that masses of people outside their borders really
want to enjoy, including an end to endemic warfare and murderous ethnic or religious conflicts.

Two kinds of empire existed before World War I: "old" landed empires, products of centuries-long expansion over contiguous territories
(and still largely agrarian and semi-authoritarian); and overseas colonial
realms. Among the first group—Russia, Austria-Hungary, the Ottoman
domains, and China—the states were empires and were vulnerable to
new forces of national self-determination. Members of the second
group—the British, French, Dutch, Spanish, and Portuguese, and more
recently the Japanese, Germans, and Americans—had empires. When
the internal crises of the first group combined with the interlocking rivalries of the second, the result was the First World War. Indeed, the
history of twentieth-century world politics was one long imperial
transition—from the domination and then the destructive rivalries of
the Europeans, to the Soviet and American spheres of influence that
emerged from the Second World War, and finally to the ascendancy of
the United States as "the only remaining superpower."

The Importance of Frontiers

Empires claim universality but accentuate divisions between inclusion and exclusion, both on a world scale and within their own borders. Consider these external and internal effects in turn. The principal preoccupation of the guardians of empire is the frontier: what the Romans called the limes. The frontier separates insiders and outsiders, citizens and/or subjects within from "barbarians" without. This does not mean that barbarians cannot enter the empire: they can and they do and they are often actively recruited—as professional soldiers in Roman days, as industrial workers, as gardeners and house cleaners, as hospital orderlies, and also as skilled professionals. But the empire seeks to control their flow, be they the frontiers of antiquity or the fences along the United States–Mexico border. (The European Union is only a supranational association, not an empire, but it has the same preoccupation, now enforced at dozens of airports under the provisions of the Schengen Treaty framework.)

A major consequence of this preoccupation with the frontier has been a new political agenda. The salient issues today have shifted from the controversies over distribution that troubled the politics of the West, indeed of developed societies more generally, from the 1950s through the 1980s: income for farmers, the relative shares for labor and capital, the creation and costs of the welfare state. They have become questions of citizenship, residence, and belonging: who will be in and who will be outside our polities, and what intermediate rights—such as employment, welfare entitlements, and local suffrage—might they be granted.

Frontiers are important, not only at the geographic edge of empire, but as social gradients within. The distinction that preoccupies contemporary citizens, however, seems less the poverty line—which focuses attention on the deprivation of the least fortunate—than the affluence line, epitomized today by the air travelers' boundary between business, first class, or economy seating. Empires can provide increasing welfare for the less well-off in the home society, can advance the democratization of taste and access to education, but at the same time they sharpen differentials of prestige, exclusivity, and wealth. Here is the irony (or the artfulness) of empire: no matter what absolute increases in educational opportunity or income accrue either to the mass of the population at home or the subjects abroad, relative stratification seems to increase—or at least hold its own. Empires reward those who run them with goods, honor, and celebrity status. And for all the disclaimers about the white man's burden or its contemporary equivalent, few of us who get the chance to share these rewards disdain them. Helping to run an empire may not be exactly fun, but it appears to be deeply fulfilling.

Empires mitigate their inequality at home through a two-level management of public life. At one level is a serious effort to debate issues of distribution, environment, infrastructure, and development. This debate is carried on among communities of experts whose decisions must sometimes be ratified by a court or legislature. Those who take part in this "conversation," even if only as public commentators, are convinced that it represents an adequate and real form of democracy. They denigrate those who are less convinced, and call them populists (which they often are). But empires also operate on a second and more theatrical level. All politics involves some public performance, but empires emphasize dramaturgy. All societies may celebrate prowess, but from the Colosseum to the Super Bowl, in the West at least, empires particularly rely on the sports of the amphitheater that reward star players with fame and fortune. They nurture a culture of spectatorship to create rituals of shared experience.

Imperial Edges and World Order

Is an American empire good for the world? Is it good for America? What does an empire mean for international politics in general? Is it a source of order or disorder, cooperation or conflict? There are always powerful justifications for the dynamic of empire: by the second half of the twentieth century, when the United States emerged supreme, the reasons included "development" and "productivity." American supremacy quickly developed a clear military component, but it emerged by virtue of more than half a century of economic prowess: the assembly line that turned out Model Ts, the "arsenal of democracy" that armed British and Russian allies and mass-produced aircraft and Liberty ships, that subsidized the reconstruction of Europe after World War II and commercially developed electronic computation.

This country, moreover, enjoyed advantages of geography and timing. Other countries had been devastated by war—not us. The Soviet Union offered enough competition to thrust Washington into a leadership role that was accepted by its allies, but not enough to overwhelm the American effort. We developed the technology to take a brief but critical lead in the new, decisive atomic weaponry of the postwar world.

There are always propagandists to point out empire's achievement: recall Virgil's *Aeneid:*

> Roman, remember by your strength to rule
> Earth's peoples for your arts are to be these:
> To pacify, to impose the rule of law,
> To spare the conquered, battle down the proud.

J.M. Coetzee's 1980 fable *Waiting for the Barbarians* suggests otherwise: "One thought alone preoccupied the submerged mind of the Empire: how not to die, how to prolong its era. By day it pursues its enemies. It is cunning and ruthless, it sends its bloodhounds everywhere. By night it feeds on images of disaster: the sack of cities, the rape of populations, pyramids of bones, acres of desolation. A mad vision yet a virulent one. . . ."

Contemporary history suggests that both Virgil and Coetzee are correct. Empires may have helped to suppress traditional wars in large areas of their domains, although many students of international politics have proposed that democratic states assure an end to war among themselves by virtue of their liberal constitutions, and still other analysts simply credit the balance of power maintained by any large-scale states. We cannot be certain which cause has been operative; nonetheless, throughout the nineteenth century and again after World War II, imperial systems helped to stabilize a balance of power within Europe and North America. An international system based on national self-determination—even though complemented by commitments to collective security, such as the Paris Peace Conference of 1919 sought to institute—remained fragile and broke down within twenty years.

No stable imperial structures reemerged until the Cold War. Then the Soviet side relied on its own enthusiastic Communist cadres and, when these were challenged in the streets, on the calculated use of force: in 1953 in Berlin; 1956 in Hungary; 1968 in Czechoslovakia. The competing U.S. model of a liberal capitalist order (or of market democracies) rested on a combination of championing economic regulatory principles (market capitalism, productivity, and growth) and of military prowess. Military action involved strategic deterrence at the European frontier and at the Thirty-eighth Parallel following an open conflict in Korea. But American administrations also intervened openly or covertly, among other places, in Iran (1953) and Guatemala (1954), and unsuccessfully in Cuba (1961) and Vietnam (1963–75).

It remains an open question whether a major imperial structure can ever work through consensual principles or economic means alone. Establishing and stabilizing a periphery seems always to require a military effort: in this sense, Coetzee's bleak indictment is correct. Empire must inevitably generate a resistance that rulers will perceive as shortsighted, bloody-minded, and even fanatic: recall the Jewish rebels at Masada. Our filmmakers may view imperial history through the eyes of Luke

Skywalker, but policymakers, or at least their intelligence agencies, tend to share Darth Vader's perspective.

Empire builders yearn for stability, but what imperial systems find hard to stabilize is, precisely, their frontiers. Historians of empire point out that colonizing countries were drawn into expansion by the disorder that seethed just outside the last domain they had stabilized. But researchers explore less often how staking out a new frontier can generate a further zone of "chaos" that requires imperial policymakers to intervene anew. The Romans wanted to pacify territory across the Rhine. Britain found itself moving ineluctably up the Nile after what it believed would be a limited occupation to sort out Egyptian finances in the 1880s. The U.S. presence in Vietnam embroiled Cambodia. Vice President Dick Cheney warns that once we have helped friendly Iraqis overthrow Saddam Hussein, we shall have to help ensure stability in the country for a long time. But the use of force that stabilizes conditions within any given boundary often upsets a precarious peace among the tribes or weakened states that abut the frontier. Can there be successful "nation-building" in just one country? Southeast Asia, the liberated African colonies, areas of Central America, and the Caucasus became in their turn areas of endemic and bloody violence with tremendous human costs. The boundaries within societies can also become sites of conflict and tragedy. Something there is that doesn't love a wall.

Americans today face choices about empire with consequences far outrunning the stakes of any immediate military action. Teachers, scholars, and the university more generally can at best help reflect on possible alternatives. The organizations of international commerce and civil society—whether McDonald's, Microsoft, and Deutsche Bank or Oxfam and Médecins Sans Frontières—may help enhance world welfare, but they will not assure world order. Empires are in the business of producing world order. But not all orders are alike: some enhance freedom and development; others repress it.

I believe that the American empire has served some beneficial functions, above all in opposing far more authoritarian and repressive contenders for international dominance and in defending ideals of liberty and opportunity. Still, no matter how benevolent the intentions, the exercise of empire will generate some violence. The problem is that for every greater inclusive effort, there must still be those left outside the expanded walls clamoring to enter, or those not willing to participate vicariously in the lifestyles of the rich and famous—and those, indeed, embittered by the values of secular consumerism (which contemporary empires rely on to generate public loyalties) and imbued with far more zealous and violent visions of fulfillment. These issues of inclusion and exclusion, belonging and estrangement, the peace of empire and the violence it generates despite its efforts, is what twenty-first-century politics, certainly since September 11, is increasingly about.

Nonetheless, one can choose alternatives likely to lead to less bitterness and less violence. For at least fifty years, Americans sought to exercise leadership by seeking to establish institutions that did not depend solely on our own force: the United Nations, the organs of the Marshall Plan, the North Atlantic alliance, and the World Trade Organization among others. Of course, Washington often had to animate their collective resolve. Still, we achieved ascendancy by accepting the need to restrain our own unilateral action (admittedly with significant lapses in our own hemisphere) and generally to persuade allies and neutrals that cooperation did not have to diminish their interests or status. Now, for the first time in the postwar history of the United States (at least for vast regions outside the Americas), our policymakers, elated by supposedly unmatchable military technology, have formally outlined a different vision. Eventually, I fear—if not this year or even this decade—historians will have fateful consequences to narrate if we persevere in this myopic option.

CONTEXT

1

Present at the Culmination:
An Empire of Righteousness?

Lloyd C. Gardner

How did we get here? How did we get to the point, first, where military force became America's answer to what the rest of the world believed, and still believes, was an issue already on the way to being resolved: the disarmament of Iraq? Since the occupation began, no weapons of mass destruction (WMD) have yet been found. What *has* been discovered is that intelligence dossiers were sexed up to include false reports of uranium purchases from Niger, and to support assertions that Baghdad could launch a devastating chemical and biological attack at forty-five minutes notice. These discoveries should have provoked an outraged public response. But so far they have not. Why?

The short answer is that the Bush administration succeeded in using WMD to scare the nation into giving it a green light to bring down Saddam Hussein's dictatorship. UN arms inspector Hans Blix, shunted aside by the Bush administration, told Agence France-Presse that the White House "over-interpreted" the evidence. True enough, Saddam Hussein's past behavior warranted a close look. "But," Blix continued, "in the Middle Ages, when people were convinced there were witches, when they looked for them, they certainly found them." It might well have been, added Blix on Australian national radio, that Hussein pretended to have kept such weapons to deter an American attack. But was the war justified, he was then asked. "No, I don't think so."

Senator Edward Kennedy, an original supporter of the war, told the Associated Press on September 18, 2003: "There was no imminent threat. This was made up in Texas, announced in January to the Republican leadership that war was going to take place and was going to be good politically. This whole thing was a fraud."

Kennedy stopped short of saying, however, that he would oppose the president's request for an additional $87 billion for the Iraqi front on the War on Terrorism, because "our troops . . . didn't make the decision to go there." The funds President Bush wanted Congress to appropriate were and are about a lot more than protecting American troops. They are about rebuilding a nation in America's image—and represent only the down payment on a mortgage that future generations will be paying off for years to come.

Secretary of State Colin Powell is said to have admonished Bush before the war about his responsibility for Iraq's future. Pottery Barn rules applied: "You break it, you own it." The Pottery Barn Company immediately objected that their policy was not to punish careless customers that way, but to absorb the breakage costs as part of doing business. Either way, the United States will own Iraq. The "handover" of power to an Iraqi "government" on June 30, 2004, signaled nothing more than the creation of a new-style protectorate, however much it was ballyhooed as bringing democracy to the Middle East. The American Embassy will be the largest in the world, housing more than 2,000 bureaucrats and counselors. They will simply change addresses from the "Green Zone" enclave in central Baghdad to the Embassy. The American army will stay for an undetermined time, charged with maintaining internal security and prisons to make sure law and order reign. It is fitting, also, that the original post–World War I mandatory power, Great Britain, whose "coalition" forces are located near Basra, has offered some serious criticisms about American methods—implying they could still do it better than the newcomers to empire.

Thus the real issue was never the disarmament of Iraq, but fulfilling the long-term goal of finding a "friendly" government to carry out the American global mission. From the time of the Truman Doctrine in 1947, through the 1952 Egyptian Revolution, the return of the shah to his throne the following year, and clandestine support for Saddam Hussein's war against Iran in the 1980s, the search has been a frustrating one. But once "democracy" is planted in Iraq, the mission will succeed. Or so it is believed. The enemies of the American mission are always labeled alien intruders or "foreign fighters" in the post–Cold War years, or, in the earlier Cold War, "agents of the Kremlin." Or, in general, as UN arms inspector Hans Blix put it, when one believes in witches, one finds evidence of witches. This "agent theory of revolution" offers policymakers unlimited opportunity, moreover, to justify whatever they wish to do in the name of national security.

American policy in the Middle East before the Cold War, before World War II, began as a "simple" quest for oil concessions. "In May of 1933, King Abdul Aziz Bin Abdul Rahman Al-Saud, who had founded the modern Kingdom of Saudi Arabia," reads the official website of Saudi Aramco, the largest oil company of the region, "listened attentively as the text of a draft agreement was read to him. After a pause, he turned to his Finance Minister Abdullah Sulaiman and said: 'Put your trust in God and sign.' " The first oil started coming in six years later, as the war began. And it never stopped coming. "As was demonstrated during the Gulf Crisis of 1990–91 when it stepped in to make up for the loss of oil exports from Iraq and Kuwait, thus averting a catastrophic global energy shortage, Saudi Aramco is, as *Petroleum Intelligence Weekly* noted, a guarantor of the 'stability and security to world oil markets that is now the hallmark of Saudi policy.' "

During World War II, the United States took up a big stake in the Middle East for the first time, challenging British dominance that had prevailed since the fall of the Ottoman Empire. We sent forces to Iran to occupy the country along with Britain, to insure the lifeline to Russia for the duration. And we sent lend-lease aid to Saudi Arabia to insure we would not lose out in the competition for oil rights. Harry Hopkins, an aide to President Franklin D. Roosevelt, joked that he had a hard time finding a way to call "that outfit" (the Saudi royal family) a democracy as required under the Lend-Lease law, but never mind—the *idea* required us to find ways around such difficulties. And it was a good bargain, because oil would fill the tanks of a consumer democracy at home. We have been protecting Saudi Arabia (or rather its ruling monarchy and Saudi Aramco) ever since, one way or another.

With Iraq and Iran in turmoil since the 1970s, Saudi Arabia has become, with its 25 percent of the world's proven oil reserves, Washington's most important "partner" in the world. It is intensely disturbing to policymakers whenever one talks about (let alone investigates) the connections Saudi Arabia has to international terrorism and the men who flew the jetliners into the World Trade Center and the Pentagon. But it is not only oil where Saudi Arabia stands out; there are also the enormous arms purchases that help to relieve dangerous trade imbalances. From the 1970s, when Henry Kissinger set up the arms-for-oil mechanism, the Saudis have purchased upward of $100 billion from the United States. "For years upon years," writes a former CIA counterterrorism expert, "the Saudis have been the world's number-one consumer of American armament and weapons systems."

Today, however, the outlook for Saudi-American relations has clouded over a bit. The American military presence in Saudi Arabia has stirred resentments, and indeed one of the reasons for attacking Iraq, we are told, was to make it possible to reduce that presence, and thereby the threat of revolution in a country that has historically been our ally—a worst-case scenario for the managers of the new empire.

During the Cold War, the "agent theory," which posited that all revolutions were the work of the Evil Soviet Empire, operating through its agents everywhere in the world, landed us in Vietnamese swamps. The same thinking has now been resurrected to justify the creation of a world empire of righteousness—with all the hubris that self-proclaimed title implies. Thus, in asking Congress for an additional $87 billion to wage the fight on the "central front" of the war on terrorism now located in Iraq, President Bush said on September 8, 2003:

> Since America put out the fires of September the 11th and mourned our dead and went to war, history has taken a different turn. We have carried the fight to the enemy. We are rolling back the terrorist threat to civilization, not on the fringes of its influence, but at the heart of its power.

The speech passed over WMD, except for one phrase in the past tense that Hussein's regime once "possessed and used" such weapons— apparently a reference to gas attacks during the Iranian-Iraqi war in the 1980s, when the United States "tilted" toward Baghdad, in preference to the Iranian mullahs, or against the Kurdish minority in the north. In a backhanded way, however, Bush conceded that the second Gulf War had opened the doors to "foreign terrorists, who have come to pursue their war on America and other free nations." And so the circle is complete: we created the link that closed it.

But it has already become a circle of fire. A person identified only as someone familiar with the latest intelligence on Iraq told a *New York Times* reporter without even a quiver of irony, "Iraq is now Jihad Stadium. It is the place for fundamentalists to go now, it is their Super Bowl, where you go to stick it to the West."

Asking other nations to come to America's aid in the task of reconstructing Iraq as Germany and Japan had been reconstructed after World War II, Bush declared, "The Middle East will either become a place of progress and peace, or it will be an exporter of violence and terror that takes more lives in America and in other free nations." It was not supposed to be this way, of course. Iraqis were said to be waiting for their liberation, while Baghdad's own oil production would pay for the war and reconstruction.

Noting the decrepit state of Iraq's infrastructure, Secretary of Defense Donald Rumsfeld observed on a fact-finding mission only two days after the president's speech that sending more troops was not the answer. That would make the Iraqis too dependent on America. Revenues from the reconstruction of the oil fields would not, however, pay the costs either. Iraq would have to develop industries like tourism if it was going to stand on its own feet again. The country, he said, could reap real benefits from national and historic treasures like the ruins of the ancient city of Babylon. "I don't believe it's our job to reconstruct the country," Rumsfeld said, again without any sense of irony that President Bush had used Germany and Japan as examples of what could be done. "Tourism is going to be something important to that country as soon as the security situation is resolved. . . . In the last analysis, they have to create an environment that's hospitable to investment and to enterprise." The reference to Iraq's historical treasures as a foundation for its modern recovery came from the same man who had reacted with avuncular nonchalance at the looting of museums and cultural sites, as little more than the naughty exuberance of newly liberated men—a minor contradiction, but a telling one about the self-understanding of the mission. Secretary of State Colin Powell, on a quick swing through Iraq, assured friendly questioners that more progress was being made than was reported in the press:

> There is just a great deal that is happening in this country, whether it's the formation of PTAs in local schools, whether it's our brigade commanders giving $500 to each school in their district as long as that school comes up with a PTA, something unheard of here before, and uses that PTA to determine how the money will be spent. That's grassroots democracy in action.

European powers were said to have given their colonies roads and schools, and now the American empire offers the addition of PTAs. For the time being, of course, the secretary could not move outside of the tight security cordon that whisked him into and out of Baghdad to see democracy in action. And reporters attending the press conference had to walk through a quarter mile of barbed wire, and along the way encounter four checkpoints, including three body searches. Overhead Apache helicopters circled the conference center, and Bradley fighting vehicles sat outside guarding all entrances.

Inside this barricade, Powell assured listeners that the United States came not as occupiers, but "under a legal term having to do with occupation under international law. . . . We came as liberators. We have experience being liberators. Our history over the last fifty, sixty years is quite clear. We have liberated a number of countries, and we do not own one square foot of any of those countries, except where we bury our dead."

As for progress toward Iraqi self-government, the secretary said, "We're not hanging on for the sake of hanging on." Everyone had to understand that it would still take some time. Elements from the old regime, common criminals, and some number of foreign terrorists (he was not sure how many but perhaps over a thousand) had entered Iraq. Asked if he was basing his analysis of progress on official reports, a la Vietnam briefings, Powell bristled a bit. "I think I've been around long enough to understand the things I'm being told and to see behind the things I'm being told."

Hanging on, nevertheless, is an interesting phrase in itself. In a separate interview with Wolf Blitzer of CNN, Powell dismissed critics who mentioned Vietnam as using "rather bizarre historical allusions." We ought to stop doing that, he insisted. The nation should concentrate on the facts on the ground. His job now was to help the Iraqi people "put together a government that they can be proud of, a government that will never again be called a dictatorship but rather a government that can be a model for this region and the rest of the world."

That Hussein was a tyrant of the first order has never been in doubt, but Washington's attitude toward him has varied over the years. For a long time, indeed, he was our man holding the line against Iranian radicalism. That radicalism manifested itself as the Cold War reached its first peak in Korea, and then again in the late 1970s when the shah we had restored to his throne was toppled.

The Iranian revolutions offer convenient book ends for a discussion of the evolution of the agent theory of revolution. When Dean Acheson undertook to write his memoirs of the early Cold War years, he chose the title *Present at the Creation*. Today we are "Present at the Culmination." In 1939, Acheson recalls, he went to Yale University to deliver an address on the world situation. A conservative Democrat, Acheson at first had feared the New Deal was a genuinely frightening experiment in self-containment, and as such, likely to produce fascism or socialism at home—particularly if the "closed" systems of Germany, Japan, and Russia somehow triumphed in the war.

His main audience was outside the university, for he was addressing all those who worried that greater participation in world affairs meant strengthening New Dealism. What Acheson told his audience was that they had it backwards: staying out of the war would strengthen the forces they disliked. Isolated, the United States would turn inward upon itself. And by the end of World War II his prophecy proved correct. Beginning the world anew forestalled any more thoughts of a radical policy at home.

The idea of a vast, unseen army working to subvert our democracy—whether it originates at home or requires that we go abroad to instill the blessings of the free-market consumer democracy on the world—is as American as apple pie and the Dallas Cowboys. Two great forces are in a constant state of tension in a liberal democracy, Acheson explained at Yale: the worth of man as an individual, and the unity of society. "And the ideal of liberty is going out across the world, as [Thomas] Jefferson said it would," he said, " 'to some parts sooner, to some later, and finally to all.' " In short, America could not ever feel secure in a world where the Jeffersonian idea was not moving forward at a brisk pace. The step from Dean Acheson to Ronald Reagan was not actually a very long one, either historically or intellectually. "We have every right," Reagan would say in his first inaugural address, "to dream heroic dreams. We are too great a nation to limit ourselves to small dreams."

In between, Dean Rusk, an Assistant Secretary of State in 1950, most famously described the 1949 Chinese Revolution, for example, as creating nothing more than a Soviet puppet state. Years later, with the United States entrenched in the Vietnam War, and with evidence of the Sino-Soviet split, Rusk was loathe to surrender that article of faith— perhaps even more than he was to "lose" South Vietnam itself.

And Secretary of State John Foster Dulles used circumlocution to try to explain the agent theory of revolution to Congress in 1957, during hearings on the so-called Eisenhower Doctrine, for aid to countries threatened by such maneuvers by the Russians. The State Department had used the phrase "countries controlled by international communism," and several legislators were puzzled by what that meant. So Dulles explained:

> Well, international communism is a conspiracy composed of a certain number of people, all of whose names I do not know, and many of whom I suppose are secret. They have gotten control of one government after another. They first got control of Russia after the First World War. They have gone on getting control of one country after another until finally they were stopped.

Whether the Soviet Union controlled "international communism," or whether it was the other way around, Dulles concluded, had been the subject of many books and articles.

Secretary Rumsfeld posits a similar premise to Congress today. Doubters that Saddam Hussein was behind the 9/11 attacks are blind to the challenge, he argues. However well-intentioned, dissent only helps the enemy, Rumsfeld scolds. Asked by a senator on the Armed Services Committee what had changed in the international situation making it necessary to attack Iraq, Rumsfeld snapped back, "What's different? What's different is 3,000 people were killed." That's it, end of discussion.

Thus the administration's greatest success so far was not on the battlefield, where Iraq's Republican Guard faded away like extras in a remake of *Gunga Din,* but in selling the idea that there was a direct connection between Hussein and al-Qaeda to a level where well over half the nation still believes 9/11 was fomented in Baghdad. The direct connection appears in Bush speeches, and floats around in Deputy Secretary Paul Wolfowitz's loose-jointed interviews: "I think everyone agrees that we killed 100 or so of an al-Qaeda group in northern Iraq in this recent go-around, that we've arrested that al-Qaeda guy in Baghdad who was connected to this guy Zarqawi whom [Secretary of State Colin] Powell spoke about in his UN presentation."

In a statement releasing his updated version of this vision on September 17, 2002, President Bush declared, "Finally, the United States will use this moment of opportunity to extend the benefits of freedom across the globe. We will actively work to bring the hope of democracy, development, free markets, and free trade to every corner of the world. The events of September 11, 2001, taught us that weak states, like Afghanistan, can pose as great a danger to our national interests as strong states."

The agent theory of revolution here updated by George W. Bush always postulates an "evil empire," as Ronald Reagan once described the Soviet Union, and makes intervention understandable to Congress and public opinion, but it essentially denies the peoples of "Third World" countries the right to make their own history.

• • •

It is well to remember that the first battle of the Cold War was fought in the Middle East, not in Europe. At the end of World War II, Russian troops remained entrenched in northern Iran, adjacent to the Soviet Republic of Azerbaijan. Their purpose, it became clear, was to pressure Teheran for an oil concession, by threatening to support an independence movement in the area. Great Britain and the United States had shelved the Russian request, and supported Teheran's authority over the northern region. Under pressure, the Russians withdrew without gaining any share of Iran's oil, long controlled by the British.

All went well—for a time. But in 1951 the young shah we had supported found himself in trouble in the face of nationalist feelings that Iranian oil shouldn't belong to Russia, and it shouldn't belong to Britain, and it shouldn't belong to America. This discontent with the share of oil revenues Iran received from the Anglo-Iranian Oil Corporation found a powerful voice in Mohammed Mossadegh, who gained control of the Iranian parliament and proceeded to nationalize the oil company.

British efforts to undo Mossadegh's work would not have succeeded without American support. At first Mossadegh hoped that Washington would offer his regime financial support so that it might resist the British economic blockade. Secretary of State Acheson promptly disabused him of such notions with a blunt statement that the United States did not look favorably upon breaches of contract. The new Eisenhower administration promised it would aid Iran—after it came to terms with the Anglo-Iranian Oil Company, and after the United States gained the lion's share of the oil wells.

Eventually the CIA took a hand, and the shah, who had gone off to exile, was returned to power as the result of a "popular uprising." The successful coup d'etat in Iran was considered a great success—until it was undone by the ayatollahs twenty-five years later. The American who engineered the coup assured Secretary of State John Foster Dulles that it had been successful because the agency had correctly assessed the situation. If we were to try something like this again, however, warned the CIA's Kermit Roosevelt, we would have to be sure that the "people and army want what we want."

"If not," he said, "you had better give the job to the Marines."

Jimmy Carter gave the job to the newly created Delta Force instead. After the shah's dethronement in 1979, the Ayatollah Khomeini presided over a harsh theocracy, and smiled benovently upon the students who charged the American Embassy and made hostages of the diplomats. In the spring of 1980, all diplomatic efforts unavailing, Carter sent in the Delta Force to rescue the hostages. The failure of the helicopters in the desert marked the beginning of the end of his presidency.

It was enough, some said, to make one wish "Old Mossy" (Mossadegh) was still in power. But back in 1953, Mossadegh was seen as a forerunner of Communist, and hence Russian, dominance over the entire area. The fear that Iranian nationalization would set off a chain reaction that would affect oil wells around the world was not unlike Eisenhower's famous Domino Theory.

From another angle, but a related one, Ike explained America's purpose to Congressional leaders:

In simple terms, we are establishing international outposts where people can develop their strength to defend themselves. Here we are sitting in the center, and with high mobility and destructive forces we can swiftly respond when our vital interests are affected. . . . As we get these other countries strengthened economically, to do their part to provide the ground forces to police and hold their own land, we come closer to the realization of our hopes. . . . We cannot publicly call our Allies outposts . . . [but] we are trying to get that result.

From 1970 to 1979, following Ike's prescription, we relied upon Iran and Saudi Arabia as the twin pillars that would uphold American interests in the Middle East. President Carter even called the shah a rock of stability, whose Savak (secret police) presumably upheld our values as well as the shah's. When the Ayatollah Khomeini threatened to undo our work in Iran, some thought was given to encouraging a military coup. But the shah's army was unreliable, and faltered before the religious fervor of the ayatollah—as he predicted it would. He also succeeded in bringing down Carter himself, as conservative critics made the case that the Democrats had subverted a friendly ruler with all the misguided claptrap about Human Rights.

Carter was stuck on the horns of his own dilemma. When the Soviets moved to intervene in neighboring Afghanistan, his response was twofold. First, he created the Rapid Deployment force, charged with protecting the Persian Gulf from the Soviet Union, and then he authorized military aid to the Taliban forces—who, when they later gained power, made the ayatollah's regime seem the essence of moderation. While Carter could not carry out a rescue operation in Iran to free American hostages, he could send aid to the Taliban and National Security Advisor Zbigniew Brzezinski to the Khyber Pass brandishing a captured Russian AK-47.

It was not enough, and the search went on for an ally. It was time for a new look at an old enemy, one who had been accused of supporting international terrorism. Brzezinski declared, "We see no fundamental incompatibility of interests between the United States and Iraq." Saddam Hussein's regime was a dubious choice—but what was there left to do? Hussein's attitude toward Israel did not make things any easier. While perhaps not the most radical of the anti-Israel leaders, he had declared himself a champion of the Palestinians in his own bid for recognition as the Arab champion. He had ties with the Palestinian terrorist Abu Nidal. This was always a sore spot for American policymakers, who had their own problems trying to present themselves as both "even-handed" and yet a staunch supporter of Israel.

Nevertheless, when Iran failed us, Reagan tilted farther toward Iraq.

A recent publication by the National Security Archive in Washington, D.C., includes minutes of Reagan's emissary's meetings with Hussein in December 1983. The emissary who assured Hussein of the administration's desire to reestablish diplomatic relations and provide all the help it could to the Iraqi war effort against Iran was Donald Rumsfeld.

When the Cold War ended in an American victory, the new pretender in the Middle East, Saddam Hussein, really had no counterpoise to the United States—that is, he could not get away with everything like he had before. When he moved against Kuwait in 1990, it was almost as if he had heard George I's prayers. A colorless president after the thrills of Ronald Reagan's stirring "It's Morning Again in America," George H. W. Bush had succeeded in getting to the presidency largely from inertia. But his administration had one great fear: that what they called the "unipolar moment" might not last. With the Soviet Evil Empire in ashes, now was the time to secure the victory. The campaign for a New World Order began with the assertion that it had not been containment that had caused the Soviet downfall, but Reagan's moral offensive labeling of the Soviet Union as an "Evil Empire." In fact Bush and his aides were not a little upset that Reagan had set some bad precedents at times when he talked about nuclear disarmament with Mikhail Gorbachev. And when he stopped talking about the "Evil Empire," neocons got a real case of heart flutters.

But when Hussein attacked Kuwait, the future started to look bright again. Here was the opportunity, as George I rejoiced, to kick the Vietnam Syndrome. No jungles here. Just open targets on the roads, and a clear path up to Baghdad—if you wanted to take it all the way there. In a sense, Hussein could claim that he had been sucked into the war by American Ambassador to Iraq April Glaspie's statements just weeks before he attacked that it was Washington's policy not to become involved. "We have no opinion on your Arab-Arab conflicts, such as your dispute with Kuwait," she told him face-to-face.

While Glaspie and her superiors strenuously denied giving Hussein a green light, and while it is also likely that the Iraqi leader thought he could discount a strong American reaction in any event, the episode revealed contradictions in Middle East policy that would not serve the empire's interests well. In the short run, Bush was probably surprised at how easy it was to put together a coalition of the willing. Russia even joined in. (And why not? With possibly the largest oil reserves next to Iraq, why support a competitor?) Around Bush were a lot of people who felt that seizing Baghdad could be the only proper way to insure the unipolar moment would become Greenwich mean time. It was, after all, the time of the grand pronouncement; it was "The End of History," as one conservative foreign-policy intellectual insisted; or as neocon Charles Krauthammer declared in *Foreign Affairs,* the elite journal all policymakers read, the unpopular moment:

> Our best hope for safety in such times, as in difficult times past, is in American strength and will—the strength and will to lead a unipolar world, unashamedly laying down the rules of world order and being prepared to enforce them. Compared to the task of defeating fascism and communism, averting chaos is a rather subtle call to greatness. It is not a task we are any more eager to undertake than the great twilight struggle just concluded. But it is just as noble and just as necessary.

To make sure everyone saw how noble it was, and how necessary, the Kuwaiti government hired a New York public relations firm and paraded a fifteen-year-old girl (daughter of the Kuwaiti ambassador to the United States) to claim before Congress that she had seen Iraqi soldiers toss premature babies onto hospital cement floors; and the administration falsely insisted that Hussein was close to gaining nuclear weapons in his quest to become the dominant force in the Middle East. President Bush compared him to Hitler, a comparison that, as critics pointed out, trivialized Hitler, exaggerated Hussein, and did little credit to the president.

Meanwhile, the Arab-Israeli issue confounded policymakers. Since the creation of the state of Israel in 1948, the United States has tried hard to finesse the situation, but it's like trying to ride two horses going in opposite directions. Powerful currents of guilt feelings from World War II—the inability or failure to do anything about the Holocaust until it had killed six million European Jews—deeply colored American thinking about the Middle East. The Arabs, on the other hand, took the position that the West, now led by the United States, was imposing a "colonialist" solution to the problem of refugees. Every question about Israel had become a contested issue, with the Palestinians in the middle.

It spilled over into the Vietnam War in 1967 at the time of the Six-Day War. In his struggles to sustain support for the war in Southeast Asia, President Lyndon Johnson needed a lot of friends. He was perturbed that many American Jews opposed his policy. With the Six-Day War, however, his appeals to Israeli officials, citing American support for Tel Aviv, met with some success. The Six-Day War thus marked a turning point in the Middle Eastern situation, with its heritage of bitter feelings at Israeli annexation of territories.

For many neocons, the removal of Hussein was supposed to make the road safe for Middle Eastern democracy and an Israeli-Palestinian agreement. Such a vision was perfectly compatible, therefore, with other American interests in securing a firm grip on Iraqi oil resources, so that it would have a strong counterforce to either Russian moves or Saudi Arabian resources should further upheavals occur across the region. It has, of course, done nothing of the kind. The continued state of near chaos forces the administration to couple its boasts that the leadership of al-Qaeda in Afghanistan has been destroyed and the "remnants" of Hussein's government are on the run, with statements that the danger to the United States and to Israel has not declined. Israel, meanwhile, has found no respite from suicide bombing attacks.

Paul Wolfowitz, who has served in both Bush administrations, was quick to seize upon the Iraq invasion of Kuwait as a turning point for American interests in the Middle East, not least because it solidified relations with Saudi Arabia and offered an opportunity for a permanent presence that would complete the transfer of power from Europe to America:

> There are two basic factors behind the Saudi decision to let American forces on their soil. One is a clear understanding of the threat they face; they realized that temporizing with an enemy as ruthless and determined as Saddam is not likely to work for long. But that conclusion by itself would not have led them to change unless there were an alternative and the alternative required somebody who could counter Saddam's military power.
>
> The Saudis have greatly changed their view of the United States over the last ten years. The very resolve we showed during the Iran-Iraq war—our policy of containing Iran—persuaded them that the United States had staying power, that we would not simply leave when the first casualties began to come in and that we had a fundamental understanding of the magnitude of our interests.

Wolfowitz also pointed out in this 1990 speech at the Wye Plantation Policy Conference that the sanctions against Hussein would weaken him over the long haul, in case military action became necessary. How things turn around in the world of the neocon utopia! If the first Gulf War was fought to convince Saudi Arabia we would always be there, Gulf War II has the opposite goal—to withdraw our military to save the Saudi regime from the anger of its own people, and the United States from new terrorist recruits.

"In late February 2003," writes Christopher Preble of the CATO Institute, "before the start of the war, Wolfowitz admitted that the price paid to keep forces in the region had been 'far more than money.' Anger at American pressure on Iraq, and resentment over the stationing of U.S.

forces in Saudi Arabia, Wolfowitz conceded, had 'been Osama bin
Laden's principal recruiting device.' Looking ahead to the post-Hussein
period, Wolfowitz implied that the removal of Hussein would enable
the United States to withdraw troops from the region. 'I can't imagine
anyone here wanting to . . . be there for another 12 years to continue
helping recruit terrorists.' "

Wolfowitz might not have been able to foresee such a situation in
2003, but the road out of Saudi Arabia is not nearly so free of dust
storms as it may have appeared in the flush of victory. Going back to
Afghanistan for a moment, the Taliban's role in bringing down the Soviet Union was much appreciated in Washington. But the hero of the
day to Taliban fighters became a wealthy member of a Saudi elite family, Osama bin Laden.

Returning to Saudi Arabia from that front in his war on the Russians, he was ready to take on Hussein himself—so that an American
"occupation" of his native country would not occur. His offer was
scoffed at and he returned to the caves of Afghanistan to launch his jihad
against the Saudi-American alliance—a series of attacks beginning in
1995 that culminated in 9/11.

Seemingly unbeatable in 1992, meanwhile, the Bush administration
was done in by an old Republican nemesis—the economy. As George I
said ruefully at a conference at Texas A&M University celebrating his
handling of the endgame of the Cold War, for all his troubles in bringing the Cold War to a successful conclusion and winning Gulf War I,
what he got was the "Order of the Boot."

The interloper Bill Clinton moved the Democratic Party to the
right, but he could have taken it all the way to pre–New Deal days without satisfying Reagan/Bush firebrands. They bided their time and developed a plan for what they called a Project for a New American
Century (PNAC). Now the campaign to make sure the unipolar moment did not expire had a platform and a program of action: Saddam
Hussein was the enemy of choice, but certainly not the only one.

As the PNAC manifesto declared, the object of American policy should be to gain dominance in the Middle East:

> The United States has for decades sought to play a more permanent role in Gulf regional security. While the unresolved conflict with Iraq provides the immediate justification, the need for a substantial American force presence in the Gulf transcends the issue of the regime of Saddam Hussein.

To get to the point where the neocons wanted to take the United States, the road led through Baghdad. As many people have said, toward this end, Saddam Hussein was a poster boy for the role assigned to him. A despot who has not hesitated to use the worst repressive methods on anyone who dared to oppose him, who had a series of projects to develop WMDs, and who has at times claimed to be the sword of Islam against Israel, he was a perfect target for the unipolars.

George II had soft-pedaled foreign policy in the millennial election campaign, but once in office he made it clear that he was a much more colorful president than his father had been. He liked to read about Andrew Jackson, it was reported, whose raid into Spanish Florida showed who was boss in the New World, and who acted unilaterally to get the Indians out of the white man's way down there in Georgia, despite treaties with the Cherokee Nation. George could go him one better, tossing aside the Anti-Ballistic Missile Treaty and getting rid of the Kyoto Treaty in the same year.

The PNAC manifesto declared that to make the "American Peace" permanent, the United States would have to engage in a whole series of constabulary actions. "They demand American political leadership rather than that of the United Nations. . . . American power is so great and its global interests so wide that it cannot pretend to be indifferent to the political outcome in the Balkans, the Persian Gulf or even when it deploys forces in Africa."

"The stakes for America are never small," George W. Bush added in his inaugural address. "If our country does not lead the cause of freedom, it will not be led." A few days after 9/11, Bush met with his aides at Camp David. Present were Secretary of State Colin Powell, Secretary of Defense Donald Rumsfeld, and Deputy Secretary of Defense Paul Wolfowitz, along with various others. Wolfowitz argued for attacking Iraq. Powell warned that this would cause the nation's allies to back away, but agreed that undermining the Iraqi regime was an important goal of policy.

Bill Clinton had pursued a similar policy towards Iraq, trying to tighten the noose around Hussein's neck. But that was not showing the results that neocons argued would be needed to change the whole picture in the Middle East.

Attacking Afghanistan, Wolfowitz argued, might lead to an inconclusive struggle tying down 100,000 troops in mountains and caves. If the War on Terrorism was to be taken seriously, we had to go after Hussein. "He estimated," wrote Bob Woodward in *Bush at War*, "that there was a 10 to 50 percent chance Saddam was involved in the September 11 terrorist attacks."

Bush turned down the Iraq option—for the moment—but he told the group, according to Woodward, "At some point we may be the only ones left. That's okay with me. We are America."

Paul Wolfowitz, the number-two man in the Pentagon but considered by most to be the number-one theoretician of the neoconservative phalanx driving the administration's foreign policies, gave an interview to a *Vanity Fair* reporter in May 2003, in which he averred: "If you had to pick the ten most important foreign policy things for the United States over the last 100 years, it [the shock and awe attacks on Iraq] would surely rank in the top ten if not number one. It's the reason why so much has changed, and people who refuse to look at that, for whatever reason, or are unwilling to face up to the implications of that then go around and look for some nefarious explanation."

Wolfowitz has also been quoted elsewhere as saying that the question of finding WMDs was a rallying point in intra-administration debates, but only one of several considerations. Diplomacy doesn't help under such circumstances: "It's just words [and] is rarely going to get you much unless you're dealing with people who basically share your values and your interests. . . . Sometimes it does help just to have a better understanding."

Saddam Hussein shared neither values nor interests—not anymore, at least. And so Baghdad had to be liberated. "I'm not blind to the uncertainties of this situation," Wolfowitz insisted at the beginning of the "postwar" turmoil, "but [critics] just seem to be blind to the instability that that son of a bitch was causing." Wolfowitz calls himself a practical idealist. You can't go around trying to change the whole world, in a caricature of Woodrow Wilson, but you can't ignore the nature of the Hussein regime, either. Or the regimes in North Korea or Iran—the "Axis of Evil."

Therefore, says Wolfowitz, President Bush asks the right question when he first wants to know how brutal a country's leaders are before he knows whether he can do business with them. "It's really important to keep in mind what this country is about. It's a lot more than just physical security or economic health." It's here, however, that the neocons get themselves in a twist. Are we involved in Iraq to liberate the people there for the sake of our immortal souls, or are we there simply to take down a regime to protect homeland security over here?

Echoing Wolfowitz in a spontaneous display of bipartisanship, President Clinton's former CIA chief, James Woolsey, declared soon after Gulf War II began that Iraq was only the first objective. We are in World War IV, he told college students in California in April 2003. It will no doubt last longer that World War I or II, but hopefully not so long as the Cold War. There were three enemies to overcome in the Middle East: the religious rulers of Iran, the "fascists" in Iraq and Syria, and al-Qaeda.

They had been attacking us for several years, but the United States only took notice with 9/11, he went on. Victory over those foes would only be the beginning. Hosni Mubarak of Egypt and the Saudi Arabian potentates on the periphery had better watch out. "We want you nervous," Woolsey continued, hitting full stride. "We want you to realize now, for the fourth time in a hundred years, this country and its allies are on the march and that we are on the side of those whom you— the Mubaraks, the Saudi Royal family—most fear: We're on the side of your own people."

Now, that was going a bit too far; in fact much too far. A little Woodrow Wilson goes a long way for the neocons and their admirers on Fox News, and like-minded "news" broadcasters who fill the cable channels with respectful elaborations of Bush's worldview. The last thing in the world the United States wants is for the Iraq War to turn into a general revolution, until we are sure how to insure the outcome will not be revolutionary anti-Americanism. There is even talk about deconstructing the old mandate-sized Iraq into three states so as to avoid a civil war, to prevent such a Kosovo-like outcome. If the already perilous situation in Saudi Arabia were to become incendiary as well, the Iraq war would become a total disaster. And Hosni Mubarak is the least of America's troubles in the Middle East.

As Cold War Secretary of State Dean Acheson once said, what America wants is a world where those who think the way we do are free to create the kind of life they wish to live. Today the United States is no longer the empire that dare not speak its name. And it is no longer even a question about whether we are an empire. That matter is settled. Writers once too afraid to speak about empire, except as Victorians once spoke about sexual matters, through euphemism and opaque reference, now openly embrace the idea across the narrow spectrum of American politics.

There is no sense at all, as in 1900, that it could be explained as an aberration when we took Cuba and the Philippines. The historical references are clear—and direct. Thomas Paine wrote in 1776 that we had it in our power to make the world anew. For the next two hundred years and more we were not the imitators of the empires of old, but embodied an entirely new phenomenon—an empire of righteousness without frontiers. Bush put it this way in his inaugural address:

> Through much of the last century, America's faith in freedom and democracy was a rock in a raging sea. Now it is a seed upon the wind, taking root in many nations.
>
> Our democratic faith is more than the creed of our country, it is the inborn hope of our humanity, an ideal we carry but do not own, a trust we bear and pass along. And even after nearly 225 years, we have a long way yet to travel.

As befitting this "mission," there will have to be sacrifices—for some. "Old Europe" may be upset, but things will right themselves once it is recognized what the outcome will be, not only for Iraqis, but for other places where the seed in the wind takes root. The monetary costs will perhaps exceed what had been anticipated by a few hundred billion dollars, but there are places in the budget where one can economize, such as for schools and medical care. Those who wrongly believe that the mission itself might create more terrorists and less security at home will understand that the PATRIOT Acts will protect them, while we preempt and root out the wannabe Osamas in Syria, Iran, North Korea, Cuba, and anyplace else.

There are only a few stubborn holdouts against the new empire. Senator Robert Byrd, for example, speaking in opposition to Senate Joint

Resolution 46, which gave George II carte blanche to use force against
Iraq, said to a nearly empty Senate chamber:

> No one supports Saddam Hussein. If he were to disappear tomorrow,
> no one would shed a tear around the world. I would not. My handker-
> chief would remain dry. But the principle of one government deciding
> to eliminate another government, using force to do so, and taking that
> action in spite of world disapproval, is a very disquieting thing. I am
> concerned that it has the effect of destablizing the world community
> of nations. I am concerned that it fosters a climate of suspicion and mis-
> trust in U.S. relations with other nations. The United States is not a
> rogue nation, given to unilateral action in the face of worldwide oppro-
> brium.

Standing in the "liberated" city of Baghdad on the second anniver-
sary of the attacks, the commander of the American forces in Iraq, Lt.
General Ricardo Sanchez, stood foursquare behind the president.
"There is no doubt in my mind that the American people are committed to winning this war." There was no early exit in sight. "It is a very
difficult issue," he said, and again like the president, he called upon the
"international community" to focus on eliminating the threat in Iraq,
the battleground for the worldwide struggle against terrorism.

Reporters asked if there was any connection between Saddam Hussein and Osama bin Laden?

"It is very possible." Oops! Sanchez realized right away that might
not sound quite right. So he added, "That was the fundamental assumption we had as we came in here, and that is what we are going on." In the
agent theory of revolution, there can be no missing links. Otherwise it
comes apart.

The Romans famously divided the world between civilization and
the barbarians, a word derived from a Greek term to describe the
strange speech of foreigners, apparently without distinction between

them. Barbarians lived outside the empire, like the blue-faced rabble on the other side of Hadrian's Wall. The way Americans talk today, however, no one lives outside the reach of the empire's power. Nothing on the scale of the American empire has ever existed before. Accordingly, our first strikes at Iraq were given the apocalyptic code name "Shock and Awe." Little wonder that the empire's boasters incorporate a millennial motif in their pronouncements, a theological tone not confined to the Christian Right, although the events since the end of the Cold War have enhanced their once-marginal position into a potent force in the nation's political life.

The American Revolution, once identified as a triumph of the Age of Reason, has been taken over by ideologues with an agenda that tolerates no dissent—no doubts, no second thoughts. A decent respect for world opinion is considered wimpish if not disloyal. It is fair to punish dissenters outside the country—those who sign the treaty creating a world court to try war criminals—by denying them military aid from the Pentagon; and it is even fair to rebuke critics inside the country, for example, by revealing the identity of a family member who served in the Central Intelligence Agency.

This ideology is married to a political economy that simply ignores—at its peril, we are discovering—any limits on the sacrifice of its own citizenry to be able to place high-tech centurions around the globe. It was all going to be so easy. Secretary of Defense Rumsfeld promised a new military, one able to strike quickly with shock and awe anyplace in the world. Moving with lightning speed, we were to keep an eye on all conflicts, and move to preempt all potential barbarian assaults. Journalist Robert Kaplan, interviewing a captain at Fort Leavenworth, Kansas, heard this comforting declaration: "We know more about Honduras than Kansas during the Indian Wars. The intelligence is more *dense*. Honduras is closer in time than western Kansas was, a few hours by plane rather than days on horseback." Kaplan concluded, "The Third

World has become like the Old West. For the army, continental frontiers—of the kind that led to the building of Fort Leavenworth and of
the nation—have grown dim."

Our old Cold War allies, except for Bush's poodle, Tony Blair, have
substantial doubts about participating in the crusades we have launched,
although presumably prepared to reap any benefits that can be garnered
around the edges whether it succeeds or fails. To police the empire,
Bush has to turn to "New" Europe for help, calling in troops from
Poland and staging pompous ceremonies to mark the transfer of
"power" in a small area of Iraq. He has also had to reemploy intelligence
agents from the Baathist regime, presumably after they have undergone
a political dry-cleaning process to make them forerunners of the new
democratic state that will emerge to provide a beacon light to those still
sitting in darkness in fundamentalist Islamic schools and mountain caves
between Afghanistan and Pakistan.

At home, meanwhile, the PATRIOT Act will allow us to uncover
those in our midst dedicated to our destruction, the tax cuts will stimu-
late the economy once again into performances that will make the
1990s go-go years seem an idle stroll beside a quiet stream, and the development of the Alaskan oil resources will power our SUVs speedily
onto the new highways of the global economy. Of course, as President
Bush said, it was the duty of all civilized nations to pay their fair share of
the costs involved in keeping the barbarians at bay. They made a mistake
in opposing the war, WMDs or no WMDs, but all is forgiven if they
will now recognize their duty. If not, well, the deficit be damned. "At
some point we may be the only ones left. That's okay with me. We are
America."

Not a flicker of doubt crosses Bush's Marlboro Man stare as he vows
that anybody who wants to do harm to American troops will be
brought to justice. He flies to a navy aircraft carrier, the champion of the
world, and declares the war over. "Bring 'em on." American troops are

"plenty tough" to deal with any security threats. This remark brought a chorus of protest from Democratic hopefuls, none of whom, however, went beyond criticizing macho one-liners and saying we needed a "plan" for protecting our military personnel.

Bush's courage seems to falter, however, when it comes to standing up to the American Farm Bureau and its allies who managed to squeeze an additional $40 billion in farm subsidies out of this administration. The costs of that failure showed up first at the Cancún meeting of the World Trade Organization, which collapsed when the United States and the European Union suffered defeat on all fronts. The usual protestors against "globalization" were there in large numbers, but it was inside the conference halls where the Group of 21, representing mainly Third World countries, walked out in protest over the American refusal to move seriously to reduce domestic agriculture subsidies that now total $300 billion worldwide and that distort the "free market" to the disadvantage of the poorest farmers in Africa and elsewhere, as well as efforts to introduce an "investment treaty" that would allow corporations to override local laws to gain an extraterritorial position. Speaking of the American delegate's performance, the head of the Farm Bureau Federation said, "The ambassador has done an excellent job."

Making the world safe for democracy and the free market will enable the "holding company" for the new empire, the Carlyle Group, to improve the profits of its famous investors and officials, which include George H. W. Bush and former British prime minister John Major (and a host of former political leaders from around the world), and the institutions and pension funds that it serves in the United States. Established in 1987, the Carlyle Group, under its dynamic leader, the former Reagan secretary of defense Frank Carlucci, moved to extend its influence and power in truly global fashion. The largest shareholder in United Defense Industries, the Carlyle Group does business with the Pentagon simultaneously on the level of advice and sales. It is the first time in

American history that a former president sits in an official position in a company that sells to the Department of Defense.

"Carlyle is a unique model," writes Eric Leser in *Le Monde,* "assembled at the planetary level on the capitalism of relationships or 'capitalism of access' to use the 1993 expression of the American magazine *New Republic.* Today, in spite of its denials, the group incarnates the 'military-industrial complex' against which Republican President Dwight Eisenhower warned the American people when he left office in 1961."

On May 1, 2003, the current President Bush announced on the deck of an aircraft carrier, where he had just hopped out of a jet fighter, that the mission was accomplished—Iraq liberated in World War II–style, by American arms. The next day he traveled to Santa Clara, California, notes Leser, where he made another martial speech in a United Defense Industries' weapons factory. On board the U.S.S. *Lincoln* he had lauded the men on the front lines; at the United Defense Industries factory he brought it all together, including the true "author" of the American mission:

> The world witnessed one of the swiftest advances of heavy arms in the history of warfare—a 350-mile charge from south to north in Iraq, through hostile enemy territory. We were able to do so not only because of the good strategy, great courage and skill, but because of the Bradleys and Abramses with which our soldiers were equipped. You're making a good product here.
>
> One of the things that people learned about your company, as well, is how useful the HERCULES tank recovery system can be. (Applause.) The guy with the sledgehammer on the statue needed a little help. (Laughter.) Thankfully, there was a HERCULES close by. (Laughter.) A HERCULES which pulled that statue of Saddam Hussein to the ground.
>
> That meant more to the Iraqi people than you can possibly imagine. It was a symbol of their future. A future based upon something that we

hold dear to our hearts; a future based upon something that is not America's gift to the world, but the Almighty God's gift to each and every individual—a future based upon freedom. (Applause.)

So would the United States ever really walk alone on the paths of righteousness, even as the coalition of the willing began to shred? Carlyle will be there. Yet the conflicts at Cancún are likely to multiply, perhaps faster (and probably more permanently) than restoring a temporary new order in the Middle East. These conflicts pit not only the United States, but Europe as well, against the rest of the world. Managing the new empire, balancing off the needs of American farmers against the goal of creating a free marketplace, making good on the promise to protect the homeland beyond displaying a confusing panoply of colored warning lights, all the while ignoring the opinions of all but the loyalist inner circle, may soon prove too much even for its founding fathers. The point where we are the only ones left may come sooner than Bush thinks. But, then, there is nothing to worry about, is there? "We are America."

2

Imperial Language

Marilyn B. Young

Cheney shot more than 70 ringneck pheasants and an unknown number of mallard ducks. The birds were plucked and vacuum-packed in time for Cheney's afternoon flight to Washington, D.C. . . . [About] 500 farm-raised pheasants were released from nets for the morning hunt. The 10-man hunting party that included Cheney shot 417 pheasants.

—Rebekah Scott,
Pittsburgh Post-Gazette, December 9, 2003[1]

If a sparrow cannot fall to the ground without His notice, is it probable that an empire can rise without His aid?
—Lynne and Dick Cheney's Christmas card (quoting Benjamin Franklin)

One must distinguish, I think, between the language of imperialism and the language of empire. The language of imperialism, of the act of creating and sustaining empire, is immediate, direct, often monosyllabic, given to slang but not to euphemism. Its dominant tense is the imperative. The language of empire is benign, nurturing, polysyllabic; its preferred tense is the future conditional. The language of empire reassures. The epigrams for the first chapter of Rashid Khalidi's new book on the Middle East, *Resurrecting Empire,* are virtually identical, though they range in time from the eighteenth to the twenty-first centuries. Napoleon Bonaparte: "O ye Egyptians . . . tell the slanderers that I have not come to you except for the purpose of restoring your rights from the hands of the oppressors." General F.S. Maude, commander of British Forces, Baghdad, in March 1917: "Our armies do not come into your cities and lands as conquerors or enemies, but as liberators." Donald Rumsfeld, Secretary of Defense, April 2003 (addressing not the Iraqis, but U.S. troops): "Unlike many armies in the world, you came not to conquer, not to occupy, but to liberate, and the Iraqi people know this."

Those whom imperial armies must subdue are given names that are easy to pronounce, easy to remember, and that transfer readily over time and space. "Gooks" opposed the United States in the Philippines in the 1890s, Korea in 1950 and, demonstrating their longevity and mobility, Vietnam in the 1960s and 1970s.[2] The change of imperial scenery to the desert almost fifteen years ago has been reflected in a new set of words to name the enemy: "rag head," "sand nigger," "camel jockey." There is some danger here, for not all "gooks," not all "camel jockeys" oppose U.S. imperialism. Some work closely with the civilian and military administrators of the empire. Or they may be defined by international law as noncombatants, innocent civilians, whose close resemblance to "gooks" and "rag heads" makes life difficult for U.S. troops. More useful is the term for the generic enemy of both imperialists and the empire: terrorists. The vocabulary of imperialism, consisting as it does mainly of imperatives, is not that hard to learn: stop, go, fast, slow. Aging veterans of old wars know how to say this in Tagalog, Korean, Vietnamese. Younger ones can say it in Arabic and Pashtun.

The two languages, of imperialism and of empire, are in constant tension, even contradiction. If it is a dialectic, it is one that must be resolved in blood. Only with the total pacification of recalcitrant imperial subjects can the more stately language of empire resume, untroubled by the grim necessities of imperialism. On a model made familiar during the Vietnam War, the journalist Peter Maass spent some time with U.S.

troops in Iraq and, in particular, with Maj. John Nagl, the operations officer in one of the armored battalions of the First Infantry Division.
Nagl, former Rhodes Scholar, Oxford-trained student of counterinsurgency, and West Point professor, was stationed near the major city of
Falluja and the smaller town of Khaldiya. Maj. Nagl did not live in either
Falluja or Khaldiya, but rather in Camp Manhattan, so named, I would
guess, because it suggests a justification for the presence of American
troops. He ventured into the narrow streets of the city and the town in
his Humvee, sometimes accompanied by tanks. The lessons of past
counterinsurgencies were fresh in his mind. Indeed, his book on the
subject, *Counterinsurgency Lessons from Vietnam and Malaya: Learning to
Eat Soup with a Knife,* was published by Praeger only last year. It is clear
from his conversation with Maass that he would like to speak the language of empire rather than the language of imperialism.

One morning last December, insurgents blew up an Iraqi police station, killing twenty-four policemen and two passersby. Nagl's troops
rushed to the site and established a perimeter around it; the mother of
one of the dead policemen shouted imprecations, not at the insurgents
who had set the bomb, but at the Americans. Later that day, first one and
then another procession passed by the station on their way to the ceme-
tery. The second group, of over 1,000, seemed especially angry, shouting
at the troops and throwing rocks. Had they turned more actively threatening, Nagl would have ordered his troops to open fire. Reflecting on
the experience later, Nagl confided to Maass: "Across this divide they're
looking at us, we're looking at them from behind barbed wire, and
they're trying to understand why we're here, what we want from them."

Although Maass does not pause here, it is important for us, if we are
to understand the language of empire and imperialism, to do so. Nagl
does not wonder what he and his troops want from the Iraqis facing
them. Perhaps the answer is too obvious: he wants them to behave
themselves, to be good. There is a further question: how has it happened

that Maj. John Nagl has the right and the power to ask hundreds of people in a country not his own to behave themselves. I will come back to these questions later.

"Almost inconceivable to most of them, I think," Nagl tells Maass, is "that what we want for them is the right to make their own decisions, to live free lives. It's probably hard to understand that if you have lived your entire life under Saddam Hussein's rule. And it's hard for us to convey that message, particularly given the fact that few of us speak Arabic."[3] Note the shift, which I'm certain was not conscious, from the difficulty Iraqis must have understanding what the Americans want *from* them, to what the Americans want *for* them. Colonel Nathan Sassaman, a battalion commander stationed fifty miles north of Baghdad, echoes Nagl's sentiments, albeit in a slightly different key: "With a heavy dose of fear and violence, and a lot of money for projects, I think we can convince these people that we are here to help them."[4]

The problem, of course, is that with or without the history of Saddam Hussein's tyranny, even were it to be told in fluent Arabic, unarmed demonstrators facing armed foreign troops across a barrier of razor barbed wire are likely to have a hard time believing it's all being done on their behalf. Nagl's troops stood behind a barrier of razor wire. Elsewhere in Iraq, entire villages and towns are wrapped in barbed wire. The 7,000 citizens of Abu Hishma, for example, live inside a barbed-wire fence that stretches for five miles; a single check point controls who enters and who leaves. The fence, "is here for your protection." "Do not approach or try to cross, or you will be shot."

"We are like birds in a cage," Abu Hishma's school teacher observed. In close and acknowledged imitation of Israeli tactics in the occupied territories, the American command has also begun to demolish the homes of suspected insurgents and to jail their relatives. "You have to understand the Arab mind," one officer explained to a reporter. "The only thing they understand is force—force, pride and saving face."[5]

The language of American imperialism is English. This is true in obvious ways: during a military operation last June, a young man told a reporter how he had been shot despite waving a white head scarf at advancing U.S. troops: "The Americans were shouting in English, and we didn't know what they were saying. . . ."[6] In some areas where insurgents are active, all men between the ages of eighteen and sixty-five must carry identity cards featuring an assigned number, a photograph of the bearer, his age, and the make of the car he drives, all in English. The Iraqi Civil Defense Corps, for example, is being trained to shout, in English, "Raise your hands!" "Drop your weapons!" A "strange choice," the reporter muses, "in a country where few people speak English."[7] Those ICDC trainees whose names prove too difficult for Americans to pronounce receive nicknames from movies like *Animal House.*[8]

Central to the task of both empire and imperialism is the invisibility of the imperial object or, for it comes to the same thing, the assumption of their simplicity, their transparency. It is not therefore necessary to ask what it is the occupier wants of them beyond behaving well; nor is it interesting to puzzle over how it came to be that the American troops alone have subjectivity. For example, forty years ago almost to the day, an American advisor in Long An Province, Vietnam, explained to a reporter the importance of the "little farmer" and the necessity of winning the "feelings" of such people. The "man who gets the support of this farmer . . . is going to eventually win this war." The advisor was dedicated to the effort and believed that "being humble and putting yourself in their position" was the best method. "I have gone out and helped them pick watermelons," he told Peter Kalischer. "I walk around with my bodyguard . . . and we go visit them and drink tea with them . . . and this is an oddity to them, because they can't imagine that an American can put himself in this position."[9] In the American way, as Maj. Nagl rides around the narrow streets of nearby towns and villages on "cordon and search" missions, he makes "a point of waving at civilians" from his Humvee.[10]

American troops stationed on the border between Iraq and Syria complain that they have not been trained to fight an insurgent war. "We're trained to fight an army face to face," Lt. Col. Greg Reilly said, "to engage in direct combat, an enemy we can see." Reilly tries to figure out what's going on in the 125 miles his troops patrol. One constant problem is that he does not have his own interpreter but must borrow from other units.[11] He and his troops patrol the streets, stop people, search houses, all without benefit of language of any kind. Working instead with unreliable local interpreters, Reilly recently contributed a substantial sum of money to the local officials in the town of Husayba. According to an American accompanying Reilly on this mission, "the mayor expressed appreciation to Colonel Reilly for all that he had done for them—opened schools and the hospital, restored power—but said the heavy presence of American forces was counteracting all that." Reilly said he understood, but that his troops would remain until "the threat is gone. . . ."[12]

The gap between Maj. Nagl's desire to win hearts and minds for the empire and the reality of the imperialist situation in which he finds himself comes up repeatedly in his discussion with Maass.[13] At one point Nagl explains that the streets through which he must track suspects have no names, the houses no numbers, and they all look the same. Obviously they do not look the same to those who live in them—but neither Nagl nor the reporter stop to think about this. Instead, Nagl expresses his yet more intense irritation with the locals. Faced with a map or satellite image, the informant would "scratch his head." "These clowns don't know how to read maps," Nagl complains.[14]

The local Iraqis are not lost in their own cities, whether or not they can read satellite images of their neighborhood, but they sometimes have the bad luck to be out and about in the presence of heavily armed

U.S. convoys. In January a family on its way home from Al-Kindi hospital in Baghdad found itself behind two Humvees just as a bomb exploded in front of the Oil Ministry. The Humvees whirled around and opened fire on their station wagon, killing two family members, one of them a boy of ten, and severely wounding several others.[15] Elsewhere in the empire, early in the new year, a helicopter attack killed eleven people in a village in southern Afghanistan. The preceding month, over a two-day period, fifteen children died as a result of U.S. attacks. The language in which these incidents are reported (when they are reported) is flat, matter of fact. They appear with some regularity on the inner page of the newspaper of record, usually carrying only an anonymous Associated Press byline. They conclude with a standard denial of wrongdoing by senior U.S. officers and/or the promise of an investigation in the future.[16] The flatness of the accounts, the absence of named reporters, the remoteness of the locale, the consequent invisibility of both victim and perpetrator remove these deaths from all orders of explanation. They are literally accidental.

The language of empire is purposive. It purports to do good. Therefore, at least as discussed in the press, expressed by politicians and perhaps believed by American citizens, it *does* good. If, nevertheless, in a place where Americans are doing good they are repaid by violence, the explanation is that the violence comes from outside. During the Vietnam War, the outside was the Communist world, including those Vietnamese who lived north of a line drawn by the 1954 Geneva cease-fire. In Iraq, "foreign Arabs" and Saddam Hussein loyalists are blamed for the ongoing insurgency.[17] These loyalists cease to be really Iraqi, as Vietnamese Communists were no longer really Vietnamese.

Despite the good intentions of empire, the tough methods of imperialism may endanger the enterprise.[18] Counterinsurgency, Peter Maass observes, "requires an excruciatingly fine calibration of lethal force. Not enough of it means you will cede the offensive to your enemy, yet too much means you will alienate the noncombatants whose support you need." [19] When the commander of American forces in Iraq, General Ricardo Sanchez, was asked whether he worried about alienating the population through the use of harsh tactics, he explained that he dealt with the problem by going back "to help the people" who had just been targeted. "When damage is done," he told the reporter Joel Brinkley, "we come back and assist the people and correct the problem. . . ." [20]

Ever since Vietnam, there has been a debate about the calibration of the use of force. Often the marines advocate a "softer touch" than the army. Maj. Nagl, the army student of counterinsurgency, expressed his doubts about the Marine approach. "I'm not really all that concerned about their hearts right now. . . . We're into the behavior-modification phase. I want their minds right now. Maybe we'll get their hearts later. . . . Over time I'll start winning some hearts. Right now I just want them to stop shooting at us, stop planning I.E.D.s [improvised explosive devices]. If they're not involved in these activities, they should start turning in the people who are." A pithy summary of this view during the Vietnam War, variously attributed to General Patton, John Wayne, and Chuck Colson, was: "Grab their balls and their hearts and minds will follow."

John Paul Vann, a much-admired advocate of counterinsurgency during the Vietnam War, underwent a similar transformation. He had always argued passionately against the use of massive firepower. In counterinsurgency warfare, the rapier, not the rifle, should be the weapon of choice. By 1972, during the battle for the city of Kontum, he called 300 B-52 strikes in one concentrated three-week period, then ordered Cobra gunships to fire on the survivors. "Anytime the wind is blowing from the north where the B-52 strikes are turning the terrain into a moonscape," he told Neil Sheehan, "you can tell from the battlefield stench that the strikes are effective. Outside Kontum, wherever you dropped bombs, you scattered bodies." [21]

A somewhat different problem, according to the journalist Robert D. Kaplan, is that "liberal empires" (he lists Venice, Great Britain, and the United States) engender changes that may create the conditions for the destruction of the empire itself. In the recent crisis over gathering a coalition to fight in Iraq, for example, several countries whose democratic reforms the United States had encouraged, refused to participate, largely because they *were* democratic. What to do? One could resort to force in such a situation. Rather, Kaplan writes, "if we are to get our way, and at the same time . . . promote our democratic principles, we will have to operate nimbly. . . ." He leaves it to Eliot Cohen of the Johns Hopkins School of Advanced International Studies to explain the nature of being nimble: "Don't bluster, don't threaten, but quietly and severely punish bad behavior. It's the way the Romans acted." The relationship between severely punishing bad behavior—or, indeed, defining it—(we are talking about sovereign governments disagreeing with U.S. policy after all) and promoting democratic principles is left to the imagination of the reader. The U.S. Trade Representative, Robert Zoellick, is equally direct in his discussion of what the United States requires of others: "countries that seek free trade agreements with the United States must pass muster on more than trade and economic criteria in order to be eligible. At a minimum, these countries must cooperate with the United States on its foreign policy and national security goals. . . ."[22]

The language of empire, of intention to control, justifies or occludes, depending on what is needed, the language of imperialism, of the implementation of empire. However, something new is happening at the present moment: a coming together of the two languages in the nostalgic recreation of a nineteenth-century Anglo-American past, a colonizing, warrior past. In stark contrast to the present, American ideology, whether realist or Wilsonian, has always insisted on its impeccable anticolonial credentials. After all, it was in a war against the British Empire that the United States became a sovereign nation. Two world wars were fought by the United States and won, in the name, if not the implementation, of self-determination. And while the United States was, for a time, greeted as a "new Rome" in the immediate post–World War II era, such references dropped out of sight with the spread of anticolonial nationalist movements the United States hoped would move in anti- or at least non-Communist directions. This seems no longer to be the case.

The most familiar idiom this emerging language speaks is militarism. Niall Ferguson is the best-known writer in the high British imperial mode, urging Americans to stiffen their upper lips, don pith helmets and puttees, and do the hard but moral work of Empire, always with a capital *E*. Ferguson has many American admirers and imitators, for one Max Boot, a journalist, currently a fellow at the Council on Foreign Relations, and the author of *The Savage Wars of Peace,* whose title is drawn from the most famous of all the poems of empire, Kipling's "White Man's Burden." Boot's description of the twenty-first-century American domain is suitably paternalistic: "[America's] 'empire' consists not of far-flung territorial possessions but of a family of democratic, capitalist nations that eagerly seek shelter under Uncle Sam's umbrella." North America, Western Europe, and Northeast Asia are at the "inner core of the American empire [no longer in quotes]." This stable core is beset by "violence and unrest" originating in the periphery—Africa, the Middle East, Central Asia, the Balkans. But why, Boot asks, should U.S. involvement in these violent and criminal regions be military in nature? The answer is that force should never be ruled out in the effort to "shape the international environment to [America's] liking." Indeed, his appeal to a quotation from the work of Thomas Friedman suggests that force must be ruled *in* from the start: "The hidden hand of the market will never work without a hidden fist. McDonald's cannot flourish without McDonnell Douglas. . . ."[23]

Robert Kaplan is another practiced hand at imperial nostalgia. His long essay in *The Atlantic* last summer (July/August 2003), titled "Supremacy by Stealth," offers ten bracing rules for managing an "unruly world." It is worth looking at his essay in some detail, for Kaplan makes explicit what more sophisticated analysts leave to the reader's imagination. Many of Kaplan's ten rules involve the honing of a military worthy of the country's new imperial reach, an army made up of those who love the soldier's life for its own sake.[24] The sort of men Kaplan has in mind resemble those he observed in Yemen, distributing large bowie knives to the local sheikhs: "In a world of tribes and thugs manliness still goes a long way."[25] Sometimes the U.S. military men he met reminded him of Roman centurions, "hard and chiseled." The special-forces trooper, a retired military man informs Kaplan, "has to be a lethal killer one moment and a humanitarian the next. He has to know how to get strangers who speak another language to do things for him."[26] He does not, apparently, have to learn another language himself:

Michael Mann, in his book *Incoherent Empire*, finds Americans ill-suited for empire. They do not have the "stomach for a long fight, especially one involving casualties," they are not "brought up to be as racist, as stoic in combat, as self-denying in crisis, or as obedient to authority, as British kids once were."[27] U.S. culture is simply not imperial. Robert Kaplan, by contrast, finds American culture in its very provincialism suited to the needs of the new empire. One retired special-forces colonel did talk to Kaplan about the joys of foreign adventure, but, he said, "at heart many of us are farm boys who can't wait to get home. In this way we're not like the British and the French. Our insularity protects us from becoming colonials."[28]

On the other hand, David Brooks, the conservative columnist the *New York Times* has added to its op-ed page, worries about this very insularity. The problem of pacifying Iraq is that "we Americans do not like staring into the face of evil. It is in our progressive and optimistic nature to believe that human beings are basically good, or at least rational." But the people the United States fights in Iraq are "the scum of the earth." Staring into "a cave of horrors" in Somalia, Beirut, or Tikrit, Americans just want to go home as quickly as possible. Amnesiac on the subject of the U.S. record in Vietnam, Brooks believes his countrymen ready to sustain casualties themselves but reluctant to inflict them. His argument then takes an odd turn: "What will happen to the American mood," he asks, "when the news programs start broadcasting images of the brutal measures U.S. troops will have to adopt? Inevitably there will be atrocities that will cause many good-hearted people to defect from the cause." America will be "tempted to . . . retreat into the paradise of its own innocence." The president, acting as the minister of his people, must "remind us that we live in a fallen world, that we have to take morally hazardous action if we are to defeat the killers who confront us." These are the "dark realities of human nature" from which Americans must not walk away, even as they preserve their "idealistic faith in a better Middle East." In sum, protected by the banner of its own idealism, America must have the courage to be brutal, even to commit atrocities in the name of scouring the earth of its brutal scum.[29]

In his new book, *The Sorrows of Empire,* Chalmers Johnson makes it clear just how far from retreating into its own paradise America in fact is. A network of military outposts spanning every continent except Antartica constitutes "a new form of empire—an empire of bases with its own geography not likely to be taught in any high school geography class." This Baseworld, built and maintained in large part by Kellogg, Brown & Root, and other private military contractors, operates in an old-fashioned, territorial colonial manner. Americans who live and work in Baseworld are almost entirely isolated from the surrounding population: they shop in their own stores, go to their own movie houses, are not subject to local laws, and, when they feel cabin fever coming on, may choose to golf at one of the 234 military golf courses, or ski at their very own resorts in the Bavarian Alps, getting there by way of their own airline. General Jay Garner, who initially headed the postwar U.S. military occupation of Iraq, placed the country firmly on the map of Baseworld, comparing its value with that of the Philippines: "Look back on the Philippines around the turn of the century," he advised a reporter for the *National Journal*, "they were a coaling station for the navy, and that allowed us to keep a great presence in the Pacific. That's what Iraq is for the next few decades: our coaling station that gives us great presence in the Middle East."[30] The overall purpose of Baseworld, one of its most ardent advocates explains, is to create "a global cavalry" that can move swiftly out of its stockades to punish the "bad guys."[31]

Where Johnson deplores, Kaplan applauds. The American empire is being built through personal relationships, especially those consolidated in the training the U.S. offers foreign militaries both at home and in their own countries. Col. Tom Wilhelm, for example, advises the local military in Mongolia, helping to transform it from defense to "international peacekeeping—as a means of gaining allies in global forums. . . ." Kaplan was confident there would be a Mongolian contingent arriving soon in postwar Iraq. He traveled around the country with Wilhelm, sleeping in local military outposts, riding camels, sharing meals of horsemeat and camel's milk with Mongolian officers.

In January, as Kaplan had predicted in his article, 173 Mongolian soldiers arrived in Iraq, commanded by a Polish general. (The last time the Mongolian military visited Iraq was in 1258, when they laid waste to Baghdad.) Whether it's the personal touch, as Kaplan asserts, or other sorts of incentives, the unwieldy coalition of the willing has been coming through with troops—however token—for Iraq. On February 3, 2004, the *New York Times* carried a small picture of weeping women and stolid men deep inside the first section. No story accompanied the picture, only a caption: "Salvadorans are Iraq-bound." The British regularly mustered their colonial subjects for military duty in other colonies as well as pacification tasks in their own country. The United States does so now as well—with the British as perhaps our best trained Gurkhas.

The most useful section of Kaplan's essay, however, is his discussion of the erosion of any distinction between U.S. civilian and military operations overseas. The special forces helped to write Paraguay's constitution; the State Department leases helicopters to the Colombian army. At the "same time that our uniformed officers are acting more like diplomats," he writes, "our diplomats . . . are acting more like generals." He finds this development admirable; he does not seem to notice the net gain is on the military side. The move toward outright militarism is as clear as it is unacknowledged: "As for international law, it has meaning only when war is a distinct and separate condition from peace." War in the twenty-first century is increasingly undeclared, asymmetrical, and unconventional, and "there will be less and less time for democratic consultation, whether with Congress or the UN." [32]

Instead of consultation, "civilian-military elites in Washington and elsewhere will need to make lightning-quick decisions. In such circumstances the sanction of the so-called international community may gradually lose relevance. . . ." Insofar as the UN represents the international community, for Kaplan it is already irrelevant. He describes the Franco-German efforts to slow the U.S. march toward war as a "diplomatic farce . . . with France and Germany working indefatigably to contain the power of a democratic United States rather than that of a Stalinist, weapons-hungry Iraq. . . ." [33]

Kaplan is brave in the face of contradictions: the aftermath of the overthrow of Allende was not pretty, "not always moral"; the achievement of a "moral outcome" in the Balkans "involved methods that were not always defensible in narrowly moral terms"; in long wars like the Cold War or the current war against terrorism, "deals will always have to be struck with bad people and bad regimes for the sake of a larger good."

Of greater interest than these fairly familiar compromises between ends and means is Kaplan's ceding of "abstract universal principles" to others. Americans once boasted they, exceptionally, acted internationally in the name of universal principles. It is a mark of the times that Kaplan reduces these to "the traditional weapon of the weak seeking to restrain the strong. . . ." Yet in his conclusion, Kaplan argues that the American imperium, to leave a "global mark," must have a purpose beyond self-perpetuation. Indeed the entire essay moves confidently between the language of imperialism and that of empire. "Speak Victorian, Think Pagan," is Kaplan's last rule for supremacy. Americans are "idealistic by nature," but the need for security requires a touch of the pagan. This is no cause for concern. "By sustaining ourselves first, we will be able to do the world the most good." [34] In a somewhat different idiom but with the same sense of satisfaction, the prominent journalist Whitelaw Reid reflected on the happy consonance of "Duty" and "Interest" in U.S. foreign policy initiatives of the 1890s.

Kaplan, like many others including the president, has found in the U.S. suppression of the movement for independence in the Philippines a suitable model for contemporary U.S. behavior. Rule 7 reads: "Remember the Philippines," by which Kaplan means the free hand allowed midlevel commanders in the field. Directing small, mobile units, these men became "policymakers in their own patch of jungle," exploiting ethnic divisions, interrogating captured guerrillas, understanding that good intentions must be laid aside in favor of the central task: eliminating the guerrillas. [35] Presumably his approval would extend to the behavior of General Jacob Smith, who had learned how to fight "savages" at Wounded Knee, and ordered his troops to kill every male over the age of ten and turn the province of Samar into a "howling wilderness."

In an address before the Philippine National Congress, Bush also appealed to the Philippines, though his version of history would have had difficulty passing muster in 1898, when debate raged in the United

States over the annexation of the Philippines. "America," declared the president, "is proud of its part in the great story of the Filipino people. Together our soldiers liberated the Philippines from colonial rule." No mention of the Filipino resistance to this liberation, which took the form of an American military occupation, mostly engaged in suppressing the insurgency. Critics of his Iraq policy, Bush observed, were skeptical about the possibility of establishing democracy in Iraq as once they had been skeptical about "the culture of Asia." David Sanger wrote in the *New York Times* that the comparison was not entirely reassuring since "the Philippine government did not gain full autonomy for five decades." Sanger could have added that even after gaining independence in 1946, the Philippines fell considerably short of democracy.

Those who have embraced the idea of American empire are impatient with former allies who find it unattractive. The tension between Europe and the United States, Robert Kagan, senior associate at the Carnegie Endowment for International Peace, argues, "is not a George Bush problem. It is a power problem. American military strength has produced a propensity to use that strength. Europe's military weakness has produced a perfectly understandable aversion to the exercise of military power." Kagan is forgiving of the Europeans. In contrast to the standard view that the United States operates in a transcendant ahistoric realm, he sees an America "mired in history," living and struggling in a Hobbesian jungle so that Europeans may lead a privileged life of "laws and rules and transnational negotiation and cooperation." To the extent that law regulates international behavior, it is because "a power like the United States defends it by force of arms." However, in order to do so, the U.S. "must refuse to abide by certain international conventions that may constrain its ability to fight . . ." A contradiction only if one fails to believe this double standard "may be the best means of advancing human progress—and perhaps the only means."[36]

More recently, Kagan's confidence in the capacity of the United

States to keep fighting in the Hobbesian jungle has begun to flag. It is time, he wrote in a recent op-ed piece for the *New York Times,* that the United States paid attention to the problem of its waning international legitimacy. The absence of legitimacy threatens to be "debilitating, even paralyzing." Among other things it raises the most fundamental questions of identity at home and abroad. "There can be no clear dividing line between the domestic and the foreign . . . and no clear distinction between what the democratic world thinks about America and what Americans think about themselves." How can legitimacy be restored? In sentences that appear entirely reasonable and rational, Kagan urges compromise. America must grant Europeans "some influence over the exercise of American power—if, that is, the Europeans in turn will wield that influence wisely." Let's look at the sentence again, for it seems to me to embody the deep unreason of empire: America must grant Europeans "some influence over the exercise of American power—if, that is, the Europeans in turn will wield that influence wisely." The assertion of American power remains absolute in this formulation.[37]

Michael Mann, Michael Walzer, and other commentators on the current state of the American empire argue that its flaws and weaknesses will ultimately doom it. I think they are right in the medium to long run. What they miss is the damage done along the way. J.M. Coetzee captures the inside of imperialism, its linguistic soul, best: In his novel, *Waiting for the Barbarians,* he writes:

> Empire dooms itself to live in history and plot against history. One thought alone preoccupies the submerged mind of Empire: how not to end, how not to die, how to prolong its era. By day it pursues its enemies. It is cunning and ruthless, it sends its bloodhounds everywhere. By night it feeds on images of disaster: the sack of cities, the rape of populations, pyramids of bones, acres of desolation. A mad vision yet a virulent one. . . . [38]

This mad vision inhabits Bush's staccato, repetitious performance as a "war president" on *Meet the Press,* as it does the clauses of fat contracts with private military corporations and the glossy illustrated federal budget the administration has just issued. It is a vision of permanent war pursued in the name of permanent peace.

3

The Drums of War

John Prados

As this is written, the Iraq "peace" is in its third month. One hundred days after President George W. Bush declared in a speech that major combat was over, Americans are dying at a rate of one or two a day. No doubt before this text sees print the number of Americans killed since the war against the Saddam Hussein regime will exceed U.S. losses in the conflict itself. Losses are mounting among Iraqi civilians as well, though so far there is no comparison to be made with the war. International views of America are highly negative, even among the publics of countries that have traditionally been our allies. The steady denial by Bush administration figures that anything is out of whack in Iraq has given way to grudging admission that plans for the postwar reconstruction of Iraq are far from fruition and perhaps not as well-prepared as the administration first asserted. The Panglossian perspective still prevails at the White House, however, which issued a report on Iraq after a hundred days of peace that presented barely started initiatives as great progress while not even mentioning the American casualties. Among the occupation forces, military commanders have only just begun to refer to the continuing fighting as an actual guerrilla war.

The current political conversation in America is about the degree to which the Bush administration deliberately misled citizens about its reasons for wanting war with Iraq, as well as the degree to which the regime of Saddam Hussein represented a clear and present danger to the United States. This is as it should be. The United States orchestrated and carried out an aggressive war against Iraq, perhaps not out of the blue but certainly based upon the thinnest of pretexts. America has a democratic tradition, and citizens tend to remember with misgivings, or to deliberately put out of mind, such past aggressive wars as the Mexican War of 1848, the Spanish-American conflict (and resulting Philippine Insurrection) of 1898, and others like them. Under the circumstances, the heat in the political debate is a reflection of the degree to which citizens feel betrayed by their government's actions, while the Bush White House expends every effort to squirm out of the crosshairs of the political controversy.

Today's debate can be viewed in many ways, for there are multiple levels of meaning and numerous fronts on which arguments, pro and con, can be deployed. There is no way to cover all the fronts in a piece such as this one. Instead we shall try to do justice to just one facet of the Iraq debate: the Bush administration's struggle to evade accountability. We shall proceed by calling up a specter the administration has been anxious to avoid, specifically the specter of Vietnam.

There are levels at which the Vietnam analogy can be rejected in the Iraq situation. America's new cockpit of conflict is desert, the old one jungle. Iraq has oil—indeed there are those who argue the Iraq war was entirely about U.S. efforts to control oil—Vietnam had rice and little enough of that (America's ally in the Vietnam war became a net importer of rice before the conflict had ended). Military technology has evolved considerably since the Vietnam era, and that is another basis upon which to reject a comparison. But there is also a dimension of similarity between Vietnam and Iraq—a key dimension—in the methods and attitudes of the very top policymakers in the United States government. *This* is the similarity we shall explore here.

The following discussion will compare and contrast the process of involvement in Iraq with the previous experience of the Vietnam War. The focus will be on the decisions leading to war and the structuring of the situation to permit engagement in the case of Iraq. For Vietnam the focus will be on the period up through the major commitment of U.S. ground forces in July 1965. For a study of Vietnam, we benefit from a wide variety of National Security Council, Department of Defense (DOD, or Pentagon), State Department, and Central Intelligence Agency (CIA) records. For Iraq, a war conducted by an administration still in power, our history must perforce be a first rough cut, but there is enough substance already to elucidate the points we shall make. This analysis will begin with the Iraq case, and then move to the past.

First Cut on Iraq

When George W. Bush assumed office as president of the United States in January 2001, American relations with Iraq had been problematic for a decade. Almost exactly a decade before, Bush's father, George Herbert Walker Bush, had led a United Nations–sponsored coalition to free Kuwait, invaded in the summer of 1990 by Saddam Hussein's Iraq. In a matter of about five weeks in January–February 1991 Iraq was defeated by the coalition, Kuwait liberated, and the Hussein regime subjected to a stringent disarmament regime imposed by UN resolution and enforced by UN economic sanctions. Throughout the 1990s the sanctions remained, as UN weapons inspectors attempted to rid Iraq of all vestiges of the programs it had had for the development of weapons of mass destruction. The Hussein regime and the UN inspectors played a cat-and-mouse game, with Iraqis attempting to hide their technology and inspectors to find and destroy it. Large amounts of Iraqi weaponry were, in fact, destroyed, but inspectors could never be certain they had gotten everything, as the UN reported in 1995 and 1998–1999. In December 1998, amid charges that the UN weapons inspections had become a front for U.S. espionage, the Hussein regime expelled all the inspectors from Iraq.

In separate but related activity, at the end of the 1991 Gulf War the United States had issued rules prohibiting Iraqi aircraft from flying over much of the southern and northern parts of the country, originally to prevent Hussein's use of aircraft against ethnic or tribal minorities in those parts of Iraq. These so-called no-fly zones were enforced by daily patrols of U.S. and British warplanes. Iraqi air defenses that attempted to interfere with the patrols were bombed in response or retaliation, leading to a constant low-intensity air campaign that persisted throughout the decade. The United States also encouraged a (failed) revolt against Hussein by Shiite Muslims in southern Iraq immediately following the Gulf War, and carried out at least two (1992 and 1995) covert operations in support of coups and/or tribal uprisings designed to overthrow Hussein. There were also three major air attacks carried out against Iraqi targets, one in 1993 responding to an alleged attempt to assassinate former President George H.W. Bush (who was visiting Kuwait at the time), the others intended to enforce the United Nations weapons-inspection regime. Until 1998 these threats or uses of force were repeatedly successful in inducing Saddam Hussein to re-admit the UN inspectors or permit them greater freedom of action. The 1998 expulsion, however, was not reversed, and from the beginning of 1999 there were no longer foreign investigators on Iraqi soil.

Through all of this the economic sanctions against Iraq were gradually eroding. Smuggling of Iraqi oil through Jordan, Turkey, Syria, and aboard the occasional tanker earned Baghdad some cash at the margin. Charges that the sanctions hurt the Iraqi people while leaving Saddam Hussein unaffected steadily gained credibility in Europe and elsewhere. Civilian casualties and destruction wrought by retaliatory bombings in the no-fly zones weakened support within the United Nations, which had had no role in imposing the no-fly zones and where member states saw the sanctions as ineffective. This was the situation when the Bush administration took office.

One high point of George W. Bush's presidential transition came on January 10, 2001, when he went to the Pentagon to meet with the Joint Chiefs of Staff. Iraq dominated the global review the chiefs presented, with discussion on this subject taking up fully half the seventy-five minute meeting (another subject, counterproliferation, would come back into the Iraq equation as we shall see presently).[1] But after his inauguration ten days later, President Bush did not take any particularly threatening measures with regard to the Hussein regime. Instead, Secretary of State Colin Powell led on administration policy, and his effort centered upon reinvigorating the flagging international support for economic sanctions. Within weeks Powell had proposed "smart sanctions," intended to make the sanctions system have an impact on Saddam Hussein without inflicting economic distress on the Iraqi people.

From the beginning Secretary Powell faced opposition from many quarters. At the United Nations, member states who had soured on sanctions needed convincing, while the Iraqi government naturally rejected any new effort to tinker with the arrangements it had found ways to circumvent. Among Republican conservatives in Congress there were figures who wanted to hold the Bush administration to its campaign rhetoric of taking stronger action on Iraq. But most important of all were those officials in Bush's own government who advocated the overthrow of Saddam. Agitation for an overthrow had begun as early as 1992 and had continued strong during the Clinton years. The lobbying group Project for a New American Century brought together a number of these persons, and its policy papers advocated an aggressive course against Saddam. As early as 1998 there was an open letter to President Bill Clinton that demanded Hussein's ouster, signed by a number of people who went on to become foreign-policy advisors to the Bush presidential campaign and then further to become prominent in the administration. These included Secretary of Defense Donald Rumsfeld, Deputy Secretary of Defense Paul Wolfowitz, Undersecretary of State Richard Armitage, Richard Perle, vice-chairman of the Defense Policy Board, Zalmay Khalilzad, special presidential envoy to the Middle East (later ambassador to Afghanistan), and others. This group, along with their allies and promoters on the outside, have come to be called neo-conservatives, or, more commonly, "the neocons."

These individuals actively opposed the smart-sanctions idea within the councils of the administration. Some went public. Richard Perle, for example, told the Senate Foreign Relations Committee in March 2001 that "the [policy] changes that are being talked about will be no more effective than what we've had in the past." Paul Wolfowitz told his Senate confirmation hearing that if there were a "real option" to overthrow Hussein, "I would certainly think it was worthwhile." [2]

President Bush reportedly created at least three interagency groups to review Iraq policy at this stage, including one on "regime change" that corresponded to the views advanced by Wolfowitz, Perle, and their confederates. The others were to review the sanctions schemes and the no-fly zones. [3] Powell won on sanctions within the Bush administration but lost the game diplomatically—Russia, in particular, with a host of commercial contracts with the Hussein government, refused to be a party to revising UN sanctions on Iraq (in view of events less than a year later, it is worth noting that France, China, and Germany were willing to proceed with the new scheme). This situation continued essentially unchanged through the summer of 2001.

On September 11, 2001, Muslim terrorists of the group al-Qaeda, with no connection to Iraq, attacked the United States, hijacking and crashing four airliners, two of them into New York City's World Trade Center and a third into the Pentagon in Washington, D.C. Due to the Bush administration's desire to take credit for its activities in the aftermath of this tragedy, analysts benefit from journalist Bob Woodward's

book *Bush at War,* which is the result of the president ordering subordi-
nates to make themselves available for interviews and throwing open to
Woodward an array of top-secret internal records of meetings, proposals, briefings, and the like.[4] The Woodward account, plus other materials, enables us to sketch in fair detail the preparations for the war to
come, and the following text necessarily relies upon it.

George Bush held his initial national security meeting in response to
the incidents at the White House on September 12. At that meeting it
was Secretary of Defense Donald Rumsfeld who raised the question,
"Are we going to go against terrorism more broadly than al-Qaeda?"
He followed that with the suggestion of action on Iraq.[5] At Camp
David, when better-prepared meetings of the National Security Council (NSC) took place on September 15 and 16, Paul Wolfowitz joined
Rumsfeld in advocating a move on Saddam. At that time, according to
the Woodward account, Vice-President Dick Cheney opposed such a
move, while President Bush is quoted as being convinced that Iraq was
involved in the attacks but wanting to reserve action against Baghdad
for a later time.[6]

In early December 2001, however, President Bush approved a memorandum of notification to the CIA, commonly known as a "presidential finding," authorizing a covert operation aimed at Saddam Hussein
and Iraq. The CIA and the Pentagon were instructed to begin planning
action.[7] The difference between this and the September view is palpa-
ble. Interviewed later about how Iraq moved so quickly up the priorities list, the proverbial "senior administration official" told journalist
Nicolas Lemann, "That's a mystery that nobody has yet uncovered. It
clearly has something to do with September 11, and it's clearly consistent with the President's speech on weapons of mass destruction in the
hands of rogues, people with a history of some terror—but, again, how
it exactly happened, and what was the particular role of Cheney, among
others, I wish you well in uncovering."[8]

Indeed the role of Vice-President Cheney is significant. A Wyoming Republican whose first government role had been during the Nixon administration (into which he was hired by Donald Rumsfeld), Cheney had served in Rumsfeld's place in the Gulf War. He had been the Secretary of Defense in the first Bush administration. When, at the tail end of that war, the first President Bush had resisted the call to topple Saddam Hussein, Cheney had gone along with it. Ten years later, this must have rankled with him. While not usually pictured among the neocons, Cheney was certainly aligned with them. In his early months as vice-president, Cheney chaired a White House panel on energy policy for George W. Bush, and among the first struggles over government accountability in the Bush II administration would be one over releasing records from that energy-policy review. In the summer of 2003, when a tranche of the records was opened by court order, it turned out that the Cheney group's records included maps of Iraqi oilfields, documents listing Iraqi oil development programs, and other material on the Iraqi oil industry. There were no similar documents covering any other nation.[9] Vice-President Cheney was known to take a dim view of Saddam Hussein, and his refusal to take an extreme position in the immediate aftermath of September 11 may have been merely a tactical move.

In late January 2002 the Principals Committee, which constitutes the NSC meeting in the absence of the president, apparently concluded that the policy of containment of Saddam had failed, and that active measures should be taken to overthrow him.[10] At that same time, President Bush made his 2002 State of the Union address, which characterized Iraq, along with Iran and North Korea, as parts of an "Axis of Evil." The initial CIA and DOD plans for an invasion of Iraq reached Bush around mid-February. "I will reserve whatever options I have," Bush told reporters on February 12. "I'll keep them close to my vest."[11]

It was around this time that the decision for war with Iraq was made. President Bush was speaking of options close to his vest by February.

Vice-President Cheney declared in a February 19 speech at a marine air base that Iraq harbored terrorist groups and that the United States would not permit "terror states" or "their terrorist allies" to threaten the use of weapons of mass destruction. Soon thereafter, Cheney left for a visit to Europe and the Middle East intended to line up international support for overthrowing the government of Iraq. On March 19, while Cheney was on this trip, reporter Bob Woodward ran into Secretary Rumsfeld in a Pentagon corridor and found him "exuding self-confidence," almost too confident. Asked how the war—Woodward had meant Afghanistan—was going, "Rummy" had chirped, "There's the war you see and the war you don't see." [12] Meanwhile sources around the CIA had told British reporters, in reference to the possibility that Iraq could defuse American hostility by admitting a fresh mission of United Nations weapons inspectors, "They will not take 'yes' for an answer." [13]

But while Washington hatched its plans, worldwide backing for war against Iraq was impossible to find, not just in the final weeks before the war but even when the subject was first broached in early 2002. The French foreign minister—a different man from the elegant character who would be seen in the UN debates a year later—told radio interviewers about U.S. policy: "Today we are threatened by a new simplistic approach that reduces all the problems in the world to the struggle against terrorism. This is not well thought-out." [14] European Union External Affairs Minister Christopher Patten publicly opposed an Iraq war in February 2002, as did United Nations Secretary-General Kofi Annan, when accepting the Nobel Peace Prize in Oslo in December 2001. Russian President Vladimir Putin, asked in December 2001 what he expected United States might do after Afghanistan, warned against any adventures in Iraq. German officials also spoke out against the possibility of war. When Vice-President Cheney made his March 2002 visit to Europe and the Middle East, almost every leader with whom he

spoke opposed any move against Iraq. This included the leaders of
Turkey, Jordan, and Saudi Arabia. Only the British were on board. After
meeting with British Prime Minister Tony Blair on April 6, 2002,
George Bush blurted out, "I explained to the prime minister that the
policy of my government is the removal of Saddam." [15]

It is a measure of the obstinacy of President Bush and the Americans
who helped him plan the Iraq war that all these warning indicators were
ignored or treated as difficulties in communication at most. In May
2002, President Bush made his own visit to Europe, in large part to reverse the opposition to his intended course on Iraq. Such successes as he
achieved were with the former Soviet satrapies of Eastern Europe. The
major allies, France and Germany, remained unmoved, even after a Bush
speech in Berlin evoked John F. Kennedy in an earlier era. When war actually came in 2003 and Bush proved unable to secure approval by the
United Nations, the constellation of opposition would be almost identical to what it had been twelve months before. Describing overall opinion among the member states of the UN's Security Council in May
2002, a reporter wrote, "The United States is alone among the fifteen
Security Council members in leaning toward a military route." [16] American officials deliberately ignored the international diplomatic opposition to their intended course in Iraq.

To the degree that there was a basis in national security strategy for
the evolving U.S. policy on Iraq, this flowed from what analysts termed
"counterproliferation." Throughout the 1990s, as the tensions of the
Cold War receded, strategists began to construct theories of national security that made drug policy, international criminal activity, and the
spread of weapons of mass destruction—most importantly nuclear
weapons—their centerpieces. Proliferation was the conventional term
for the spread of nuclear weapons, so efforts to stem the tide came to be
called "counterproliferation." During the Clinton years and earlier,
counterproliferation embodied diplomatic, intelligence, and export-

control activities combined with economic incentives or sanctions. More alarmist analysts began to push for "proactive" counterprolifera- tion beginning in the mid-1990s, including on their menus such things as ballistic missile defenses or even military strikes. The foreign-policy advisors to George W. Bush's presidential campaign embraced these views, increasingly using the word "counterproliferation" to denote the most militant approaches.

Soon after September 11, Secretary Rumsfeld suggested that Presi- dent Bush insert the possibility of Iraq having weapons of mass destruc- tion into a speech he was planning, arguing this would be a rallying point for Americans. According to Bob Woodward, Bush rejected this course at the time.[17] However, on April 17, 2002, Bush addressed a group of honor students at the Virginia Military Institute and began ar- ticulating his desire to move beyond traditional deterrent approaches. The president referred to "outlaw regimes" that possessed and are de- veloping chemical, biological, and nuclear weapons, asserting that "these regimes constitute an axis of evil and the world must confront them."[18] Then, shortly after returning from his European trip, President Bush gave a speech at the U.S. Military Academy at West Point. Speak- ing on June 1, the president spoke of a strategy of preemptive action against threatening states, to "confront the worst threats before they emerge," as Bush put it. The president presented much the same speech before a group of active military persons at Fort Drum, New York, on July 19. This preemptive war doctrine would be formalized in a national security strategy document the administration would issue in early Sep- tember, and reiterated in another paper released in December 2002. The strategy formalized a concept of attacking first, exercising what the military mavens call "full-spectrum military dominance." By using the term "preemptive defense," administration spin doctors were deliber- ately attempting to evoke the traditional sense of preemption, which re- ferred to the act of responding to an attack by striking back just before the enemy's strike hits. As Iraq would show, the new meaning of pre-emption is "unprovoked, aggressive attack."

The Bush speeches were the portion of policy that Americans saw. What they could not see were the war plans secretly being refined inside the administration. The plans were created in close coordination between the Pentagon and the U.S. military's Central Command (CENTCOM), the headquarters responsible for Iraq and South Asia. General Tommy Franks led CENTCOM and developed plans first briefed to President Bush in the late spring of 2002. Franks assembled a plan for an invasion of Iraq. This compared poorly with schemes current among the neocons outside government and within Bush's own NSC staff, where Counterterrorism Director General Wayne Downing advocated the use of small numbers of U.S. special forces, plus airpower, to make an initial penetration into Iraq in support of anti-Saddam exiles armed and trained by the CIA. The exile group, in a plan very similar to the Kennedy administration's Bay of Pigs fiasco, would presumably be joined by Iraqi citizens rising up to overthrow the dictator. The U.S. military, particularly the Joint Chiefs of Staff, had no confidence in the notion of using exiles to spearhead an uprising. On the other hand, Secretary Rumsfeld was impressed and liked the way this option used techniques that had succeeded recently in the U.S. campaign in Afghanistan. When the Franks plan was presented, Rumsfeld took the lead in complaining that it was too conventional.[19]

On June 19, just a couple of weeks after the Bush speech on preemptive war, General Franks was at the White House for a full-dress briefing of a revised war plan. The new plan continued to be rejected as flawed. Pressures were put on CENTCOM to design a war plan that might disrupt Iraqi defenses by simultaneous attacks from the west and north (coming from neutral Jordan and Turkey), not merely from Kuwait in the south, where the United States had bases and could assemble troops. General Franks traveled to Jordan in late June, immediately after the

White House discussion of his plan, and Rumsfeld and Deputy Secretary Paul Wolfowitz visited Turkey in July. There can be little doubt these visits were attempts to enlist those countries in the Iraqi invasion plan.

At the Pentagon the Joint Chiefs of Staff labored mightily against what they considered Rumsfeld's misconceptions about attacking Iraq, and achieved some success. By the end of July, the Secretary of Defense was telling a hearing of the Senate Foreign Relations Committee that airpower alone would not suffice to defeat Iraq. The Joint Chiefs themselves compromised somewhat in encouraging CENTCOM to come up with a "light" invasion option that utilized fewer troops and could presumably be executed more quickly. The revised plan also became necessary once it was clear that neither Jordan nor Turkey had any interest in participating in a U.S. invasion of Iraq. President Bush convened the NSC to consider the latest plan on August 5. The senior leadership all favored invasion, with the exception of Secretary Powell, who warned President Bush against any effort to attack unilaterally.

Unaware of nuances or details, the public did perceive the trend of policy from the stream of denunciations of Iraq that kept coming from U.S. officials. There were also news leaks regarding planning for war against Baghdad. By August there was such concern among the public, including political leaders, former officials (both Republican and Democrat), and opinion-makers, that vocal opposition to any war with Iraq grew dramatically. President Bush acted to counteract this criticism, declaring in remarks at a Mississippi school he visited on August 6 that "We owe it to our children to deal with these threats." [20]

From August 2002 through the onset of the Iraqi war on March 19, 2003, the entire course of events with regard to Iraq consisted of the process of President Bush making feasible the decisions made during the earlier period. A characteristic pattern of action emerged: each time diplomatic obstacles, domestic or world public opinion, or internal difficulties within the military surfaced, Bush would make conciliatory gestures and appear to back away from his course, pocket concessions made by others as a result, and then proceed with his preparations out of public view. In August, Bush responded to the great revolt of opinion-makers by asserting that war was a last resort. In response to protests against administration claims that the president had inherent authority to order the war, Bush promised to seek congressional approval. Criticisms of his unilateral action similarly led Bush to promise he would seek United Nations approval.

On September 12, President Bush addressed the General Assembly of the UN and asked for a resolution that would mandate yet another weapons inspection of Iraq, but that would additionally authorize members to use force if Saddam failed to comply. Bush could not obtain a UN resolution on those terms and had to settle for a formula that required further consideration by the UN Security Council in the event of a breach. The U.S. put immense pressure on UN weapons inspectors to report to the Security Council in terms favorable to the American construction of events, and when that failed, made its own claims of Iraqi activity as a means of justifying a second request for a UN resolution authorizing war. In February and March 2003, the U.S. failed to obtain the second resolution, which was opposed by many of the same nations that had warned the Americans against the war the year before. The Americans proceeded to war anyway.

Through September and October, a major political debate took place in the United States over allegations of an Iraqi threat and the alleged need for immediate action to disarm Baghdad. President Bush began to make claims about Iraqi possession of weapons of mass destruction, and administration officials played the same keys in their public statements. This occurred in the Bush United Nations speech and in a speech he gave in Cincinnati just as Congress was considering a resolution that would grant the president the power to go to war without further Con-

gressional approval.[21] The CIA put out a report to the Congress sub-
stantiating claims made by the president, supposedly based upon its best
intelligence estimate but artfully contrived in a number of ways. Congress gave Bush his resolution and the administration never looked
back.

Public opinion rose mightily in the form of protests and marches in
cities, towns, and schools all over the world. There were major waves of
protest in October, December, January 2003, February, then March. On
one memorable weekend, more than eleven million demonstrators
filled the streets in ninety cities worldwide. Cities all over the United
States passed official resolutions condemning the war that had not yet
happened in their effort to turn Bush aside. There was massive public
criticism of administration plans for the war, and for postwar Iraq. The
administration response was to claim repeatedly that it had prepared
fully for all eventualities, and Bush personally assured the world on numerous occasions that war was not his desire and was necessary only to
enforce UN mandates if Iraq did not disarm. President Bush then
launched the war after the UN inspectors reported they could not find
Iraqi arms to speak of, and after it became apparent that Security Council views of a resolution authorizing a war were so negative that the
United States abandoned the very idea of seeking such an authority.

On the military side, President Bush placated the Joint Chiefs of Staff
by encouraging Secretary Rumsfeld to modify the war plans to provide
a more robust force for the invasion of Iraq. Rumsfeld sanctioned an increase in the field army involved to roughly 140,000 ground troops,
while rejecting and even ridiculing the public comment of army Chief
of Staff General Eric Shinseki that a force of up to 300,000 would be
necessary to occupy Iraq even after a successful war. The Joint Chiefs
also warned of the untenability of the feature of the plan that required
dispatch of major U.S. forces through Turkey, but Rumsfeld insisted
upon preserving that portion of the operation, which led to a huge

diplomatic and military fiasco in the war. Once war came, Rumsfeld's light force proved adequate to defeat a decrepit Iraqi military, but woefully understaffed for the subsequent occupation.

In summary, President George W. Bush was far from ignorant. The obstacles to war with Iraq at the international level were apparent long in advance. Flaws in war plans were pointed out in good time by U.S. military officers, as were the dangers in the postwar occupation (NSC officials from the White House actually bragged about how well they had prepared for an occupation of Iraq). Political opposition to Bush's desired course was obvious. The president proceeded purposefully, carefully structured the evolving situation to provide the option he desired, and then ordered the war and subsequent occupation of Iraq. All of this shows startling similarities to the process of U.S. involvement in the Vietnam War, as we shall now see.

Marching into a Quagmire

Where Iraq has been a conventional war that is becoming a guerrilla conflict, Vietnam started as a guerrilla war and went conventional later. In this respect the two conflicts are different. Presidents John F. Kennedy and Lyndon B. Johnson presided over the most intense phase of commitment, during which the United States went from an ally associated with the government of South Vietnam to the leading partner in a full-scale (though, to the United States, limited) war. From 1961 through the end of 1965 the number of American troops in South Vietnam went from 685 to 184,300. Casualties rose from zero to dozens per week. Fighting became generalized. How did American leaders and their senior advisors conduct themselves in making the decisions that led to this situation?

President Kennedy followed his instincts on Vietnam. His predecessor, Dwight D. Eisenhower, had warned Kennedy coming into office that the biggest problem was with the neighboring nation of Laos, a landlocked country in the middle of Southeast Asia. Kennedy felt it made no sense to fight a major war in Laos, where troops could hardly be supplied or supported. In South Vietnam, the southern rump of what had been part of the state of Vietnam associated with France, at least there were ports, cities, roads, and a large local military. But Vietnam was already threatened by a guerrilla adversary. Kennedy looked to his military leaders for ideas. Secretary of Defense Robert McNamara, in a reflection many years later, writes of Kennedy's assumption of office: "Within a few weeks it became evident that trouble was developing . . . faster than we had anticipated."[22]

President Kennedy swiftly ordered a policy review, led by McNamara's deputy, Roswell Gilpatric, which came up with a menu of over forty actions the United States could take to augment South Vietnamese capabilities. Kennedy chose cautiously, approving an increase of 100 advisers plus 400 special forces troops plus other measures. Increases in funding for the South Vietnamese army permitted Saigon to increase the size of its military. Before 1961 was out, the exercise had to be repeated again, with Kennedy sending his Deputy National Security Adviser, Walt Rostow, and his personal military representative, General Maxwell Taylor, to do a survey mission on the ground. The Taylor-Rostow Report of November 1961, contained a fresh menu of options that included sending American combat troops to Vietnam. By his account, McNamara initially supported the recommendations, then became more impressed with the complexities of the situation and sided with Secretary of State Dean Rusk in opposing the dispatch of combat troops. Kennedy again chose cautiously, ruling out combat troops while approving many other aid measures.[23]

President Kennedy's actions of 1961 set the pattern for many subsequent American decisions in the Vietnam War. Options always came to the NSC from field commanders, the U.S. ambassador, the Washington bureaucracy. Presidents listened to the discussion at the National Security Council and consulted their security advisors and NSC staff privately. The options always ranged between the unattainable and the unacceptable, with something thrown into the middle. The president consistently selected a moderate course, but every time there had to be a choice, the stake in Vietnam grew ever so slightly. Thus, from 1961 to 1963, without ever choosing a maximum option, President Kennedy committed over 16,000 American troops in South Vietnam, sent constituted combat units (of air, combat support, intelligence troops, and special forces), had Americans directly engaged in combat with the adversary (by bombing and in covert operations), and almost doubled the size of the South Vietnamese army.[24] By November 1963, when the United States assumed an even greater responsibility for the Vietnam War by collaborating in a South Vietnamese military coup that overthrew the dictator Ngo Dinh Diem, there had been seventy-eight Americans killed in action in Vietnam.

All of this occurred without much questioning of the basic commitment. In a celebrated incident in 1961 and 1962, the economist John Kenneth Galbraith, a JFK friend who served the president as ambassador to India, wrote Kennedy a letter advising that more U.S. troops would solve nothing, that only changing the South Vietnamese leadership could accomplish anything, ultimately questioning the U.S. commitment. Kennedy's advisors, from McNamara and Rusk to Walt Rostow, General Taylor, and National Security Advisor McGeorge Bundy, uniformly rejected the advice. The president's men had an assured, can-do attitude, they knew the answers, they were, in the words of author David Halberstam, the best and the brightest.[25]

President Lyndon B. Johnson made the series of decisions that actually brought Americans to a shooting war in Southeast Asia, culminating in July 1965, when he commanded huge increases in the number of U.S. troops in South Vietnam and freed them to engage in offensive combat operations. As with Kennedy, LBJ had someone to whisper caution in his ear, in the form of Undersecretary of State George Ball. As with Galbraith, the president's advisors joined ranks to dismiss the alternative views that went against the course they wished to adopt. McNamara, Rusk, and Bundy went to the length of together crafting a joint memorandum to President Johnson intended to refute a lengthy dissent paper Ball had sent to LBJ. Bundy also separately wrote a nine-page exegesis of the Ball paper for LBJ. The memorandum reads even more ominously today, in the light of the decisions made in Iraq, for it illustrates the impact one can-do presidential advisor had, through his simple denial of the historical and political points Ball had made in his memorandum. Bundy rejected Ball's argument that the United States in Vietnam would replicate the experience of the former colonial power, France. Instead, Bundy maintained, France had sought to fight for colonial rule using conventional military tactics, where the United States had no such interests and its forces would be a source of stability and strength. Bundy denied the point that a war would engender significant domestic opposition leading to political instability. And in conclusion, the National Security Advisor asserted that the United States had options now that had not been available before.[26] President Johnson accepted Bundy's reasoning, not Ball's. The United States went on to be defeated in Vietnam in exactly the way George Ball had foreseen. When the United States withdrew under a ceasefire agreement signed in Paris in January 1973, there had been 58,191 Americans killed in Vietnam (of which roughly 10,000 were nonbattle deaths).

Of course the process of engagement in the Vietnam War has a much lengthier history than outlined above. There were numerous policy reviews, constant survey visits to South Vietnam along the lines of the Taylor-Rostow mission, national security directives, meetings, and memoranda. The declassified record permits recounting this process at any desired level of detail. Our aim here is a comparison to Iraq, however, and this outline is sufficient for that purpose. In the Iraq case there is certainly a similar collection of materials, though one that will be held secret for as long as the current incumbent of the presidency can contrive to do so. To return to the Ball paper and the Bundy memorandum, these contain the essence of a truth for history: the dangers of the war, and of the United States' style for managing that war, were *specifically* foreseen *before* the major troop commitment.[27] That was not only true inside the Kennedy and Johnson administrations. Outside the government, those members of the attentive public alert to the dangers of deeper involvement had issued similar warnings. In the Iraq case, as has already been seen, this is true in spades.

The Best and the Brightest

In his reflection on Vietnam, Robert McNamara confesses: "Over and over again . . . we failed to address fundamental issues; our failure to recognize them was not recognized; and deep seated disagreements among the president's advisers about how to proceed were neither surfaced nor resolved."[28] The day that the inside accounts and the declassified documents of the Bush administration become available, I submit that McNamara's description of the Vietnam policy morass will be seen to apply precisely to the Iraq case as well. And in much the same way that Washington's collaboration in the overthrow of Ngo Dinh Diem made the Vietnam quagmire inescapable, the American capture of Baghdad in April 2003 did the same for the Iraqi imbroglio. This is where the Iraqi war cements its parallel to Vietnam. The question in both these American tragedies is why.

For Vietnam, Robert McNamara proposes some reasons. He maintains that Washington lacked the necessary experts on the local situation, that senior officials had to deal with Vietnam alongside all their other business, forcing them to divide their attention among a host of other vital issues. The first argument is simply not true; the second is a truism, as accurate for Iraq as for the Vietnam War. McNamara adduces a number of other explanations, including misjudging adversary intentions, the South Vietnamese allies, and the power of nationalism; failing to recognize the limitations of modern, high-technology weaponry; failure to draw Congress and the American people into "a full and frank discussion and debate of the pros and cons of a large-scale U.S. military involvement"; unanticipated events that changed the course of action; failure to seek multinational support; failure "to recognize that in international affairs, as in other aspects of life, there may be problems for which there are no immediate solutions"; and not recognizing that "neither our people nor our leaders are omniscient. . . . We do not have the God-given right to shape every nation in our own image or as we choose."[29]

Almost every one of these explanations can be applied to the Iraq case. There is no evidence that Saddam Hussein intended to attack the United States. Bush administration authorities misjudged the response of the Iraqi people to an American conquest. Iraqi nationalism and ethnic and religious issues played differently than anticipated by Bush administration officials. The effect of the "shock and awe" Bush commanders expected from their weapons did not deter people from using their simple rifles to oppose America. President Bush deliberately attempted to avoid insofar as possible any "great debate" on attacking Iraq, hiding estimates of forces, costs, and international support behind platitudes. Obviously there have been unanticipated events that have changed the course of the occupation. And most clearly, the Bush people went into Iraq with the specific intention of remaking that country along lines they had selected.

These propositions fit Iraq very well, but they are largely second-order explanations. *Why* is still the question. The answer lies in President Bush, Vice-President Cheney, and the people around them. They, too, assumed themselves to be "the best and the brightest." *They* had the answer to terrorism—make an example of some other country. *They* knew how to solve the Palestinian problem—start a democratic revolution in Iraq. The ideological blinders were on tight, not only did the neocons refuse to deal with any objections to their intended course, but administration officials and their political allies often responded to questions raised about their course by impugning the patriotism or motives of the questioner. They knew how to fight a "light" war, and how to conduct an occupation of Iraq; they had foreseen everything. Except that they had not. Just like Vietnam. These were proud, arrogant men and women. The quandaries George W. Bush faces in Iraq today are purely of his own making.

CHANGED RELATIONSHIPS

4

American Hegemony and
European Autonomy, 1989–2003:
One Framework for Understanding the War in Iraq

Thomas McCormick

Things fall apart; the centre cannot hold.

—W.B. Yeats,
"The Second Coming"

This was an attack on Europe, and that is why Europe responded the way it did.[1]
—Immanuel Wallerstein

The 2003 American war on Iraq was also, in part, an indirect war on the European Union. That latter conflict was, in turn, the result of an extraordinary paradox that has characterized American foreign policy since the end of the Cold War—the paradox of unparalleled American power and diminished American hegemony.[2]

Certainly, America's preponderance of power has never been more overwhelming—indeed, it is a hyperpower, to use the French designation. Particularly awesome is its military might. It possesses, after all, a military budget bigger than its next eight nearest competitors combined and holds a technological advantage in weaponry, logistics, and communications that seems unchallengeable for the foreseeable future. Likewise, American economic strength, while lacking the awesome dominance it enjoyed in the golden age of the 1950s and 1960s, still functions as the most important economic locomotive for the global economy, providing other nations with a vast, lucrative market in which to sell their goods and invest their money. As the world's only super-power—perhaps the greatest in history—the United States is able to treat any probable enemy with near impunity.

Hegemony, on the other hand, is not about the power to vanquish one's enemies but about the ability to translate that power into influence over friends and allies. It means being able to manage them in a manner that persuades them to defer to the hegemon's global leadership and accept its rules for the international game, even at some expense to their own sovereignty and autonomy. To achieve that kind of hegemonic relationship would require the dominant power to make a tacit social compact with its friends and allies, promising that it will provide them with greater peace and prosperity than they could otherwise achieve by acting unilaterally in their own behalf. Meeting the promise of greater security would require a system of military alliances and the capability to honor them. Meeting the promise of larger material rewards would require it to serve two masters—both its national economic interests and that of the global economy. Given the dominance of its economy, the construction of an open-door free world would benefit its interests the most, since its goods and capital would fare well competing in a global market where goods, services, capital, and technology were relatively free to move. But it would also have to persuade its allies that such a free world system (which we now call "globalization") would benefit them as well. Since some of its allies might be skeptical of the free-trade ideology that a rising tide lifts all ships, and since the invisible hand of the global market does not always work as perfectly as that ideology would imply, the hegemon would also have to supplement its system with a willingness to provide so-called public goods in a pinch. By public goods, one means such items as "a market for distress goods, a steady if not countercyclical flow of capital" and "liquidity when the monetary system is frozen in panic." As the late Charles Kindleberger put it: "For the world to be stable, it needs a stabilizer."[3]

In the aftermath of World War II, the United States made just such a social compact with Western Europe. Its essence was indeed an exchange of European deference for American delivery of peace and security. To be sure, there were limits on American hegemony, and beneath European deference, there always existed a kind of suppressed urge for autonomy based on Europe's sense that its culture, its form of capitalism, and at times its self-interests were not identical to America's. Of course, this was less true of Britain, whose "special relationship" often made the British seem more American than European, but it certainly was true of much of continental Europe (on which this essay will focus). Nonetheless, despite occasional episodes like France's departure from NATO in 1966, continental Europe generally followed wherever America led. And it did so because America's nuclear shield and America's promotion of global economic expansion enabled it to deliver on its promissory notes of peace and prosperity to a continent that had known neither for four decades.

From the early 1970s onward, however, the social compact between the United States and Europe began to erode. The issue of European security seemed less pressing as the Cold War gave way to détente and Western Europe began to calculate that entente with the Soviet half of Europe was less costly and risky, and potentially more enduring, than the Cold War had been. And even the revival of that Cold War in the late 1970s and early 1980s proved too ephemeral to alter that calculation. Likewise, the two decades between 1973 and 1993 were to see the prior golden age of capitalism give way to declining productivity and a global economic slowdown, especially in Europe and America, that some have termed the "Quiet Depression." Without an expanding pie to divide, each sought to take unilateral actions to cut a larger slice for itself, producing a kind of low-intensity economic war that flared on and off. The United States retreated from its historic, hegemonic responsibility to provide a stressed global market with the necessary "public goods" of a stable exchange-rate system and steady, countercyclical lending. Europe, for its part, attacked the overvalued American dollar and, at the same time, began the first halting moves toward the 1992 Maastricht Treaty that would create the European Union, lay out the roadmap to a common Euro currency, and establish its long-term goals of economic parity with the United States and the capacity to act with a more unified voice in matters of foreign policy and security.

This essay will focus on the erosion of America's social compact with Europe. It will posit that the end of the Cold War and the collapse of the Soviet Union tended to accelerate that erosion, and will argue, nonetheless, that the United States made a concerted effort in the 1990s to reverse that trend and to restore America's hegemonic leadership and Europe's deference toward it. America's strategy was the traditional one: demonstrating to Europe that acquiescence in American leadership was essential for both its security and its prosperity. Cognizant of Europe's heavy dependence on Persian Gulf oil, the United States emphasized its crucial role as stabilizing protector of that region—not only in the Gulf War of 1991, but also in the low-intensity war of sanctions and no-fly zones against Iraq that followed in the 1990s. More important than military power, however, was economic might. Both the administration of George Bush and the first administration of William Clinton sought to derail any autonomous European trade bloc by trying to demonstrate, with considerable success, that the market forces of globalization, protected by American open-door rules of the game and driven by the American high-tech economy, would renew global growth, revive the Euro-American social compact, and give the EU greater material rewards than they could garner from semi-autarkic regionalism.

This essay will then argue, however, that such success was ephemeral, especially in the economic sphere; that it began to wither in the face of the widespread backlash against globalization, Japan's deflation after 1997, the Asian financial crises of 1997–1998, the collapse of the American technology bubble, and a return in the United States and especially Europe to the flat economic growth pattern of the 1970s and 1980s. In that context, the second Clinton administration moved away from its primary emphasis on economic strategy and looked to its military power to cement a division-of-labor that would insure European dependence on and deference to the United States. Resuscitating NATO through expansion into Eastern Europe and broadening its mandate to act "out-of-theater" beyond NATO's borders, the United States attempted to make clear to Europe that an autonomous voice in security matters (and by extension, foreign policy) was impossible without the coordinated help of American air power, logistics, and high-tech communications.

The 9/11 terror attacks on America in 2001 offered the new administration of George W. Bush an opportunity to continue that existing policy of using NATO to co-opt Europe and, by so doing, secure both Europe's help and its renewed obeisance. It chose not to do so. Instead, it said "Thanks, but no thanks" to NATO's historic invocation of Article V and its implicit offer of European help, proceeding instead to make both the Afghanistan War of 2001–2002 and the Iraq war of 2003 into unilateral American undertakings, welcoming only a measure of support from Uncle Sam's British cousin. Indeed, the Bush administration sanctified its choice by adopting the so-called Bush Doctrine that arrogated to itself the right to identify threats to global well-being and the right to act preemptively against such threats as it saw fit. Corollary to that right of preemption was the tacit abandonment of permanent entangling alliances like NATO in favor of a more pragmatic approach creating ad hoc "coalitions of the willing," in or out of NATO, at America's discretion. In sum, instead of restoring its hegemonic relationship to Europe through a co-opted NATO that would be its partner in the War on Terrorism, the Bush administration tried to marginalize it in a divide-and-conquer policy of playing "New Europe" (especially the new NATO members from Eastern Europe) off against the "Old Europe" led by France and Germany.

Why the shift in U.S. policy toward Europe? And what role was the 2003 Iraq War designed to play in that shift? In the absence of firm archival evidence, no definitive explanation is possible and speculation is necessarily the order of the day. But some hypotheses can at least be entertained, and the final part of this essay will advance a number of them for consideration, some contradictory, some not. First, the Bush administration, especially its neoconservative elements, may have regarded Europe as a null and void factor in their run-up to the Iraq war. Less respectful and fearful of Europe than the Clinton administration had been, it took European support of its Iraq policy for granted; and when that support proved not to be there, it launched a crude, heavy-handed, balance-of-power effort to divide so-called Old Europe from New Europe. Second, and perhaps at odds with the first, the Iraq war was designed to neutralize EU policies in the Middle East—policies that had come to be viewed as serious obstacles to the success of America's own policies in the region, especially by neoconservative "transformationists" who sought a grandiose new order for the region. Third, and as a consequence of the first, the war on Iraq was to give America the vital leverage in the oil-rich region to roll back the French-led EU drive for an autonomous military and foreign policy, thus restoring European legitimization of American hegemony. And the Franco-German effort to derail that war and place some limits on the exercise of American power resulted, in part, from their understanding of American purposes. Finally, and perhaps subsuming all the rest, the Iraq war signaled that the United States had abandoned hegemony as it had been practiced since the end of World War II—that is, as a reciprocal social contract some now call "stakeholder hegemony."[4] Instead, it sought to replace it with a more unilateral mode that accepted the contraction of globalization and economic multilateralism, and which saw its military superiority as the only remaining basis for its global leadership.

Life after the Cold War:
Challenges to American Hegemony

Contrary to conventional wisdom, the Cold War's demise and Soviet collapse made the task of hegemonic revival even more difficult. To be sure, America's much-trumpeted, new-found status as sole superpower emancipated American military power from any shackles, like Prometheus unbound. But the Cold War's demise also released a horde of destabilizing, centrifugal forces that the conflict had held in check. After all, for all its seeming chaos and quite real dangers, the Cold War—especially after the Cuban Missile Crisis—had evolved into a reasonably stable, symbiotic system (the "imaginary war" as Mary Kaldor termed it) in which each superpower, in tacit complicity, manipulated the fear of "The Other" to maintain hegemony over their Third World client-states as well as their allies and/or satellites in NATO and the Warsaw Pact.[5] The end of the Cold War, however, coupled with the collapse of the Soviet Empire, significantly diminished that control and introduced a new era of instability and volatility.

First and foremost, the new era deprived the United States of a single and identifiable enemy (Communism), whose apparent and continuous threat could be used by American policymakers to mould foreign-policy support at home and provide the crucial lever for hegemony abroad—the need for other nations, like its European allies, to accept American rules of the game in exchange for protection against alleged Communist threats. In the post–Cold War period, however, every new foreign policy initiative had to be justified by an ad hoc rationale, each having to be sold anew as credible and legitimate to both American citizens and American allies—for example, drug trafficking, rogue dictatorship, famine, warlordism, ethnic cleansing, and genocide. Not until the attacks on September 11, 2001, did the war on terrorism seem to provide the U.S. government with a "one-size-fits-all" rationale that could be used in almost all times and places to justify America's primacy in global affairs. And as it turned out, this rationale was far more readily accepted at home than it was abroad.

In the meantime, the unstable decade that preceded 9/11 saw a number of new threats raise their frightening heads. Among them was China's emergence as an economic powerhouse in Asia with ambitions of regional hegemony in the Pacific Rim. So too were the regional adventures of former Soviet allies no longer constrained by conservative Soviet instincts—dramatized most vividly by the Iraqi effort to project its power into the oil-rich Persian Gulf in the Kuwait invasion, and by the North Korean efforts to develop missile and nuclear programs. Similarly, the disintegration of the Soviet Union, already preceded by its military defeat in Afghanistan, produced a band of independent but unstable new governments in Central Asia that, in turn, fueled the centrifugal forces of tribalism, ethnicity, religion, and nationalism—all this in proximity to the new oil and gas fields and pipelines being developed in and around the Caucasus/Caspian Sea area. Finally, the triumphant sweep of globalization, characterized by a free flow of goods, capital, services, people, culture, and ideology, showed strong signs that it had reached its limits and created its own antiglobalization backlash—both because the economic fruits of globalization were not shared equitably, thus creating losers as well as winners, and because its homogenizing, secularizing effects threatened traditional cultures and religions. Nowhere was this more dramatically apparent than in the wave of Islamic militancy that swept in an arc from West Africa to Indonesia.

Eclipsing those problems, however, was the challenge of Europe embodied in the Maastricht Treaty of 1992, which subsumed the former European Economic Community (EEC) into a much larger and bolder enterprise now called the European Union. In the economic sphere, the European Community (EC), as the EEC was now renamed, vastly broadened its goals to include a common currency (what became the Euro) and a more fully integrated common market, not only for trade, but eventually for finance, mergers, competition policies, labor migration, and the like. In the political sphere, the European Union created new transnational political institutions like the Council of Ministers and the European Commission, to advance the goals of a common security and foreign policy. These developments, while still in their embryonic stages, presented the United States with an immense challenge. Could it keep this European Union firmly coupled to the United States—that is, committed to the American-led NATO alliance and to an American-led globalized market? If it could, then the preconditions for American hegemony would still remain in play. If not, the United States could eventually face a relatively autonomous European competitor, politically as well as economically, that stretched from the British Isles to the Ural Mountains. The prospect of a Europe dominated by a single power, be it Germany or the Soviet Union, had always been America's worst nightmare in the twentieth century. So even the phenomenon of the European Union, while still a problematic work-in-progress, had to be immediately countered, contained, and channeled in ways acceptable to the United States.

Countering the European Challenge, 1989–1997

In confronting that task, both the administration of George Bush and the first administration of Bill Clinton pursued two strands in their effort to translate Cold War victory into sustainable hegemony over Western Europe. The first was political-military and centered on Iraq and on the Balkans. During the post–Gulf War period of 1991–1998, the Bush and Clinton administrations followed a consistent policy toward Iraq, which was simultaneously a de facto policy toward Europe as well. On one hand, they sought to maintain Iraq's boundaries intact and sustain the authority of the central government in Baghdad. To be sure, they would have preferred that central government have someone other

than Saddam Hussein at its head, since he had proved to be too unpredictable to be controllable. But the Baathist regime itself had the twin
advantages of being a secular government in a sea of religious ones like
those in Iran and Saudi Arabia, and of maintaining order, however brutally, in a country otherwise divided by ethnic and religious loyalties.
Without a stable, central regime, American leaders feared that the country would degenerate into civil war (like Yugoslavia had) and become
weak, inviting prey for interference or even intervention by neighboring countries. That fear, compellingly articulated by Colin Powell in
1991 when he was Chairman of the Joint Chiefs of Staff, was the principal reason why the Bush administration did not take the Gulf War to
Baghdad after vanquishing the Iraqi army in Kuwait. As a consequence,
American policy after 1991 sought to contain the Baathist regime in the
Persian Gulf without bringing it down, while hoping that an internal
coup would put someone more acceptable than Saddam Hussein at its
head. To those ends, the United States, aided by Great Britain, conducted a low-intensity war consisting of economic sanctions, UN inspections for weapons of mass destruction, a heavily patrolled no-fly
zone in northern and southern Iraq, and periodic bombings to degrade
the Iraqi military, especially its radar and communications divisions.
Aside from weakening Iraq while keeping its government intact, this
"containment" policy had the added virtue of giving the United States
the excuse and opportunity to maintain a permanent military presence
in the Persian Gulf. Just as the Gulf War itself had been a "resource war"
to remind Europe that it still needed America to maintain access to
global raw materials in a post–Cold War world, so the low-intensity war
on Iraq acted as a continuing reminder to EU nations (and Japan) that
they still needed American protection to maintain the stability of the
Persian Gulf region and its oil production, on which they depended.
And needing American protection meant they still needed to maintain
their deference to American hegemonic leadership in global affairs.

The Balkan crisis provided the other political-military opportunity to bind Europe more closely to America. Like the Soviet Union, Yugoslavia began to disintegrate into multiple nations based largely on ethnicity and religion. The process was a violent one, producing a series of civil wars that shook the Balkans throughout the 1990s, beginning with the Slovenian and Croatian secession in 1991, followed by the Bosnian secession in 1992. While American policy early on was largely passive, in principle it favored maintaining the territorial and administrative integrity of Serbian-dominated Yugoslavia—out of the same fear of instability that had prompted it to dread the break-up of the USSR. But the European Union, led by Germany, undercut that policy by recognizing the independence of both Slovenia and Croatia in 1992, leaving the United States watching on the sidelines. The Bosnian crisis of 1992–1995, however, proved too bloody, too complex, and too intractable for either the EU or the UN to resolve. As such, it offered the new Clinton administration the chance in 1995 to kill two birds with one stone—for starters, to overcome the legacy of its disastrous 1993 intervention in Somalia, which had left the American public reluctant to support military ventures abroad; and moreover, to give the European Union a graphic demonstration that military and diplomatic successes were possible only when undertaken with America and under its aegis, not on their own.

First, the United States led NATO in launching an air war on Serbian positions in Bosnia; indeed, more than two-thirds of the air strikes were American. Second, the successful air war produced a diplomatic settlement that was hosted and brokered by the United States—appropriately, in Dayton, Ohio, where the narrative of American air power had begun nearly a century earlier in the Wright brothers' shop. Finally, in implementing the Dayton Accords, the United States made itself an integral part of the multinational force that was to maintain the problematic peace, contributing a third of the 60,000 troops involved.

The American government also pursued a second strand—an economic strategy—in its effort to keep the European Union firmly coupled to American leadership. That strategy, more vigorously pursued than the military one, had two main elements—a regional "stick" and a global "carrot." NAFTA (the North American Free Trade Agreement) was the major component of the regional, coercive element. While its purposes were many, a major one was to counter the European common market by using NAFTA as a bargaining chip (a "stick") to insure that the European Union would forgo any autarkic tendencies and remain integrated into a multilateral global market. The move to NAFTA began during the last year of the Reagan presidency with the signing of a free trade agreement with Canada; and it climaxed in 1994 when NAFTA's birth included Mexico in the arrangement. Explicit in NAFTA's formation was the long-term goal of broadening it to include the whole western hemisphere. Arguably, this regional expansion of the U.S. market gave America more clout in its periodic bouts with the European Union in the 1990s over the proper rules of economic behavior governing farm subsidies, merger policies, offshore banking, and the like.

The global carrot was the other face of America's economic diplomacy—the exploiting of American financial power and market size to advance the process of globalization, demonstrating to the European Union (and others) that the flat global growth of the 1970s and 1980s was over, and that more was to be gained from an open-door world market for its trade and investment than could be realized, once more, through any autarkic organization of the European market. Two instances illustrate the American effort. One was the Clinton bailout of the Mexican economy that dramatically demonstrated America's renewing willingness to meet its hegemonic responsibility of providing "liquidity when the monetary system is frozen in panic." The second was the negotiation of a Sino-American agreement intended to pave the way for China's membership in the World Trade Organization, signaling the willingness of that giant, dynamic economy to join in and play by the rules of a multilateral, global economy. The essence of those rules, known as the Washington Consensus, was the necessity of debt reduction, balanced budgets, reduced spending, free trade, and an open door for foreign investment.

Between 1993 and 1997, this economic defense of American hegemony seemed to succeed beyond anyone's wildest expectations. The extraordinary American bull market offered foreign investors a profitable outlet for capital when such was sometimes hard to find closer to home. Similarly, America's booming consumer demand offered a market of last resort to absorb global overcapacity, helping Asia to export its way out of its late 1990s economic crisis. Moreover, its economics rules of the game—summed up in synonyms like globalization, neoliberalism, and Washington Consensus—were enshrined in almost every country and zone of the world economy. So too were the lifestyles and mass culture often associated with American consumerism. By most criteria for hegemony, America superbly fulfilled its systemic responsibilities even as it served its own national interests—market for distress goods, lender of last resort, and governor of international rules of economic behavior. Moreover, American economic supremacy and its productivity miracle suggested that it could continue to fulfill those hegemonic responsibilities ad infinitum. Presumably, an economic locomotive possessed of such enduring dynamism could pull a whole trainload of global trading partners, including the European Union, into a new era, a new economy—especially, so it was argued, if they were wise enough junk their rigid, over-regulated labor and capital markets (Europe's social capitalism) in favor of flexible, deregulated ones (American free-enterprise capitalism).

The Failure of America's Economic Response to Europe

The era of triumphant globalization proved, however, to have a short shelf life. First, NAFTA proved not to be a very useful lever in keeping the EU committed to a globalized economy; instead, it encouraged the EU (and other countries) to negotiate their own FTAs (free trade agreements) to compete with NAFTA. The consequence was a shift in world trade away from a multilateral pattern of integrated, global trade to a complex set of bilateral patterns that made trade more regionalized than global. Moreover, while NAFTA may have been meant as a parallel response to the EU, it was in fact a horse of a different color. The EU's core (e.g., Germany and France) subsidized the infrastructural development of Europe's poorer periphery (e.g., Ireland and Portugal), closing the gap between rich and poor. NAFTA did no such thing, trusting the invisible hand of the free market to do the job. Since it did not, Mexico's president, Vincente Fox, began to criticize NAFTA and urged that it be reformulated along the lines of the European common market. His criticism did nothing to make NAFTA attractive to Brazil and Argentina, the next targets of American hemispheric expansion.

Second, like the first wave of globalization at the end of the nineteenth century, the current wave created its own hostile backlash, most visibly in the surge of protests against the WTO.[6] Despite the usual free-trade promise that a rising tide lifts all ships, globalization had short-changed many of the world's economic participants. In part, the deficit was economic: the continuing gulf between rich nations and poor; the volatile capital flows and outflows that destabilized emerging markets in Asia, Latin America, and Russia; the outsourcing of jobs from G7 countries to China and the Pacific Rim; and the competition for jobs and social benefits intensified by mass migration of people from the Third World to the EU and the United States. In part, as well, the deficit was social and cultural: the impact of environmental degradation on the

lifestyle, aesthetic sensibilities, and public health; and the impact of ho-
mogenization and secularization on traditional ways of viewing and
doing things, evident in a range of responses from growing xenophobia
against Muslim migrants in Europe and America to French attacks on
American fast-food enterprises to Indian charges of toxicity in American soft-drink colas to Islamic crusades against Western secularization.

Such hostility might have been overcome, however, had it not been
for the conspicuous failure of globalization to meet the American
promise of a sustainable high growth rate that would permanently rescue the world economy from the decades-long economic malaise of the
Quiet Depression. Trouble in paradise began in the emerging markets,
especially in Asia. Long trumpeted as showcases of capitalist success, the
Pacific Rim had been one of the few consistently dynamic parts of the
global economy since the 1970s. But the roiling wave of financial crises
in South Korea, Taiwan, Hong Kong, Singapore, Thailand, and Indonesia brought that story line to an abrupt end in 1997–1998. At the same
time, with its markets and investments badly damaged by these crises,
Japan drifted into a deflationary spiral after 1997 of declining prices and
declining profits from which it has not yet emerged. And in the United
States, investors awash in capital, who had fled Asia in the crisis and were
now besotted with the alleged productivity miracle of America's New
Economy, sent a tidal wave of speculative investment flowing into
telecommunications, internet technology, venture capital, and hedge
funds. The end result of that manic behavior (like the tulip-style manias
of the past) was the spectacular bursting of America's IT bubble, the parallel collapse of the stock market (the tech-heavy NASDAQ lost 75 percent of its value), the U.S. recession of 2001, an uncertain, jobless
recovery, whose slow pace seems to suggest that the American economy
has returned to the flat growth of its pre-bubble years before the 1990s,
and the specter raised by the Federal Reserve Board that America could
find itself adrift in the same deflationary boat as the Japanese.

Nor would they be alone. The German economy—linchpin of the European Union—also began to show signs of meeting the same fate. For the first time since the 1930s depression, all the G7 areas of the world (North America, Europe, and Japan) seemed to suffer from the same fundamental problem of surplus capital, excess capacity (overproduction), and a declining rate of profit. Such circumstances tempted economic blocs like the European Union to look outside the multilateral world of the WTO, and to challenge American economic rules of the game.

The Beginnings of Militarization: The Second Clinton Administration

The failure of economic diplomacy was to militarize American foreign policy, in part as the vehicle to reestablish European dependence on American power. In a move reminiscent of the military buildups of NSC-68 in the early 1950s and of the Reagan Doctrine in the early 1980s, the United States commenced another such effort after 1997 to use a heated-up global situation and a beefed-up American military as the means to sustain its hegemonic position in the world system. That shift to a latter-day militarization began gradually in the second Clinton administration. Three developments illustrate it best—the expansion of NATO, that quintessential military alliance during the Cold War; the war with Yugoslavia (Serbia) over Kosovo; and Operation Desert Fox in Iraq. All three steps were as much about the European threat to American hegemony as they were about the Balkans or the Middle East.

The expansion of NATO into Eastern Europe was the first step in this evolution of U.S. policy. Initially proposed in 1994, that expansion became a reality when Poland, the Czech Republic, and Hungary joined the Brussels-based treaty organization in 1998. Already in the pipeline were additional proposals to add seven other nations from the area, which would mean that ten of the twenty-six members of NATO would be from the old Soviet sphere of interest that had been used as a counter to NATO. This NATO expansion was not primarily about containing any future Russian threat, but rather about containing and co-opting our old allies in Western Europe.

Throughout the Cold War, NATO had functioned as an American protectorate, and as such gave the United States the leverage to deflect any efforts by Western Europe (especially by France and sometimes by Germany) to create a greater degree of European autonomy from the United States or to seek closer ties with Russia and Eastern Europe. The end of the Cold War, however, threatened to undermine that relationship as Europe moved toward its own defense industry with the creation of EADS (the European Aeronautical and Space Company), the world's third largest military manufacturer, whose stock and leadership was 80 percent controlled by German and French companies.[7] At the same time, Europe took the first, tentative steps toward creating its own rapid defenses force, whose 60,000 personnel could become the instrument of a common European security policy, possibly acting independently from NATO. These actions foreshadowed the possibility that the United States might eventually face a relatively autonomous global rival able to address its own security needs without looking to the United States. In this context, the expansion of NATO into Eastern Europe, just at the moment when the same area was about to join the European Union, was a sophisticated American effort to use those countries as a Trojan horse. Still insecure about their Russian neighbor, they welcomed NATO membership; and because they owed their inclusion largely to the United States, it tended to make them proxies for U.S. policy in that military alliance. Moreover, because NATO membership required modernization of their military forces, American companies like Boeing and Lockheed were able to pad their profits from military sales while further cementing the region's ties to the United States.

The Clinton policy, while trying to blunt Western European instincts for autonomy, nonetheless still sought to co-opt that region rather than isolate and marginalize it. To that end, it sought to make expanded NATO into a junior partner of the United States, relying on a division of military labor between the technology-heavy American military (especially its air power) and the troop-heavy European armies. But to make that partnership real rather than theoretical, the United States had to persuade its European allies in NATO to accept the alliance's responsibility to operate "outside of theatre" in this new era. Since the organization's original raison d'être had vanished with the Cold War's end, its new remit had to include areas outside NATO's boundaries—in the Balkans, the Middle East, or areas of the old Soviet empire, like the oil-rich Caucasus. And the crisis in Kosovo, the second step in American militarization, provided just that opportunity.

NATO had, of course, exercised its political muscle in the Bosnian conflict, in both the American-led NATO bombings and the peace-keeping enterprise that followed the Dayton Accords of 1995. But Kosovo also provided the precedent for NATO to intervene even in the internal affairs of an out-of-theatre country—not unlike America's current intervention in Iraq. Unlike Bosnia, a semiautonomous part of the old Yugoslavia federation, Kosovo had simply been a province of Serbia and the repository of hallowed sites in Serbian history. In a legal sense, then, NATO's intervention in Kosovo was intervention in the internal affairs of a still-sovereign country, however unsavory that country's regime might appear to be. And unlike Bosnia, the NATO bombings in early 1999, again U.S.-dominated, targeted not simply the area in question (Kosovo), but Serbia and its infrastructure as well. Though the given reason for the intervention was a humanitarian one—saving Kosovo's Albanian majority from genocide—another major American purpose was to cement Europe's role as America's junior partner in NATO, operating in geographic areas far removed its original borders.

At the same time, however, Kosovo illustrated the limited scope of Clinton's conversion to military diplomacy. Unlike his friend Tony Blair, the British prime minister, Clinton remained reluctant to consider the possibility of a ground war to augment the air war on Serbia/Kosovo. Partly influenced by his National Security Advisor, Sandy Berger, and still mindful of the public response to the Somalia debacle in his first administration, the president wished to avoid situations where he might put American ground troops at battlefield risk. In this, he was supported by the Chair of the Joint Chiefs of Staff, Colin Powell, whose so-called Powell Doctrine warned against interventions not undertaken with overwhelming force, with a clear objective achievable within a specified time frame, and with a workable exit strategy. Only Secretary of State Madeleine Albright demurred, having already tweaked Powell that she saw no reason to spend such treasure on high-tech toys for the military if they were not willing to use them.[8]

The final example of the tilt toward militarization came, perhaps appropriately, in Iraq. As we noted, the earlier policy of sanctions, inspections, no-fly zones, and sporadic bombings had served to remind Europe that it needed American protection to maintain the stability of the Persian Gulf region and its ocean of oil. In late 1998, however, that Clinton policy appeared to escalate with a concerted military action against Iraq called "Operation Desert Fox." Opposition politicians denounced it as a contrived effort to divert attention from the Clinton–Monica Lewinsky debacle, but this trivializes an important turn in American foreign policy in Iraq (and elsewhere). For seven years, the containment of Iraq had worked quite well, but by the end of 1998 it had reached a point of diminishing returns. Saddam Hussein had not been deposed; his noncooperation with UN inspectors had led to their final withdrawal from the country; and intelligence accounts from Iraqi exiles, some with suspect credibility, suggested he was trying to upgrade Iraq's military and revive its weapons programs. At the same time, he parceled out future concessions on oil and infrastructure to France, Russia, and other European countries, while mounting a diplomatic offensive to bring an end to UN economic sanctions. In short, the 1990s containment strategy began to look rather shaky.

To offset this impression, both Clinton and Tony Blair launched a ferocious air war on Iraq featuring the BI bomber in its first combat deployment. Centered first on communications in southern Iraq, it eventually hit infrastructural targets in Baghdad as well. To be sure, the onslaught lasted only four days before the two allies declared success in the goal of degrading Iraq's military—suggesting that Clinton was not yet willing to go to all-out war as his successor would. Nonetheless, it was a precursor of things to come in two ways. First, as Thomas Friedman of the *New York Times* reported in early 1999, "the Clinton administration says it has decided to focus its energy now on producing the ouster of Hussein, rather than on just containing him."[9] Second, three members of the Security Council—France, Russia, and China— roundly criticized both the wisdom and legality of the Anglo-American actions, offering a clear preview of their stance four years later in the run-up to the 2003 Iraq war.

Militarization Accelerated: The Emergence of Imperial Hegemony, 2001–2003?

While George W. Bush's foreign policy had more in common with Bill Clinton's than either man would like to acknowledge, it did seem to diverge from prior policies in two obvious ways. First, it seized upon militarization with a vengeance far beyond that of its predecessor. Certainly the Bush Doctrine, with its affirmation of preemptive war and America's unilateral right to determine its usage, went well beyond any previous presidential doctrine. And the Afghanistan war and the Iraq war both served notice that the doctrine was not empty bombast. Second, the Bush administration seemed to abandon the Clinton policy of co-opting Europe through a NATO expanded both in numbers and mandates. Rather than view Europe's invocation of Article V of the NATO charter (that an attempt on one was an attack on all) as an offer of support, they regarded it, perhaps rightly, as a European effort to gain some influence in putting limits on how and where America would conduct its War on Terrorism. Instead of accepting Europe's offer of tacit support, it proceeded to marginalize or neutralize Europe's input—reflecting another maxim of the Bush Doctrine that pledged the United States to thwart any real or potential rivals to American hegemony.

Again, why this shift in U.S. policy toward Europe—especially continental Europe? And what role was the Iraq war of 2003 designed to play in that shift? The paucity of solid, primary-source historical documents requires that the answers to those essential questions must necessarily be speculative—hopefully, of course, of an informed variety. And in particular, it is difficult to access, from the outside looking in, which element in the Bush administration was dominant at one particular time on any given issue; like all administrations, it has its bureaucratic, factional, and ideological divisions. One can, however, advance some hypotheses for consideration, even if it is not entirely possible to weigh their plausibility or rank-order their importance.

The first hypothesis posits that thoughts of Europe played little role in America's Iraq policy. This approach rests on an assumption that the Bush foreign policy was ideologically determined and that the ideologues who led it regarded Europe more with contempt that apprehension. Believing that Europe needed America more than the reverse, they felt they could take European support for granted. This explanation sees a foreign policy team largely dominated by so-called neoconservatives—avid opponents of détente in the 1970s, eager devotees of Reagan's war on the Evil Empire in his first administration, and savage critics of Clinton's foreign policy (and more tempered ones of Bush the Elder for failing to finish off Iraq in 1991 and for his support of the Oslo peace process). After spending the 1990s in the nooks and crannies of right-wing think tanks and journals, they found themselves catapulted into power by the contested election of 2000. It was not until the 9/11 terror attacks, however, that neoconservatives were free to push their agenda. In this, they were powerfully aided by Vice President Richard Cheney, Defense Secretary Donald Rumsfeld, and White House advisor Karl Rove, who embraced much though not all of the neoconservative agenda, but had their own economic, bureaucratic, and political reasons for allying with it.

For the dominant neoconservatives in the administration, Robert Kagan's best-selling book, *Of Paradise and Power: America and Europe in the New World Order,* was alleged to be Holy Writ.[10] Rather than inhabiting a North Atlantic community together, different historical experiences and sharp contrasts in the military power of each were said to have made the United States and the European Union inhabitants of two different worlds—a European world of diplomacy, consensus-building, and conflict resolution; and an American world of exuberant power, a sense of its own exceptionalism, and a conviction that the use or threat of military power produced clearer and quicker results than endless palaver. Put more crudely, neoconservative ideologues saw Europe as a skittish wimp, militarily weak and wholly dependent on American power to do their work for them (as the Balkans had demonstrated), and unable to articulate or implement a common foreign policy on any topic of consequence. France, with its delusion of grandeur, might rail against American hyperpower, but Great Britain, the dominant military power in Europe, and Germany, the dominant economic power on the continent, both believed they enjoyed a "special" relationship with the United States, and both could be counted on to support or at least acquiesce in America's policy toward Iraq. Not wishing to be isolated and left out of the spoils of war, even France would, in the end, join in. This presumption of European docility produced an unfathomable diplomatic neglect by the United States that then turned to shock and finally anger at European opposition to America's Iraq strategy. Focused on France, even the anger missed the point that Germany's choice of France over America, of the European Union over transatlantic unity, was the truly extraordinary development—a development that some might blame on the exigencies of German electoral politics, but whose choice actually reflected a more fundamental decision to value the autonomy of an expanding Europe over obeisance to American hegemony. As the German newspaper *Die Zeit* put it: "Germany doesn't feel that old strategic dependence on the U.S. anymore." [11]

Failing to get unquestioning EU support, forced to go to the UN for a resolution it did not want, and then faced with the prospect of securing yet a second UN resolution to legitimize its planned war on Iraq, the United States retaliated with a divide-and-conquer tactic that tried to exploit the very real divisions that Europe was experiencing in its growing pains of expansion and restructuring. Essentially, the divisions were between the core of the European Union, a small but powerful inner group anchored by the Franco-German axis, and the more numerous nations on the Union's periphery: the United Kingdom, which remained outside the Eurozone and tried to use its "special relationship" with the United States to counteract Franco-German domination in the European Union; the southern flank of the EU, principally Italy and Spain, that felt their size, status, and needs were insufficiently respected by the Franco-German core; the Scandinavian bloc, which remained outside the common currency; and the new members from Eastern Europe, who often felt that the Franco-German axis had driven overly hard bargains in the prices they had to pay for EU admission. Understanding these divisions, the U.S. administration tried to exploit them by playing off the periphery of "New Europe" against the core of "Old Europe," enlisting the aid of the former in legitimizing and executing its war on Iraq. As UK columnist Philip Stephens saw it, the assumption was simple—"A cohesive Europe is one tempted to answer back. A divided one cannot challenge U.S. power."[12]

America's European policy of balance-of-power diplomacy had mixed results. It kept the UK firmly tied to U.S. policy and enlisted some small but symbolic force contributions to the Iraq occupation, especially from Eastern European countries like Poland. On the other hand, the vigorous opposition of Old Europe to America's Iraq strategy deprived the United States of UN approval and legitimization. Moreover, the practical requirements of America's war on Iraq ultimately necessitated help from Old Europe as well as New. The aftermath of the Iraq conquest, for example, quickly demonstrated that a combination of simplistic assumptions, amateurish planning, and unanticipated developments required the Bush administration to seek significant outside military and financial support to effect the pacification and reconstruction of Iraq. But the continued opposition of the Franco-German axis made it difficult not only to secure their help, but again to secure the UN mandate that other countries like Turkey and India required as political cover at home if they were to lend their support.

In the short term, then, America's divide-and-conquer policy toward Europe did not produce a great dividend. To be sure, it may do so in the future if it is still pursued, but for the moment, it has underestimated both the will and the power of Old Europe; and it has failed to understand that New Europe is facing a terrible dilemma—however much its leaders want to stay in America's good graces, their own domestic constituencies demonstrate in poll after poll that they are far more favorably disposed toward the European Union than they are toward the United States and, indeed, often view America as a dangerous, destabilizing force in world affairs. Only the UK, lead by Tony Blair, is willing to buck public opinion and cast its lot unequivocally with the Americans.

But leaders in Eastern Europe, where such negative views of the U.S. are even stronger than in Western Europe, have seen no great reward for taking such political risks and therefore have lent America only small-scale, almost token support. As one Czech diplomat put it: "We lived on the periphery for years, while geographically we were at the heart of Europe. Now that we have the opportunity to join, we don't want to be back on the periphery again." [13]

A second way to think about the relationship between America's European policy and the Iraq war also rests upon an assumption about the ideological nature of Bush foreign policy, but draws an opposite conclusion: that neoconservative ideologues saw Europe as a serious rival rather than as a docile ally to be taken for granted. This approach particularly stresses the role of so-called transformationists, who took issue with the skepticism about nation-building evident in traditional realpolitik conservatives like Defense Secretary Rumsfeld. While they thought the process of globalization was both real and significant, they believed its results were not; and nation-building was required to create the circumstances in which the consequences could be beneficial. For starters, they were committed to refashioning Iraqi society into a regional model of democratic, free-market capitalism. Some might dispute their stated commitment to democracy, though some transformationalists had started out as Henry Jackson Democrats in the 1970s, committed not only to big military spending and an aggressive foreign policy, but also to traditional Democratic concerns for social welfare. But one can hardly dispute their commitment to free enterprise. Ignoring the earlier failure of "shock therapy" in Russia and its mixed record in Eastern Europe, the CPA (Coalition Provisional Authority), headed by American proconsul L. Paul Bremer III announced a sweeping series of economic reforms for Iraq that reflected this transformationist perspective. Seeking to transform Iraq's semi-command economy into a free marketeer's notion of heaven, it proclaimed a low 5 percent import tariff, an equally low 15 percent ceiling on all forms of taxes, a de facto opportunity for an American banking consortium to take over Iraq's banking system, and an open door for almost all forms of foreign investment. The absence of a social safety net for Iraqis suggested, however, that either the transformationalists had lost their former affection for social reform or other corporate interests had tipped the scales to effect a transformation more to their own views on nation-building in Iraq.

Nation-building, however, was not to end with Iraq, but was to extend to the whole Middle Eastern region—an approach that almost guaranteed conflict with the European Union. Prior administrations during the Cold War had sought to stabilize an acceptable status quo in the Middle East and to prevent outsiders like the USSR or indigenous forces like Pan-Arab radicalism (secular or religious) from challenging that status quo. But neoconservatives in and out of the administration seemed committed to playing the role of revolutionary, seeking to destroy the status quo rather than preserve it. If one can take their rhetoric at face value, it sought to use regime change in Iraq as a kind of regional multiplier to reorder the whole Middle East—to use its control of Afghanistan and Iraq to intimidate Iran and encourage its youthful reformers to rise up against the mullahs; to pressure Syria to walk the straight-and-narrow; to frighten Saudi Arabia into reining in its Islamist militants; to place curbs on OPEC; and to maintain Israel's nuclear monopoly, secure it against Hamas and Hezbollah terrorism, and enable it to settle the Palestinian issue overwhelmingly on the terms of its own choosing. In the judgment of the *Financial Times,* the strategy was so "breathtaking in its audacity," yet so lacking in sober thought, that it even transcended "wishful thinking." [14]

The question of whether this region-building required further American military intervention was left unanswered, though the option apparently remained on the table. On the other hand, neoconservatives

like Richard Perle were "optimistic that we'll see regime change in Iran
without any use of military power by the U.S.," and William Kristol
agreed that "it is right to think we have got a good chance of getting
[regime change in Iran and Syria] without military action."[15] The
whole grandiose project for the region reminds one of Joseph Schumpeter's classic concept of "creative destruction"—destroying the old in
order to build the new upon its ashes. But it may also remind one of
JFK's "best and the brightest" in Vietnam, and their extraordinary
hubris—the "arrogance of power" as Senator J. William Fulbright
termed it—that led them to embrace the illusion that American social
engineering could recast a complex and foreign world into a prefabri-
cated mould.

Even before the war, even before the venture in region-building had
to face its own contradictions and shortcomings, it had to confront one
hard reality—that the European Union was a major obstacle to its realization. Had America not intervened in Iraq, European companies—
concession contracts in hand—stood at the ready to do business in Iraq
if and when UN sanctions were lifted. In Iran and Syria, the European
Union bucked America's policy of confrontation in favor of constructive engagement. Most dramatically, the European Union dispatched
several missions to Iran to speed negotiations on a proposed free trade
agreement between that country and the EU. And when the issue of
Iran's nuclear program escalated, the EU (like Japan) tried the diplomatic track in trying to persuade Iran to cooperate with the IAEA (International Atomic Energy Agency)—in part out of their own fear of
an Iranian-Israeli nuclear arms race that would destabilize the region,
but also in part to forestall any American military adventurism against
Iran that might itself provoke regional destabilization. Similarly, in the
Israeli–Palestinian conflict, the European Union counteracted
America's pro-Israeli tilt by providing the Palestinian Authority (the
PA) with its major source of external funding; it continued to recognize

the political arm of Hamas even as Israel and the United States demanded that the PA do all in its power to destroy it and other terrorist
groups; European diplomats continued to display deference toward
Yasser Arafat even as Israel and the United States tried to neutralize
him; and when the United States did make clear its intent for war on
Iraq, Europe did exact a price that America join the EU, Russia, and
the UN (the so-called Quartet) in using the moment to establish an
evenhanded blueprint for a peace settlement. Even America's closest
supporter, Great Britain, stood as an obstacle to neoconservative region-
building. UK Foreign Secretary Jack Straw made four visits to Iran in
pursuit of constructive engagement; Prime Minister Tony Blair had two
head-of-state visits with Syria's president on behalf of a similar policy;
and Blair, joined by Spain—another American ally—pushed America
as hard as any European leader to sign on with the Quartet and its blueprint. All these hard facts of life made it clear that Europe—far from
being a wimp to ignore or an ally to take for granted—was a serious
rival in the Middle East, and that its policies had to be overcome if U.S.
region-building was to succeed. And that made for a powerful incentive
to marginalize Europe in general and exclude it specifically from any
role in the Iraq war and the occupation to follow.

A third hypothesis assumes that the Bush policy rests less on ideology
than it does on traditional, historic American tactics of using American
leverage in the Middle East to heighten the likelihood that Europe will
acquiesce in American hegemony. With the exception of North Korea,
the other members of Bush's Axis of Evil—Iraq and Iran—are located
in the same geographic region, as is that lesser evil, Syria. Taken together
with Afghanistan and the former Soviet republics in Central Asia, they
are all part of what Carter administration National Security Advisor
Zbigniew Brzezinski termed in the late 1970s "the Arc of Crisis,"
which runs from southwest Asia to northeast Africa through the Middle East. It is a region that every American president from Harry Tru-

man onward has marked out in solemn, sacrosanct doctrines as an American sphere of influence—from the Truman Doctrine that led to eventual alliance with Turkey to the Eisenhower Doctrine that prompted the 1956 U.S. intervention in Lebanon, to the Nixon Doctrine that anointed the special relationship both with Israel and Iran under the shah, to the Carter Doctrine that pledged to use any means necessary to keep the Persian Gulf open against Iran's clerical revolutionaries or Soviet incursion, to the Reagan Doctrine that took its war against the Evil Empire once more to the beaches of Lebanon, and finally to the Bush Doctrine of unilateral preemptive war. In some ways, then, Bush merely walked in the footprints of his predecessors—all of them committed to prevent the emergence of any rival to American regional dominance; all of them committed to maintain access, at stable and profitable prices, to the ocean of oil in the Persian Gulf and Caspian Sea regions—not only against rival nations, but against any OPEC temptation to inflict oil shocks on the West as it did in the 1970s. All of those past presidential initiatives were cognizant that America's role as regional policeman made Western Europe (and Japan), who are more dependent than America on the region's oil, far more likely to defer to American leadership and American rules of the global game.

The Bush administration's initiative, however, seems likely to go a step further than his predecessors' did. While its long-term plans for Iraq are deliberately opaque, there is evidence to suggest that it seeks to create a permanent protectorate in Iraq—drawing less on its historical experiences in post–World War II German and Japanese occupations than on its earlier occupations of Cuba and other Caribbean and Central American countries. If so, American troops will leave in due course (it took four years in Cuba), but only after a constitution is written that legitimizes a permanent, special relationship with the United States. That relationship will probably involve military bases to replace those in Saudi Arabia, an obligation to consult with the United States on matters of security and foreign policy, American dominance of Iraq's banking system, and an open door for goods, capital, and raw material access.[16] For example, both Paul Bremer and a spokesman for the World Bank, participating in the Middle East economic summit in Jordan, pledged themselves to "economic liberalization" in Iraq to "replace failed socialist and bureaucratic models."

But the American presence will probably not end there. American leverage inside Iraq's oil ministry in the postwar protectorate will give America a virtual place in OPEC, where it can either moderate its policies or, in a crisis, even break the producers' "cartel." (The *Financial Times* said the decision had already been made that postwar Iraq would stay in OPEC, but not be bound by its quotas.[17]) That strategic placement might even strengthen the U.S. hand in dealing with Russia and Western Europe in the rough-and-tumble economic and diplomatic warfare being waged over the oil and gas resources of the Caspian Sea and the Caucasus, and the pipelines that carry them. In any case, if successful, that strategic placement would certainly magnify Europe's necessity to depend on the protection and good graces of the United States for its vital access to the energy resources in the Middle East and the larger Arc of Crisis.

The final hypothesis is the broadest. It speculates that the Iraq war signified that America had abandoned past hegemonic practices honed throughout the Cold War and embraced a more unilateral mode that made little room for social compacts with permanent allies like Europe; one that relied instead on pragmatic, temporary arrangements with an ever-shifting "coalition of the willing"—what British commentator Philip Stephens saw as "not quite unilateralism; more multilateralism *a la carte.*"[18] Judging by its actions rather than its rhetoric, this administration may have reached an even firmer conclusion than its predecessor that globalization has reached a point of diminishing returns, and that the time might well be at hand to pay less attention to America's systemic responsibilities and pay more heed to the need to serve its unilateral national interests.

Certainly in the economic sphere, the administration's notion of national interests produced a tilt away from multilateralism to managed protectionism and bilateralism. While the administration continued to preach the virtues of free trade, for example, it imposed high tariff duties on steel imports and passed an enormous farm subsidy bill that was, per capita, higher than the European Union's. While it proclaimed support for developing countries, it joined the EU at the WTO's Cancún summit in blocking more liberal access for their agricultural exports to developed markets. While its trade representative, Robert Zoellick, often reaffirmed the Bush commitment to liberalize trade through comprehensive global pacts, in practice he warned other trading nations after the WTO collapse at Cancún that the United States would soon add many more free trade agreements to the four it already has in operation. And indeed, negotiations were already underway or planned with twenty-one other countries in Asia, Africa, and Latin America, with the further prospect down the line of a hemisphere-wide Free Trade Agreement for the Americas (FTAA). To be sure, administration rhetoric always proclaimed this bilateralism to be consistent with global multilateralism, but the clear intent of American bilateralism was not to lower trade barriers for everyone, but to secure special privileges for itself. As the *New York Times* described it, America was "returning to the pre-1922 practice of awarding preferential trade treatment to some countries and regions."[19] All this intensifies an existing tendency to replace a multilateral global market with a series of regional trade blocs in which most goods and capital move within the blocs rather than between them. These trends of managed protection at home and targeted bilateralism abroad suggest an administration more inclined to view Europe as a rival trade bloc than part of a larger, multilateral whole.

The apparent U.S. retreat from multilateral trade, however, suggests something further. American hegemony had always rested on the twin pillars of its economic and military power; its ability to deliver greater prosperity and security to its allies than they could secure on their own. If the economic prospects of the European Union were, however, increasingly derived from its own common market and its FTAs in the Middle East and Africa, and not from an American-sponsored, multilateral global market, then the United States no longer had quite the same economic leverage over Europe to help secure its obeisance to American policy and American rules. If that was the case, then American hegemony would have to depend more heavily on one pillar than on two—that is, on its awesome and unchallenged military supremacy. And the doctrine of preemptive war, the size of the American military budget, and its wars on Afghanistan and now Iraq certainly suggest, as noted earlier, a decided tilt toward further militarization of American foreign policy.

If economic leverage over Europe is contracting, can militarization make European security sufficiently dependent on U.S. protection that it alone can constitute the basis for American hegemony? The Communist menace that once worked so well is now a thing of the past. The threat of terrorism, while new to American soil, is one Europe has known repeatedly since the Munich Games of 1972; and one they generally think can be contained without recourse to preemptive wars. The threat of nuclear proliferation, to be sure, is one of far greater concern to Europe, and a U.S. capacity to prevent that proliferation through preemptive action would carry great weight with Europe. But the Anglo-American manipulation of the WMD issue in Iraq has made Europe even more suspicious of U.S. motives; and moreover, America's preemptive wars in Afghanistan and Iraq may have had the opposite of their intended effect by accelerating nuclear proliferation as both North Korea and possibly Iran perhaps conclude that only possession of nuclear weapons can deter the hostile American actions that are threatened implicitly in the designation of these countries as members of the so-called Axis of Evil. Which brings us back to an earlier theme—the one crucial form of security that America has to offer Europe is that of secure access to the vast energy resources, both present and future, in the so-called Arc of Crisis that extends from the Caspian Sea through the Persian Gulf to the Arabian peninsula, and then westward to Libya and southward to the Gulf of Aden. And the Iraq war was the linchpin of that regional policy.

A Brief Summing Up

The end of the Cold War increased American power, but decreased American hegemony. In particular, the erosion of America's post–World War II social compact with Western Europe produced a diminution of Europe's deference to America's global leadership and an acceleration of Europe's drive for greater autonomy in matters of security and foreign policy. In response, American foreign policy in the 1990s attempted to reverse those tendencies by demonstrating anew that acceptance of American policies and international rules would provide Europe with more prosperity and security than it could manage on its own. While low-intensity confrontation with Iraq reminded Europe of its need for American protection of Middle Eastern oil, the major U.S. tactic was to stymie European tendencies toward economic autonomy by demonstrating that American-sponsored globalization could restore the world economy to a pre-1970s level that would be far more profitable to Europe than any EU emphasis on regional markets.

The backlash against globalization, coupled with the financial crises and economic slowdown after 1997, tended to undermine that economic strategy of the United States and produced a decided tilt toward emphasizing military power instead. During the second Clinton administration, that new strategy sought to reinvigorate NATO through ex-

pansion of its membership into Eastern Europe and by broadening its
mandate to act "out of theater" beyond NATO's boundaries. The reen-
ergized NATO would revive its former status as an American protectorate; give the United States the internal leverage to retard any
European tendencies toward an all-European army or an autonomous
foreign policy; and demonstrate to Europe, as it did in both Bosnia and
Kosovo, that Europe was so deficient in air power, technology, and logistics that it had no choice but to remain simply a junior partner with
the United States. In addition, the United States under Clinton also escalated its low-intensity war against Iraq with Operation Desert Fox in
1998, underlining its reminder to Europe that it depended on the
United States to protect its essential access to Persian Gulf oil.

   After 9/11, however, the administration of George W. Bush took the
tilt toward a militarized foreign policy to new limits with the so-called
Bush Doctrine, which embraced the principle of preemptive war in its
War on Terrorism. Rather than co-opt and use NATO in that venture,
the United States ignored a tacit European offer to lend its NATO support. Instead, the United States—with support from a compliant British
government—made Afghanistan and Iraq, in essence, into unilateral
wars. Seeing the NATO offer as a subtle European effort to place limits
on the exercise of American power, the administration sought to marginalize Europe's input. And that decision put it on a collision course
with Europe, and especially with the dominant Franco-German axis,
that would be played out in the UN prior to the war, and would result
in an American divide-and-conquer effort to play so-called New Europe off against Old Europe.

   Several speculations have surfaced regarding the relationship between this new policy toward Europe and America's policy in Iraq, in
the Middle East, and in the whole so-called Arc of Crisis area between
the Caspian Sea and the Red Sea. There are four primary hypotheses
advancing different ways to think about that relationship, some of them

contradictory, some not. All of them, in the absence of firm historical evidence, are tentative. First, that Europe was so weak and divided that it was a null factor whose acquiescence could be assumed in Iraq and elsewhere. Second, that Europe was a serious threat to America's transformationalist strategy of using an American protectorate in postwar Iraq as the initial lever to remake the entire Middle East region into a more controllable U.S. sphere of influence. Third, that the Iraq war was simply a further escalation of the Clinton strategy in Operation Desert Fox to strengthen and perpetuate Europe's dependence on American protection of its crucial oil access to the region. And finally, that the Iraq war signaled the U.S. abandonment of hegemony as it had exercised it since World War II and with it the reciprocal Euro-American social contract on which that hegemony largely rested.

Some Additional Thoughts

The great historian Fernand Braudel, writing about the cycles of the world system, rightly observed that "each time a decentering occurs, a recentering takes place."[20] That cyclical process, however, is not a seamless one, and the transition between decentering and recentering is awkward, contentious, and quite dangerous. Hegemony, whatever its sometimes terrible excesses, has always played a stabilizing role in squaring the circle between the political nationalism of nation-states and the economic internationalism of capital.[21] The essence of hegemony was to reconcile those contrary tendencies by persuading nations to give up some of their sovereign autonomy in return for the hegemon's promise that collective security arrangements and economic globalization would give them greater security and prosperity than they could provide for themselves. Despite the dreadful costs of the Cold War and Asian hot wars, American hegemony in the late twentieth century had created a world order that was more stable and prosperous than the world wars and depression produced by the unstable balance of world power that preceded it.

The decline of hegemony gradually deprives the world system of the necessary mechanism (the visible hand) to deflect each nation from pursuing only its narrow, economic-political self-interests. That deprivation develops even more rapidly when the hegemonic nation itself abdicates its responsibilities and increasingly places its self-interests over systemic interests. Not only does it not restrain other nations, it does not restrain itself. America's current tendency certainly runs that risk in its experiments with managed protectionism, bilateralism, preemptive war, and its tacit retreat from permanent alliances like NATO.

It is possible, of course, that America's hegemonic decline might yet be reversed. Obituaries have been written for U.S. hegemony before, and proved premature. Nonetheless, the revival of American hegemony is at least problematic. Globalization seems to have reached its likely limits, and militarization seems too blunt an instrument to be effective save in special instances. Moreover, the United States may prove unable to fulfill its promise of guns and butter (Iraq *and* tax cuts) to an uneasy American public. Indeed, it may produce, as Vietnam did, another "fiscal crisis of the state," where the State is unable to provide for both welfare at home and warfare abroad.[22] So it may well be that no strategic choice is likely to sustain American hegemony over the long term.

Even so, it is possible that the decline of America's hegemony need not be as calamitous as that of Great Britain's a century ago. Circumstances, after all, are very different at the start of this century. First, America's decline will probably be more gradual and more incomplete than Britain's. The latter never possessed the absolute and relative preponderance of power enjoyed by the United States; moreover, it had to battle serious contenders for potential hegemony waiting in the wings. As a consequence, Britain lost both its economic and military dominance in little more than a generation at the end of the nineteenth century, to the United States and Germany respectively. Today, however, both of America's great rivals, the European Union and China, face enormous internal difficulties, whose resolution (if it is even possible) will be a long time coming; until then, neither can seriously compete with American economic and/or military power. Even then, it is hard to imagine either functioning as a hegemonic replacement in the century to come. Second, the world system is not cursed for the moment, as it was a century ago, by a European continent riven by nationalism, militarism, and authoritarianism. Whatever the present failings of the European Union, and however uncertain its future course, it has already achieved something of a miracle, not only in political and economic integration, but in its collective consciousness and worldview. The continent that gave the system two world wars, fascism, and the holocaust now offers itself as a role model of how to build a new system on the ashes of a moribund one.

Finally, the world now possesses international institutions that it did not a century ago—institutions that can potentially perform some of the tasks heretofore performed by the United States. The economic institutions, to be sure, are problematic, given the deadlock in the WTO and widespread criticism of the IMF's past policies. Circumstances, however, can change, and policies can alter, and those institutions may yet be able to play a useful role in preventing the current drift toward regional trade blocs from degenerating into outright economic warfare. Likewise, the United Nations, the world's leading political institution, has had a checkered past as well. But the manner in which Europe has played the UN card to resist American military preemption, and the way in which the United States felt compelled to use the UN as well in response, has given that organization an importance and a potential that it never managed to achieve in the Cold War era.

Despite these more propitious circumstances, however, the process of decentering is still likely to be an awkward and dangerous one. And if that decentering is to avoid past perils of major war and depression, the major players of today's world order may well have to imagine and create a world beyond hegemony—perhaps some more collaborative entity to perform hegemony's essential role of being stabilizer to an otherwise unstable system. And that frankly utopian task of replacing hegemony with some new kind of center will require, for starters, an American recognition of the impermanency of its hegemony and the grace to settle for the still-vital role of being first among equals. And it will require of America's critics, domestic and foreign, that they focus not merely on ways to limit and tame American power, but on some concerted and constructive thought about what kind of alternative to offer in its place.

5

Anti-Americanism and Anti-Europeanism

Mary Nolan

In the immediate aftermath of September 11, there was an outpouring of European sympathy, solidarity, and support for America. Citizens held candlelight vigils, states promised cooperation in the fight against terrorism, and NATO invoked its self-defense clause for the first time. A shocked and understandably self-absorbed United States appreciated Europe's support, which it regarded as self-evident and appropriate. The transatlantic relationship, uncertain and at times frayed in the post–Cold War era, seemed assured, yet a new period of Euro-American cooperation and understanding failed to emerge. The Afghanistan war, the new United States National Security Strategy, the divisive negotiations preceding the Iraq war, and the deteriorating situation within American-occupied Iraq mark milestones in the conflictual relationship between major European countries and America, as well as within Europe itself. Charges of vitriolic, unjustified European anti-Americanism and widespread, nasty American anti-Europeanism are hurled across the Atlantic by politicians and pundits; they pervade the media and popular consciousness and are the object of anguished analysis by those seeking to restore or reform the Euro-American partnership. While the charges America and "Old" Europe make against each other—of self-interested actions, unfulfilled responsibilities, duplicitous desires, and absurd, unfair criticisms—differ, both sides acknowledge that relations have deterio-

rated, rhetorical attacks have escalated, and the future of transatlantic
cooperation remains uncertain.

The ubiquitous term anti-Americanism and the less familiar one,
anti-Europeanism, are admittedly both polemical and problematic.
They are defined and deployed in contradictory ways and often conflate
indiscriminately sober criticism, genuine differences, rational discourse,
deep-seated prejudices, petty jealousies, and exaggerated insults. They
fail to attend to often-acrimonious divisions among European governments as well as within the political establishments and between governments and their citizens on both sides of the Atlantic. Nonetheless,
these capacious and provocative concepts provide a convenient shorthand for constellations of attitudes and emotions, analyses and predictions that have emerged with a new intensity and ubiquity and that are
lauded or condemned as expressing the dominant attitudes of America
and Europe toward one another. Why have they emerged in the last two
years, and what precisely are their themes and tropes? To what extent do
they mutually construct one another and to what extent do they draw
on long-standing sentiments, prejudices, and evaluations that have historically structured their perceptions of one another? Are European
anti-Americanism and American anti-Europeanism responses to the
contingencies of the moment, or do they reflect historically rooted disagreements between, and developments within, Europe and America?

Some scholars of European anti-Americanism, such as Dan Diner,
insist that America is resented now, as in the past, for what it is and not
for what it does, and many American officials, politicians, and political
analysts insist that jealousy of America's military might, economic influence, cultural hegemony, and/or superior values alone motivates criticism.[1] Others, such as Stanley Hoffmann, Tony Judt, and Claus
Leggewie, view European anti-Americanism as a new response to the
altered post–Cold War world and America's claimed place within it.[2] A
2002 Pew Survey of Global Attitudes concludes that "in general, an-

tipathy toward the U.S. is shaped more by what it *does* in the international arena than by what it *stands for* politically and economically." [3] The current manifestations of anti-Europeanism and anti-Americanism are the product of the upheavals and uncertainties of the post–Cold War order, of shifting American policies and perceptions of itself and the world after September 11, of intensified American demands for material and moral support from Europe, and of the divided European responses to them. Anti-Americanism and anti-Europeanism reflect differing assessments of dangers and challenges that each side of the Atlantic faces at home and abroad. The tropes and targets of Europe's anti-Americanism have changed substantially over the course of the Cold War and in the wake of its demise. In a departure from the pre- and immediate post–World War II eras, politics plays a much more central role than culture; economic critiques, which are shaped by social and ecological concerns, occur on the terrain of capitalism rather than being anti-capitalist or anti-modern.

With the fall of the Soviet Union and the growing economic power and unity of Europe, American anti-Europeanism has also reoriented itself. The claimed requirements of Cold War anti-Communism can no longer be invoked to critique and cajole; the relegation of Europeans to the status of feminized or childish junior partners is no longer rhetorically persuasive or politically productive. American anti-Europeanism alternates between trying to deploy anti-terrorism as it once did anti-Communism, appealing to realpolitik, and ridiculing Europe's idealism and anxiety as immature and unmasculine. In a reversal of earlier positions, America is appealing for aid (and finds itself a debtor state), while many European states are equivocating or refusing, and this neediness on the part of the global hegemon imparts a singularly shrill and emotional tone to its anti-Europeanism.

The current upsurge in anti-Americanism and anti-Europeanism also results from a constellation of disagreements between Europeans and Americans about foreign policy and the economy, energy and ecology, social policy at home and development abroad. These disagreements have erupted periodically from 1968 on and were articulated sometimes by protest groups, sometimes by political parties, sometimes by states, and increasingly by all three. Both specific issues of dispute and the more amorphous but pervasive resentments they arouse have proven much more difficult to manage without the disciplining force of the Cold War, for which the war on terrorism has not proven to be an effective substitute. Past and current policy disagreements and new forms of anti-Americanism and anti-Europeanism have been fueled, in turn, by the similar and sharply different ways in which American and European societies and cultures have developed. Europe has borrowed from and negotiated with the American models of economy, culture, and politics; it has been more fascinated with than repelled by the capacious and contradictory category and ideology of Americanism. Yet, despite the Americanization of Europe in the decades following World War II, capitalist modernity in Europe differs in profound ways from its counterpart in America.

Differing European and American views on nationalism, multilateralism, power, and law, differing assessments of the present danger and preferred future lie at the heart of current controversies. Whether American foreign policy has fundamentally changed under Bush II or marks only an intensification and modification of earlier forms of interventionism has been debated by scholars, but popular and governmental perceptions in Europe and the self-presentation of the Bush administration emphasize a deliberate rupture with previous perceptions and policies. In Europe, America once had, to borrow Geir Lundestad's phrase, an "empire by invitation." It was, according to William Wallace, "a self-consciously liberal hegemon, operated through multilateral institutions that disguised, legitimized, and moderated its dominance and provided a narrative (or rationale) of common values shared by the 'free world,' which were declared to be universal in their application." Now the Cold War is over, the Soviet Union gone, and America is the world's only superpower, and ". . . the rhetorical justification for this dominant position is more often couched in realist than in liberal terms; with reference to American national interests rather than to shared global values and concerns."[4] These shifts are neatly captured in the National Security Strategy, the official government statement of purpose and vision published in September 2002, which declared emphatically that the United States would pursue "an American internationalism that reflects the union of our values and our national interests."[5] Before, during and in the troubled aftermath of the Iraq war, the Bush administration has reiterated its new commitment to unilateralism, preemptive and preventative war, regime change, an extreme variant of neoliberal capitalism, and a Pax Americana to which the rest of the world is told to accommodate itself or suffer irrelevance if not worse.[6]

The Bush administration and its many neoconservative and mainstream supporters presented the case for war in Afghanistan, in Iraq, and against terror everywhere as a necessary and virtuous battle of good against "evildoers," and chastised "unwilling" Europeans for failing to understand the moral and civilizational stakes in the struggle. Many European governments and most of the populace west and east were narrowly and selfishly absorbed in such secondary European issues as economic unification and a possible EU military force. America raised the now-discredited specter of weapons of mass destruction, angrily warning Europeans that UN inspections could not be relied on to ward off such an imminent danger. Members of the administration and the media insinuated—and a majority of the American public believed—that Saddam Hussein was linked to September 11. Europeans who hesitated and questioned were ridiculed and rebuked; those who refused to

join the coalition of the willing were publicly threatened with retaliation in the form of troop withdrawals, economic boycotts, and diplomatic marginalization. NATO and the UN were told to reform and
cooperate with the only superpower, or become marginalized. When
Germany, France, Belgium, and Luxemburg discussed plans for the
headquarters of an EU military force, a U.S. State Department
spokesman belittled "the little bitty summit" of "the chocolate makers."[7] Europe was reminded of American military power, economic
prowess, and cultural hegemony, and told—sometimes in the rhetoric of
the reluctantly assumed, burdensome responsibility of power, sometimes in the enthusiastic discourse of a new benevolent empire—that
the only alternative to an America-controlled world order was chaos.

For many in Europe, the American defense of unilateralism in theory
and practice, its instrumental and often dismissive attitude toward the
United Nations, and its rejection of the constraints of international law
and permanent alliances arouse great anxiety and so feature promi-
nently in the oppositional discourses labeled "anti-Americanism" in the
U.S. and, to borrow Günter Grass's phrase, *"Amerika Kritik"* abroad.[8]
Anti-Americanism and anti-Europeanism do agree on the crucial substantive issues that are at stake, but they are committed to different principles and paths. In a scathing critique of the American right's
far-reaching aspirations, Anatol Lieven has expressed postnational
Europe's fear of America's aggressive nationalism and postimperial
Europe's skepticism about America's newly stated imperial ambitions.[9]
The Bush administration claims to be realist, but to Europe it seems sur-
realist. Europe is worried not just by the Iraq war but by America's
hubris, its lack of clear priorities, its refusal to compromise on any of its
conservative and unilateral goals. The United States' withdrawal from
the Kyoto Protocol on global warming, the Anti-Ballistic Missile
Treaty, and the Comprehensive Nuclear-Test-Ban Treaty, its refusal to
sign the land-mine treaty or CEDAW (the Convention to End All Dis-

crimination Against Women), its rejection of the International Criminal Court and its reluctance to sell anti-HIV/AIDS drugs at prices the
global south can afford are constantly cited in the anti-American critique of unilateralism. America defends such actions as vital to its independence and self-interest, insisting that constraining agreements can be
embraced by smaller, weaker nations but not by the world's only superpower. Finally, if Europe was and remains divided about Iraq, it is united
on the question of Palestine. Europe believes that it is possible to criticize Israeli policies without being anti-Semitic and believes that European pleas for rapid movement toward a fair two-state solution fall on
deaf ears in Washington.

These differing European and American positions on issues of policy
and the principles underlying them are bolstered by the different tales
Europe and America tell about World War II and the reconstruction of
Europe. For America, World War II was the good war, the just war
against totalitarian violence and injustice, the war that is the proclaimed
model for the Iraq intervention. American anti-Europeanism is filled
with harsh reminders of how easily Europe succumbed to the totalitarian temptation in its fascist and communist variants, how nobly America came to the rescue, and how blind Europeans are to the ostensible
recurrence of similar conditions in the Middle East.[10] The cowardly
French are labeled "cheese-eating surrender monkeys," a phrase that
impugns their masculinity, denies their humanity, and ridicules their
culinary culture even as it distorts history.[11] The Germans are reminded
of their complicity in the twentieth century's worst crimes, and the
once-powerful British are complimented for recognizing the need to
continue a political and military collaboration solidified in World War
II. (The Russians fit most uneasily in this American narrative of European wartime weakness, cowardice, and complicity, and in Cold War
fashion their wartime contribution is passed over in silence.)

As American politicians and the media constantly remind Europeans, American generosity continued with massive Marshall Plan aid, the maintenance of a vast American military presence, and after 1989, support for the reunification of Germany and the construction of capitalism and democracy in Central and Eastern Europe. All these American measures are presented as altruistic efforts to promote European prosperity and anti-Communism, while their benefits to American economic and global power are overlooked. So why, American critics of Europe ask in tones of wounded surprise or indignant protest, are so many European nations ungratefully withholding political support, moral approval, and material aid? As one Frenchman aptly noted, "What's important about the American attitude is the emotional dimension. . . . You hear about betrayal and ingratitude." [12]

Europeans also refer back to World War II, but the war had different meanings for them, regardless of whether they were victors or vanquished, extracting an enormous toll on human life, material resources, social cohesion, political institutions, cultural traditions, and moral values. The romance of war that pervaded American society until Vietnam and returned with the Gulf War has no European counterpart after two world wars and the costly struggles to thwart decolonization. Europeans are wary of a speedy resort to military force, preferring containment to open conflict, nuclear-arms limitation to proliferation, and multilateral negotiation to unilateral intervention. As German Chancellor Gerhard Schroeder noted in a recent interview, Germany's experiences in World War II made it look at issues through a different moral prism and be extremely careful when considering the use of force. [13] Europeans are profoundly appreciative of the system of international institutions and law that the U.S. was instrumental in establishing after World War II, but their loyalty is to the values and practices embodied therein, not to the changed priorities of the system's chief designer.

Anti-Europeanism and anti-Americanism reveal very different conceptions of what sort of international order is possible and desirable.

Americans now talk about Europe in the way the Europeans used to talk about America—naïve about power and conflict, and idealistic because cushioned by too much prosperity and peace. When signing the Congressional resolution that gave him the power to use military force as he deemed "necessary and appropriate," Bush reminded Europeans that "those who choose to live in denial may eventually be forced to live in fear."[14] Robert Kagan, a neoconservative commentator close to the Bush administration, elaborated on this theme in a widely cited article and book. "Europe is turning away from power . . . it is moving beyond power into a self-contained world of laws and rules and transnational negotiation and cooperation. It is entering a post-historical paradise of peace and relative prosperity, the realization of Kant's 'Perpetual Peace.' " Europe, in short, is accused of embracing the morality of the weak, a Nietzschean slave morality. By contrast, Kagan continues, "The United States remains mired in history, exercising power in the anarchic Hobbesian world where international laws and rules are unreliable and where true security and the defense and promotion of a liberal order still depend on the possession and use of military might."[15] Such depictions of America and the European "other" mark a radical departure from the heady post–Cold War days when Francis Fukuyama predicted that Europe and America would lead the entry into a peaceful posthistorical era of triumphant liberal capitalism.[16] They are a dramatic reversal of the way Americans represented themselves to Europeans in the immediate post–World War II decades. At that time Americans saw themselves and were seen as pragmatic, optimistic, rational, reliant on technological cures, and committed to international cooperation.[17] Now they present themselves as pessimistic realists, rightly skeptical of internationalism, and appropriately committed to military solutions.

Whether the defenders of American foreign policy claim to be idealist champions of democracy and human rights or reluctant bearers of the (imperial) burden of restoring world order, they claim to embody a new masculinity of a sort they argue is sorely lacking in Europe. American men are strong and tough, unafraid to make difficult decisions, eager to compete, and willing to resort to force. As *The American Enterprise* argued in a special issue revealingly entitled "Real Men: They're Back":

> The awesome display of masculine courage shown by the firemen and policeman at Ground Zero, the heroic soldiers fighting in Afghanistan and Iraq, the focused determination and exemplary leadership of President Bush, Vice President Cheney, Defense Secretary Rumsfeld, and General Tommy Franks, have rekindled in Americans an appreciation for masculine virtues.[18]

According to the highly sexualized rhetoric of anti-Europeanism, Europeans don't understand that "fighting enemies and protecting the nation are overwhelmingly male projects."[19] The low European birthrate is certain proof that Europeans lack virility, but so too is the widespread preference for negotiation and cooperation. When not espousing a utopian idealism, European men are accused of either the crass pursuit of material self-interest or cowardice. *New York Times* columnist William Safire claimed that the "old Berlin imperiousness" was combining with French ambitions to dominate the small democracies of Europe.[20] The *New York Post* labeled France and Germany "The Axis of Weasel," and Thomas Friedman condemned the French for wanting the U.S. to fail in Iraq.[21] The American media is replete with references to Euroweenies, wimps, and EU-nuchs, suggesting that homosexualization has become a popular rhetoric of insult.[22]

In the immediate post–World War II period Americans often viewed Europe, especially Germany, as feminized, dependent, and in need of aid and guidance.[23] Although France remains as ever female, femininity now connotes irrationality, duplicity, and danger that evoke unrestrained American ridicule and anger. Given the economic clout and political influence of Germany, France, and the EU, however, they cannot be completely feminized, infantilized, or marginalized.[24] Instead, European men—and it is only men who are targeted by conservative anti-Europeanism—are rebuked for refusing to be tough, independent, adult men, willing to take on the political and military responsibilities commensurate with their economic wealth. Simultaneously, they are chastised for failing to display the filial piety due America, which provided economic and political tutelage. Germans are the particular recipients of America's hurt disappointment in this regard.

Anti-Americanism, by contrast, focuses more on the substance of American unilateralism and preemption than on the style of masculinity that imbues them. To be sure, there are caricatures of Bush as a wild cowboy and critiques of his willful ignorance of the world outside of America that build on long-standing European prejudices about American men's lack of culture and education due to their devotion to pursuit of the almighty dollar. To varying degrees, Europeans have moved away from the militaristic and moralized masculinity that is now in vogue in America. They seem less interested in promoting European variants of masculinity, perhaps because they fail to see the connections between gender and politics, perhaps because they separate their critique of the Bush administration from their assessment of American society and culture.

Anti-Americanism and anti-Europeanism emerge most sharply in the discourses produced by politicians and government officials, pundits and policy analysts, and the elite and popular media. To what extent do they reflect or find popular resonance? A sampling of demonstrations, spontaneous actions, and public-opinion polls suggests that popular anti-Americanism is a potent political force throughout Western and to a much smaller degree Eastern Europe, but its biting political critique of Bush is combined with an openness to American culture and a clear separation of Americans from their government. This distinction is often denied by Americans, who charge that European anti-Americanism represents not a critique of policies, but rather a rejection of America in toto, and with that of capitalism and modernity. In some formulations, anti-Americanism is held to code America, capitalism, and modernity as Jewish, and to attack them as well as Israel in an all-encompassing and anti-Semitic manner. Anti-Europeanists explicitly critique both governments and societies; they mirror and encourage a mixture of suspicion, resentment, and superiority toward those who dissent, while according only condescending thanks toward those states that have joined the coalition of the willing.

The millions of European demonstrators who took to the streets on February 15, 2002, to protest the impending U.S. attack on Iraq represented every possible position in the spectrum of anti-Americanism. In Europe, as in America, there were peace flags and Bush caricatures, pleas to give peace a chance and protests of "no blood for oil," reasonable slogans and sectarian claims and comparisons. Demonstrators came not only from the ranks of usual suspects—i.e., the till-then virtually dormant peace movements, left and Green political parties, and universities and schools—but also from church groups, trade unions, and community associations. To a surprisingly high degree, they represented people who had never before attended a demonstration. Anxiety about war and instability, dislike of Bush, a broader critique of American foreign policy, and a desire for greater European autonomy and power mixed in proportions that are impossible to estimate from numbers and slogans alone.

American anti-Europeanism has no such popular mobilizing power. There have been no large protests outside the French and German embassies, for example, but hostility is expressed in petty, more spontaneous ways. Anti-European—above all, anti-French—insults and jokes abound on TV and radio to apparent popular support. The House of

Representatives' insistence that its cafeteria henceforth sell only "freedom fries" in place of that now unmentionable other sort, won popular applause and inspired others to imitate. Some restaurants dumped their merlot in the gutter, and an informal boycott of French wine and cheese has had notable effect. (European threats to boycott Coca-Cola, ketchup, and Esso gas stations, by contrast, have found little support.)[25] Such anti-European actions reflect less an informed critique of French or German policy than a resentful reaction against anyone who is "not with us."

Opinion polls are more informative about popular anti-Americanism and to a lesser extent anti-Europeanism. According to a Pew survey taken in 2002 before the war was imminent "criticism of U.S. policies and ideals such as American-style democracy and business practices are also highly prevalent among the publics of traditional allies. In fact, critical assessments of the U.S. in countries such as Canada, Germany and France are much more widespread than in the developing nations of Africa and Asia." The British, Germans, and French believed that Iraq represented a great or moderate danger in only somewhat lesser proportions than Americans did, but Europeans, unlike Americans, suspected that the United States might intervene as much if not more because of oil rather than because Saddam was a threat.[26] A March 2003 Pew survey of public opinion in nine European countries concluded that Europeans blamed Bush rather than Americans in general for U.S. policy. The June 2003 Pew survey showed that whereas 70 percent of the British continued to have a favorable image of the United States, fewer than 50 percent of those interviewed in Germany, France, Spain, and Russia did. Over three-quarters of French people, nearly two-thirds of Spaniards, Italians, and Russians, and nearly 60 percent of Germans favored more independent relationships with America.[27] A recent Eurobaromenter public opinion survey, comparing attitudes within the fifteen EU member countries and the thirteen candidate countries revealed surprising agreement despite differing stances on the Iraq war. While a mere 23 percent in the EU thought the US was a positive force for peace in the world, the figure for the candidate countries (CC-13) was only 34 percent. The CC-13 ranked the EU well above the United States on everything from fighting terrorism and poverty to protecting the environment and promoting world economic growth.[28]

A recent BBC poll suggests that widespread European criticism of American politics is accompanied by admiration for aspects of American culture. It also reveals how poorly Americans assess how others see them. Despite their different relationships with America, nearly two-thirds of the French, Russian, and British interviewees described Americans negatively as arrogant and positively as free. They also highlighted American religiosity. Americans overwhelmingly believe that "America is a force for good in the world," while Europeans—even the British—are highly skeptical. On the cultural front, the British and the French, but not the Russians, view American music, TV, movies, and products (food aside) positively, even as they judge their own countries as overall more cultured. Perceptions of the desirability of American and European societies diverge wildly. Sixty-nine percent of Americans believe the United States is the best place to live, and 96 percent assume that most non-Americans are eager to live there. In fact, if offered the chance, only 21 percent of Russians, 15 percent of Brits and 7 percent of the French want to live in America.[29]

These samplings of anti-Americanism from below suggest the prevalence of critical attitudes toward American policies, even in countries whose governments, such as those of Spain and Italy, joined the "coalition of the willing." They suggest the breadth of issues on which disagreement exists, and the strong European desire for a more autonomous and equal transatlantic partnership. But they indicate as well a differentiated attitude toward American society and culture. There is an openness to American products and mass culture, an admiration for American freedom and economic opportunities, but simultaneously a clear preference for European culture and society, Americanized as it in many ways is. Popular anti-Europeanism seems to be less nuanced, less knowledgeable about European goods and culture, and more dismissive of alternative European values and institutions. The American people display "an intense solipsism" and "a general ignorance of the world beyond American's shore," argued Anatol Lieven. Most "are not nearly as militarist, imperialist or aggressive as their German equivalents in 1914; but most German people in 1914 would at least have been able to find France on a map."[30]

On the elite and popular levels, anti-Europeanism is divided about whether Europe remains essential to America's global interests, whereas Europe, however much it wants a more equal, multilateral relationship with America, does not desire and cannot afford a complete break. To be sure, many Americans accuse the French of clinging to Gaullist fantasies of an independent Third Force and suspect the Germans of wanting the EU as a counterpole to America, but most Europeans seem to aspire, in Schroeder's words, to a partnership on equal footing, built on the basis of a strengthened and integrated Europe.[31] The end of the Cold War has given America the freedom to prioritize non-European areas, but it has simultaneously given Europeans the freedom to push their disagreement with America more forcefully. What is new about anti-Americanism and anti-Europeanism is less the substantive issues in dispute, which have been rather consistent over the past two decades, than the context in which they are being articulated.

The current forms of anti-Americanism and anti-Europeanism have evolved in fits and starts. The late 1960s witnessed a new anti-Americanism that neither rejected American capitalism nor anguished about American culture and gender relations; rather it singled out American interventionism, above all in Vietnam but also in Iran and

Latin America. For the '68 generation in Western Europe, vitriolic attacks on American foreign policy (think of the infamous USA-SA-SS slogan in Germany), went hand in hand with a "passion for American culture."[32] If there was criticism of how well the Social Democratic welfare state functioned, there was a shared commitment to Keynesianism, regulatory social policies, and industrialism.

Anti-Americanism of a somewhat different sort emerged in the 1980s. On the one hand there was a growing critique of the norms, forms, values, and costs of the model of industrial capitalism, capitalist rationality, and obsession with growth that the United States had pioneered and much of Western European has adopted. On the other hand, and closely related in terms of program and personnel, was the growing opposition to nuclear weapons and U.S. nuclear policies that came to a head with bitter disputes over the stationing of Pershing II and Cruise missiles in Europe.[33] Europeans and Americans found themselves at odds over the desirability of détente, the threat represented by the Soviet invasion of Afghanistan, the wisdom of boycotting Iran, and the possibility of delinking North-South issues from East-West ones. In good Cold War fashion, those favoring more conciliatory policies and expressing concerns about war and the environment were accused of objectively serving Soviet interests. German opponents of Euro missiles were accused of pursuing "self-Finlandization." To a degree not seen in the earlier postwar decades, Europe and America disagreed about global threats and developmental possibilities, about the relative weight of military and diplomatic solutions, as well as about social policy, the environment, and religion.

Although defense and security were the primary foci, other issues, such as the regulation of seabed mining, the marketing of baby formula in the Third World, abortion, and neoliberal economic policies played a role as well. According to Sanford Ungar's diagnosis, America had become estranged from an increasingly complex world, was unwilling to try to understand or negotiate with even its economically powerful European allies, and insisted that others accept its policies and priorities, its definition of a world simplistically divided into good guys and bad ones.[34] From the perspective of the present, both the unilateral behavior of the United States and the political anti-Americanism of Europeans sound strikingly familiar. But the Cold War context contained rhetoric and reactions on both sides, disciplining European dissent but not bitterness, and limiting U.S. willingness to launch a full-scale critique on countries and international institutions that failed to do its bidding.

The end of the Cold War resolved one set of Euro-American tensions, but left unresolved a host of environmental, social, and development disagreements, while opening up vast uncertainties about the future of NATO, the importance of Europe, and the dangers facing the now geographically expanded West. The Gulf War provides a window on the altered context. The Gulf War of 1991 is remembered by America as a good war because it was fought with a UN resolution and a broad coalition, ended quickly, entailed few American casualties, and required no costly occupation. Yet, in the run-up to and ultimate participation in the Gulf War, old themes reappeared and the questions and tropes of the Iraq war were foreshadowed. Forgotten was the long and bitter wrangling, after the Iraqi invasion of Kuwait, about whether war was necessary or whether diplomacy might prevail; over who should provide troops, who would command them, and what the war's ultimate purpose should be. While the French supplied both troops and money—a collaboration overlooked by Francophobe Americans—Germany footed a large portion of the bill but refused to send troops, citing constitutional prohibitions on operations outside the NATO area. American critics impatiently admonished Germany (and Japan as well) to grow up, behave like a sovereign nation, and assume its adult responsibilities in the world. America had facilitated German reunification and it was the rankest ingratitude for Germany not to support

America in its hour of need. Money alone was insufficient thanks. No longer concerned about potential German militarism, Americans complained bitterly about a feminized anxiety that pervaded Germany, an overwrought fear of war, an inability to overcome past traumas. Hiding behind the fig leaf of constitutional clauses was pure cowardice.[35] The disintegration of Yugoslavia provided occasions for both disagreement and cooperation between Europe and the United States, but when the Iraq conflict erupted again, the barely repressed disagreements about policy and principles that had surfaced in the early 1980s and the Gulf War burst forth again.

This sketch of the shifting articulations of anti-Americanism and anti-Europeanism tells a Western European and American story of repeated disagreement on policies and principles, even as the context and rhetoric of dispute have altered. It ignores some of the deeper divergences between Europe and America in the last three decades that have enhanced conflict and inhibited mutual understanding. Whereas America has become ever more religious over the last three decades, Europe, New as well as Old, has become increasingly secular.[36] The messianic rhetoric of Bush, his tendency to divide the world simplistically into good and evil, arouse discomfort if not ridicule in Europe. There is dismay that Bush's religiously based radicalism is used by those "fundamentalists of power" Cheney and Rumsfeld for "imperial power politics" justified as a divinely ordained mission.[37] Since the 1980s, environmental politics play a much greater role in Europe than they do in America, reflecting a clearer recognition of limited resources and a greater willingness to adopt conservation measures. The "greening" of Europe has also generated sustained criticism of America's selfish refusal to end its love affair with gas-guzzling cars or to impose higher taxes despite repeated energy crises, growing reliance on foreign oil, and a disproportionate consumption of nonrenewable resources. Finally, although the European welfare states have been dramatically curtailed, outside of Britain, social policy remains much more extensive than in America. Unlike the Anglo-American model of capitalism, which tolerates insecurity and high levels of inequality, much of Europe embraces the Rhenish model, which gives priority to social integration and the minimization of poverty. Capitalist modernity in Europe and America has diverged, and many parts of Europe embrace a different conception of social justice and not just a different conception of international law and cooperation, and of postnational development. America has not been marginalized by any means—how could a country with so much military and economic power be ignored?—but it has been decentered as an economic model, a cultural mecca, and a political beacon. The new anti-Americanism both reflects and is intensified by Europe's tendency to look to the real and imagined Europe, rather than to America, when debating its modern future.

Does the current upsurge in anti-Americanism and anti-Europeanism indicate a permanent breach in the transatlantic partnership or only a temporary rough spot in a committed relationship? Can the transatlantic partnership survive only if fundamentally revamped? It is easier to outline the options than predict the outcome. Many neoconservative Americans who see the interests of America and Europe diverging advocate reliance on ad-hoc coalitions, believe the UN is useless unless reformed to serve American interests, and oppose any EU military force. Others, such as the policy analysts Charles Kupchan, Joseph Nye, and Clyde Prestowitz, and former members of the Clinton administration, insist that America must return to multilateralism, treat Europe as a vital, equal partner, and rely on soft power rather than military might alone.[38] Western Europe favors a renegotiation of the partnership in ways that enhance its influence and autonomy, while Blair, despite his growing unpopularity at home, clings to his special relationship with America. "New" Europe oscillates nervously between courting American attention and funds and cultivating ties to Western Europe with whom its economic future lies.

As the situation in Iraq deteriorates, Germany, France, and America talk of reconciliation, but the terms remain most unclear, as the ongoing discussions about an Iraq resolution illustrates. Europe has no interest in seeing Iraq descend into chaos, even with many Europeans opposed to the war. French President Jacques Chirac has promised not to veto a UN resolution, while Schroeder and Bush have announced that past differences are behind them. Nonetheless, France insists on a speedy transfer of sovereignty to the Iraqi people, Germany vows not to send troops, both demand that the UN be in control, and neither has as yet committed funds for reconstruction. As a sequel to unilateral intervention, America wants a multilateral restoration of order, but while it requests money and troops, it still refuses to share power. While some sort of UN resolution may well be hammered out, it will do no more than paper over differences. The anti-Americanism and anti-Europeanism, which preceded the war and survived its aftermath in less rhetorically charged forms, are not likely to disappear.

ANALOGIES

6

Iraq Is Not Arabic for Nicaragua: Central America and the Rise of the New Right

Greg Grandin

It is a breeding ground for international terrorism, according to America's envoy to the United Nations, "the most important place in the world." Years before the Republican administration launched a war to topple a vilified regime, New Right defense activists warned of a grave threat to America's national security emanating from the region, calling on Washington to initiate a crusade against a militant ideology in the name of democracy and freedom. Sound familiar? It is not the Middle East today. It's Central America two decades ago.

It is often noted in passing that a number of the current administration's advisors and officials—such as Elliot Abrams, the National Security Council's Middle East expert; John Negroponte, President George W. Bush's new ambassador to Iraq; and Robert Kagan, an ardent advocate of U.S. global hegemony—were all involved in administering the Contra War, Ronald Reagan's effort to undermine Nicaragua's revolutionary Sandinista government. Yet the links between Reagan's hard line in Central America, which many at the time found to be inexplicably excessive, and the current Bush administration's foreign policy are even more intriguing. Central America in many ways can only be understood as a dress rehearsal for what is going on now in the Middle East, a place where New Right militants had near-free rein to bring the full power of the United States against a much weaker enemy in order to exorcise the

ghost of Vietnam. Many imperial hawks now take Reagan's accomplishment in Nicaragua, as well as in El Salvador and Guatemala, as proof of
the virtuousness of America's values rather than of the powerlessness of
its opponents, contributing to their dangerous swagger across the global
stage. That Republican strategist William Kristol dares to describe the
ruin that today afflicts Central America as an "amazing success story," as
he recently did, should trouble those who now call for an expanded
American empire to help stabilize a shaky world.

Pablo Neruda once described the narrow slip of land separating the Atlantic from the Pacific as America's "sweet waist," a place too small to
bear its outsized history. For nearly two centuries, Central America and
the Caribbean have served as a workshop of empire; endless military interventions there schooled the United States both in imperial self-
assuredness and in extraterritorial policing. In 1855, the Tennessee
freebooter William Walker invaded Nicaragua, proclaimed himself president, and reinstituted slavery, an institution Nicaraguans had abolished
three decades earlier. (U.S. President Franklin Pierce quickly recognized
the presidency of Walker, who previously had attempted to install himself as ruler of Baja, California.) In the early twentieth century, U.S.
troops invaded Honduras, Mexico, Guatemala, and Costa Rica, annexed
Puerto Rico, and occupied Haiti, Cuba, and the Dominican Republic.
In 1902, Theodore Roosevelt teamed up with J.P. Morgan to shave off a
piece of Colombia—Panama became both an important global transit
route and, as the home of SOUTHCOM headquarters, the forecastle of
U.S. hemispheric might. The frequency of these military incursions
steadily increased until 1927, when the marines landed in Nicaragua and
became ensnared in a protracted guerrilla war. After five years of fruit-
lessly chasing Augusto Sandino and his rebels through mountainous jungles, the marines withdrew, leaving behind a newly created national
guard, which successfully defeated Sandino.

From this experience, the United States learned an important lesson: the value of proxies. For the next five decades, until the end of the Cold War, the United States would rely mostly on foreign strongmen, troops, and police to administer the hemisphere, training Latin American security forces to counter real and perceived threats. True, the United States at times strayed from this strategy. It sent the marines to the Dominican Republic in 1965 and to Grenada in 1983 in order to prevent political crises from producing more Castros. Yet the debacle of the United States direct involvement in Vietnam underscored, for many, the effectiveness of its surrogate strategy in Latin America.

By the late 1970s, however, the United States' hemispheric strategy showed signs of strain. In South America, Washington had responded to a growing left by supporting or orchestrating a series of military coups—Brazil in 1964, Bolivia in 1971, Uruguay and Chile in 1973, Argentina in 1976—that turned the Americas below Costa Rica into a fortress continent. Closer to home, U.S. power seemed vulnerable. With Cuba joined by left-leaning governments in Jamaica, Guyana, Panama, and Grenada, a rising cohort of New Right cadres identified the area as the place where the United States needed to salvage a foreign policy wrecked in Vietnam. In Central America, leftist insurgencies gained in El Salvador and Guatemala, and won in Nicaragua, prompting Jeane Kirkpatrick to declare that the isthmus was more important to the United States than Europe, Asia, and the Middle East.

Just as Paul Wolfowitz, Richard Perle, and think tanks such as the Project for a New American Century laid the groundwork for the war in Iraq long before the current Bush administration took office, conservative experts outside the political establishment charted the path Ronald Reagan would take in Central America during his predecessor's reign. In a series of articles and manifestos, a group of disaffected hawks challenged what they perceived as Jimmy Carter's complacent and morally askew foreign policy. On the heels of Nicaragua's Sandinista revolution, would-be policymakers organized the Committee of Santa Fe to produce "A New Inter-American Policy for the Eighties."[1] Condemning Henry Kissinger's power politics and Carter's human-rights diplomacy, they warned of an imminent U.S. defeat in the Cold War unless the country changed course. Under the cloak of détente, the Committee claimed, the Soviet Union had encircled China, positioned itself to seize control of much of the West's oil and ore supply, and had begun to penetrate the western hemisphere. Carter's tolerance of Castro and the Sandinistas put U.S. access to the Panama Canal in jeopardy and threatened to turn the Caribbean into a "Marxist-Leninist lake." The Committee identified Central America and the Caribbean—"our Balkans"—as the place to take a last stand against international Bolshevism. The crisis confronting the United States, they argued, was more than strategic; it was "metaphysical." The "inability or unwillingness" of the United States "either to protect or project its basic values and beliefs has led to the present nadir of indecision and impotence and has placed the very existence of the Republic in peril." In the same way that Wolfowitz's 1992 Defense Policy Guidance papers were dismissed at the time as too extreme, so was the 1979 Santa Fe manifesto repudiated. Yet a number of its authors, such as Roger Fontaine and Gordon Sumner, took important posts in Reagan's White House, preparing the way for today's neoconservatives.

The Committee of Santa Fe was part of a larger firmament of militant New Right intellectuals and foundations dedicated to revitalizing America's purpose in the world. While they criticized Nixon as ethically bankrupt, they dismissed Carter as terminally befuddled. In an influential article published in *Commentary* in 1979, Kirkpatrick—who would go on to serve as Reagan's ambassador to the UN—lambasted the paralysis of the Carter administration, a paralysis derived, she argued, from defeat in Vietnam. Such self-doubt led the administration to mistake friends for foes in El Salvador, Guatemala, South Africa, the shah's

Iran, and Anastasio Somoza's Nicaragua. She attacked Carter's language, singling out his tendency to talk about politics and history in abstract, impersonal terms, as "forces" or "processes." "What can a U.S. president faced with such complicated, inexorable, impersonal processes do?" Kirkpatrick asked. "The answer, offered again and again by the president and his top officials, was, Not Much."

What made Central America so important to New Right activists was its unimportance. Unlike the Middle East, it had no oil or other crucial resources. Nor did Washington's opponents in the small, desperately poor countries of Nicaragua, El Salvador, and Guatemala have many consequential friends, except perhaps Cuba. Unlike Southeast Asia, the region was in America's backyard—the USSR would not support Nicaragua's Sandinistas or the rebels in El Salvador and Guatemala to the degree it did its allies in Vietnam. Central America's very insignificance, in fact, made it the perfect antidote to Vietnam: "Mr. President," Secretary of State Alexander Haig assured Reagan, "this is one you can win." [2] It also made the region a cheap reward to the conservatives who helped elect Reagan; Reagan's hardline was largely dictated by a group of individuals—Kirkpatrick, Haig, and Abrams, along with John Poindexter, Caspar Weinberger, and CIA director William Casey—with little or no experience in Latin America. "They can't have the Soviet Union or the Middle East or Western Europe. All are too important. So they've given them Central America," remarked a Senate staffer. [3]

Ronald Reagan took up the Kirkpatrick's call for a resolute realism with a vengeance. [4] The White House lobbied successfully to restore counterinsurgent aid to Guatemala, partially cut off by Jimmy Carter, even as the Guatemalan military was committing over 400 massacres, killing more than 100,000 Mayan Indians, destroying 600 villages, and driving nearly a million people from their homes—just between 1981 and 1983. Soldiers beat children to death on rocks while their parents watched. They extracted organs and fetuses, amputated genitalia and limbs, committed mass rapes, and burned victims alive. A 1999 UN-administered Truth Commission report deemed these acts to be part of a larger campaign of genocide.[5] Recently declassified documents leave no doubt that the Reagan administration was aware of the killing. "The military continues to engage in massacres of civilians in the countryside," reported the officer in charge of Inter-American Affairs to the Secretary of State in November 1982.[6] Nevertheless, a month later, Reagan met with José Efraín Ríos Montt, who presided over the most severe phase of this campaign, and publicly declared that Ríos was getting a "bad deal" from his critics and that he was "totally committed to democracy."[7]

In El Salvador, over the course of a twelve-year civil war, Washington provided the government with roughly six billion dollars in financial aid, equipment, and training. Security forces there murdered approximately 60,000 people—an average of 1,000 a month during the early years of the war. And in Nicaragua, Reagan organized remnants of Somoza's National Guard into the Contras, a surrogate army that routinely decapitated civilian supporters of the Sandinistas. The slaughter was so horrendous that Reagan's Assistant Secretary of State for Inter-American Affairs, Thomas Enders, who helped carry out Nixon's massive, covert aerial bombing of Southeast Asia, urged the White House to pursue an alternative course of negotiating with the Sandinistas and the Salvadoran rebels. He was dismissed for his efforts.

The first generation of New Right intellectuals walked a fine line between realism, calling for a robust use of military force, and idealism, which justified that force. Kirkpatrick, for example, argued that U.S. principles should guide foreign policy but also insisted that that policy should be used only to defend U.S. national security. She warned against trying to be the "world's midwife" to democracy. In classic conservative terms, she urged the United States to support allegedly organic dictators such as the Somoza and Shah Pahlavi dynasties of Nicaragua and Iran, and counseled against the conceit that it was "possible to democratize governments, anytime, anywhere, under any circumstances." Reagan's uncompromising rhetorical stance toward Central America notwith-standing, political constraints often forced him to a more unassuming role. For Reagan, like Carter, was still hamstrung by the antimilitarism generated from the U.S. experience in Southeast Asia. Public opinion polls consistently showed that voters did not favor an invasion of Nicaragua, while bumper stickers reminded the electorate that "El Salvador is Spanish for Vietnam." High-level U.S. military officers, believ-ing that the Sandinistas had too much popular support, strongly advised the president against direct military involvement. So, despite occasional saber-rattling, Reagan was forced for the most part to stick with the well-proven proxy strategy. The Committee of Santa Fe called for the United States to lead a "war of national liberation" against Castro; Rea-gan gave them Grenada instead.

Yet despite shunning, either by instinct or by necessity, the kind of ambitions expressed today by neoconservatives such as Wolfowitz to re-make the world in an American image, Reagan did use Central Amer-ica to portray the Cold War as a moral struggle between good and evil. In so doing, he moved the Republican Party away from its foreign-policy pragmatism. It was Reagan, after all, who rehabilitated Abraham Lincoln for the Republican Party, citing the Great Emancipator's lofty rhetoric in his recurrent fights with Congress to fund the Contra War and the Salvadoran and Guatemalan militaries. Continued aid to the Contras, he claimed, would keep faith with the "revolutionary her-itage" of the United States, a heritage that, borrowing from Lincoln, be-stowed a "hope to the world for all future time."[8] Reagan consistently picked up the torch of idealism traditionally borne by Democrats like Woodrow Wilson and John Kennedy. This marked a break from previ-ous Republican administrations, which had little sympathy for the word "revolution." "I never believed we should compete with revolutionaries," said Thomas Mann, a high-ranking Republican career foreign service officer, in reference to Kennedy's promise to "transform the American continent into a vast crucible of revolutionary ideas and efforts."[9]

It was in Central America, then, where the Republican Party first rolled out a foreign-policy philosophy described as "hard Wilsonianism" or, as Wolfowitz recently dubbed it, "democratic realism"—an unapologetic willingness to use the full spectrum of American power to both defend our national interests and to export our moral values.

Perhaps more than any other American conflict, Vietnam highlighted the porous border between foreign and domestic policy. Escalating domestic dissent, much of it linked to a reinvigorated leftist internationalism, not only helped end the war but led to legislative measures that curbed the power of government security institutions, most notably the Central Intelligence Agency. Throughout the 1970s, Congress issued a number of reports that described in detail the U.S. government's role in the executions of foreign leaders and in the surveillance and harassment of domestic dissenters, generating a deep culture of distrust and cynicism among American citizens. The Central American conflicts provided an opportunity to reverse this trend. In the face of persistent and growing opposition to its policies in El Salvador and Nicaragua, the White House countered with a series of actions that eroded the boundary between imperial policies and national politics. Making little distinction between foreign enemies and domestic opponents, Reagan used the Central American wars to reinvigorate the national security state in ways that resonate to this day.

The White House launched a three-pronged approach to winning the war at home. First, it sought to influence popular domestic opinion by improving "public diplomacy." Members of the administration were keenly aware that the Vietnam conflict signaled a new kind of war, one where the enemy was successful at waging not just a military but a propaganda battle. As one 1983 RAND Corporation analysis put it, "today's revolutionaries" have abandoned isolated guerrilla strategies and have adopted a policy of "deliberate internationalization." They seek "allies, resources, and volunteers from around the world and are building sympathetic support networks within the United States."[10] In response to the successful efforts of the Salvadoran rebels and the Sandinista government to establish ties with church groups, human-rights organizations, the media, some unions, and solidarity committees in the United States, the White House established in 1983 the Office of Public Diplomacy for Latin America and the Caribbean. Staffed with members of the intelligence service, including members of the CIA whose expertise was the dissemination of propaganda in foreign countries, the office's first task was to undertake polling to determine what "turns Americans against the Sandinistas" and to identify "exploitable themes and trends."[11] After coming up with such useful topics such as "drugs," "terrorism," "persecution of church groups," "anti-Semitism," "Soviet ties," and "racism" toward native Nicaraguans, the office launched a public-relations campaign designed both to justify Reagan's policies and erode support for the Sandinistas and the Salvadoran insurgents. Administration officials, conservative pundits, and think tanks repeated a number of damning charges: the USSR, Vietnam, and Ethiopia had shipped hundreds of tons of arms to the Salvadoran rebels, the Cubans and the Sandinistas were fomenting terrorism in Costa Rica, the Soviets were building a deep-water port in Nicaragua to dock nuclear submarines; high-level Sandinista officials trafficked in cocaine; Nicaragua was harboring terrorists from the PLO, Libya, the Red Brigades, ETA, even the Baader-Meinhof Gang—claims as false, yet no less effective, as those now-famous sixteen words in Bush's State of the Union address.

Second, the administration countered left internationalism by cultivating its own grass-roots support for its foreign policy, mobilizing its evangelical Christian base in the struggle against the kind of Marxist Christianity advocated by the Central American Left.

Third, the administration sought to revive an intelligence operation crippled by the scandals of the 1960s and 1970s. This revival was partly accomplished through the creation of alternative institutions—the Office of Public Diplomacy, for instance, and ad-hoc working groups within the National Security Council (such as the one responsible for the Iran-Contra Scandal)—which could circumvent Congressional oversight. Reagan also issued a number of executive directives, which once again authorized covert operations and allowed interagency intelligence sharing. Worse yet, intelligence agencies—both the FBI and those authorized exclusively for foreign espionage—again turned their attention on domestic dissenters, carrying out a far-reaching operation against church groups, human-rights organizations, and solidarity committees. This activity went beyond surveillance to include the harassment of activists in their homes and workplaces. In one of the more outrageous examples of government schemes to circumvent the right of due process—particularly chilling in light of today's revocation of constitutional rights of designated "enemy combatants"—the National Security Council, through the office of Oliver North, drafted plans to hold antiwar activists in detention centers in the event of a U.S. invasion of Nicaragua.

In many ways, then, the government's actions on the domestic front during the Central American crisis were not only a response to the antimilitarism generated by Vietnam but helped pave the way for the domestic initiatives taken by the Bush administration in the current War on Terror. This administration has been highly effective at garnering support for its imperial policies through the orchestration of public spectacles, the dissemination of dubious intelligence, the management of major media outlets, and the containment of dissent. Furthermore, the government, through the USA PATRIOT Act, the Department of

Homeland Security, and other initiatives, has consolidated surveillance capacities to an unprecedented degree, eroding the firewall designed to separate domestic and international intelligence gathering.

Jeane Kirkpatrick promised that U.S. actions in Latin America, though designed to protect our national security, would also "make the actual lives of actual people . . . somewhat better and somewhat freer." [12] And in his many appeals on behalf of the Contras, Reagan urged the United States not to abandon Nicaragua. But after the war, that is effectively what happened, not just in Nicaragua but throughout the region. The United States spent roughly $10 billion in Nicaragua and El Salvador throughout the wars of the 1980s, yet refused to take responsibility for postwar reconstruction. Instead, it delegated the job of demobilizing combatants and political and judicial reform to the United Nations. While the United States financed some of these efforts, it quickly grew bored and turned its attentions elsewhere, mostly to Colombia and the War on Drugs. Washington's involvement in Central America today is largely limited to issues of illegal immigration and drug trafficking. It has taken few substantial steps to fulfill Reagan's thunderous pledges of democracy and development other than promoting and profiting from free trade. (In 1986, the International Court of Justice ruled that U.S. aggression toward Nicaragua constituted "an unlawful use of force" and ordered the United States to pay between $12 and 17 billion in reparations to Managua. Washington refused to pay, instead giving Nicaragua's post-Sandinista government a $60 million direct aid payoff in exchange for dropping the claim.)

What has become of the place now that Washington has moved on? Political terror has certainly abated. Nicaragua, Guatemala, and El Salvador are all nominally constitutional democracies, holding regularly scheduled elections. Yet the devastation that began a quarter century ago has not been reversed. In fact, it has accelerated.

A few months ago, U.S. and Western media paid much attention to a

United Nations Development Programme report, which highlighted the growing gap in education and development between the Middle East and the rest of the world. For neoconservatives, the report was proof positive of the need for increased U.S. involvement in the Middle East. Had they—or their allies in the media—bothered to compare countries like Iran and Syria, both slated for imperial reform, to today's Central America, however, they might have thought twice about the wisdom of their policies. In terms of education, for example, 10 percent of Iranian women between the ages of fifteen and twenty-four, and 21 percent of Syrian women of a similar age, are illiterate. In Guatemala, by contrast, nearly 30 percent of women in that age range cannot read or write. In Nicaragua, illiteracy rates among all men and women stand at 33 percent, a sharp increase since the electoral defeat of the Sandinistas in 1990.

In Iran, 40 percent of the population lives in poverty, while in Syria, that number is approximately 20 percent. According to CIA estimates, two-thirds of the inhabitants of Nicaragua, Guatemala, Honduras, and El Salvador—roughly 20,000,000 people—live below the poverty level, a situation that has grown worse since the wars ended.[13] In Guatemala, almost six million people survive on less than $2 a day. After Haiti, Nicaragua is the poorest country in the hemisphere. In Guatemala, the infant mortality rate is 38 deaths for every 1,000 live births—a rate more than five times greater than that of the United States. At the same time, wealth inequality is at an all-time high.[14] Privileged elites live in garrison communities, with private, heavily armed security guards protecting them from the constant threat of kidnapping for ransom.

The recent emergence, financed by the World Bank, of Vietnam as a major coffee exporter has led to a steep drop in coffee prices and hard times for a number of Guatemalan planters—an irony not lost on them: "We were faithful to Washington during the Cold War, and this is the way the U.S. repays us, by funding its enemy," one complained to me last year. The fall in coffee prices has made an already-dire situation even worse for those most vulnerable. In some rural areas, hunger, infectious disease, and malnutrition is routine, and starvation has become common.[15] For many, the only viable escape from such wretchedness is to travel north to Mexico or the United States, but increased U.S. border patrols—in response to the war on terror—have made that route more hazardous than ever. Environmental degradation—deforestation, soil erosion, poisoned water, and polluted air—has reached crisis proportions.

All through Central America, even in reputable Costa Rica, violent crime has skyrocketed to wartime levels. In El Salvador, the murder rate is 120 per 100,000 inhabitants, besting even Colombia. In Guatemala, more than 700 women, mostly from poor families, have been kidnapped, tortured, raped, and then stabbed to death since 2001. The police have made few arrests, and the killings go on, unexplained and unsolved. Sixty people are murdered each week in Guatemala City, mostly connected to car thefts, kidnappings, illegal timbering, bank robbery, and, most important, drugs. The isthmus has become the key transit point for drugs coming into the U.S. from the Andes, with high-ranking military officers moonlighting as import-exporters. A clandestine globalization has fueled this violence, with gangs such as Mara Salvatrucha and Mara 18 operating throughout El Salvador, Guatemala, Honduras, and Los Angeles. It is estimated that these gangs are responsible for 10 percent of the region's homicides. In Guatemala, shadowy groups affiliated with the military operate in much the same way that the death squads did in the 1980s. Reinforced with information supplied by a wartime intelligence apparatus, they do the frontline work for cliques headed by military officers. While mostly involved in common crime, they occasionally eliminate activists attempting to bring to justice those responsible for political repression.

The history of Central America sounds another note of caution to those who would hold up empire as the executor of progress and liberal democracy. For the simple fact is that whatever degree of democracy and human rights the region today enjoys is due not to the actions of the U.S. empire but to the struggle against that empire. While sympathizers and opponents of the Nicaraguan revolution continue to debate its degree of authoritarianism, there is no doubt that it acted as a catalyst for liberalization that, despite today's high levels of apathy and poverty, created a culture of mass political participation and expectations of social justice. Perhaps for that reason, the Sandinistas, though plagued by divisions and charges of corruption, remain the single largest political party in the country. In El Salvador, the Frente Farabundo Martí para la Liberación Nacional fought the U.S.-backed military to a draw, and in so doing managed to extract real concessions from the oligarchy and the military in the 1992 peace accords, such as land reform, the cashiering of some human-rights violators from the ranks of the army, and the restructuring of security forces. While many of these concessions have not been adequately implemented, the FMLN has successfully passed from the bullet to the ballot and now represents a diverse array of social movements in the political arena. In general, the Central American countries with the most vibrant civil societies are those, like Nicaragua and El Salvador, where the former enemies of the United States still have some social power.

By contrast, Guatemala—intended as a "showcase for democracy" after the Eisenhower administration ousted its democratically elected president—suffers from a septic political culture. State repression there was the worst in the region, leaving little but an ineffectual scrap of an opposition. The initial excitement generated by the emergence of a postwar Mayan cultural rights movement has dissipated. Intimidation of peasant-, labor-, and human-rights activists, while greatly decreased from wartime levels, continues. Close to thirty political activists were assassinated in the run-up to the recent presidential election. The power of the military remains unassailable. Aside from a few notable exceptions, those responsible for the genocide continue not only to enjoy impunity but to hold high public office. Ríos Montt, for example, just completed a term as president of the congress—though he did recently lose a bid to return to the national presidency, a bright spot in an otherwise desolate political landscape.

There are, of course, many important differences between Central America and the Middle East, not least of which is the nature of Washington's opponents in both places. In Guatemala, Nicaragua, and El Salvador, the United States fought against democratic movements. In the Middle East, this is clearly not the case.

There is another critical distinction between the two conflicts that this governing cohort of neoconservatives, perhaps blinded by their self-reported success, has ignored. Reagan's revolutionary claims notwithstanding, his interventions in Central America were designed either to defend or restore the region's old regimes. Indeed, nowhere in Latin America during the Cold War did Washington ever set out to set up a government from scratch. In fact, it was the burden of the hemisphere's genuinely revolutionary regimes—in Cuba, Nicaragua, Chile, and before that, in Guatemala—and its revolutionary movements—in El Salvador and elsewhere—to attempt this difficult task, and we know the outcomes of those efforts. But creating a new regime is precisely what the Bush administration is now attempting to do in the Middle East, and it now seems that they will not have an easier time of it than did, say, the Sandinistas.

The Contra war provides an illustrative example. Seeking to demonstrate to a wavering rural population that the Sandinistas could not establish effective sovereignty, the Contras destroyed cooperatives, schools, health clinics, and power stations, and murdered civilians, including foreigners who were helping to rebuild Nicaragua. The Contras and their U.S. patrons felt no need to establish ideological legitimacy. All they had to do was wear down a fledgling regime through unpredictable yet persistent acts of terror. With the Sandinistas unable to deliver security, much less a better life, popular support and goodwill tipped to their enemies, who started out, we should not forget, as a rump of discredited old regime repressors—"dead-enders," to apply Rumsfeld's description of the Baathist remnants who reportedly are organizing the resistance to the U.S. occupation of Iraq.

A year after the fall of the Baathist regime, the Bush administration lost its bid to win legitimacy in Iraq. Now in its hurry to find an exit out of the mess it has made, Washington is dusting off tactics it first perfected in Latin America. The Pentagon and the CIA are reportedly creating a paramilitary force made up of Kurds, Shiites, and ex-members of Saddam Hussein's intelligence apparatus to hunt down and presumably assassinate members of the Iraqi resistance. These plans echo tactics used by the United States in Vietnam and by Israel in its occupied territories. Yet they are also similar to Washington's proxy strategy in Central America. American advisors coordinated the activities of the police and the military, set up command centers that could quickly analyze and archive information gathered from diverse sources, and trained domestic security units to execute rapid-response raids. The hope in Iraq is that such a force—operating independently yet beholden to Washington—will prevent the country from being taken over by extremists or degenerating into civil war, as the CIA now says is a distinct possibility. But in Central America, that is exactly what happened.

Death squads first appeared in the region in Guatemala in the mid-1960s, in response to an armed insurgency that had its roots going back to the CIA's 1954 overthrow of President Jacobo Arbenz, an economic nationalist who expropriated United Fruit Company land and appointed Communists to positions in his administration. Despite

Arbenz's easy ouster, Guatemala in the 1960s stood on the brink of chaos, plagued, as Iraq is today, by bombings, bank robberies, sabotage, murders, and kidnappings. In an effort to restore order, the United States helped create a paramilitary unit that went on to wage a campaign of extrajudicial kidnappings and assassinations. By 1967, death squads affiliated with this unit were, according to the American embassy, "running wild." They killed or "disappeared" hundreds of thousands of individuals—political activists of all stripes, Communist or not—and drove, by the CIA's own estimation, "usually moderate groups to violence." By 1968, political repression had grown so acute that Viron Vaky, the deputy chief of the American embassy, felt compelled to issue a warning to his superiors in the State Department: "Society is being rent apart and polarized," he wrote. "Official squads are guilty of atrocities. Interrogations are brutal, torture is used and bodies are mutilated." Vaky blamed the crisis on the "conceptual tactic of counter-terror," which called for the fighting of terrorism with more terrorism: "Murder, torture, and mutilation are alright if our side is doing it and the victims are Communists. . . . I have literally heard these arguments from our people." The problem, he argued, was not just moral but strategic, for Washington's support for paramilitaries had created a culture of violence that undermined the rule of law, radicalized potential democratic allies, and discredited the United States throughout Latin America. "The credibility of our claims," Vaky cautioned, anticipating Kirkpatrick's hollow promises, "to want a better and more just world are [sic] increasingly placed in doubt." [16]

The first insurgent generation of neoconservatives only had to tear down a tottering power—and a U.S. foreign policy already discredited from failure in Vietnam. They were able to play out their fantasy of revolution in an inconsequential sweet waist of a land where the wreckage of their actions could be easily ignored. Yet Iraq is not Arabic for Central America—the stakes are much higher and the task of establishing a governing consensus much greater than anything the United States ever faced in its own hemisphere, a fact that this administration has been forced to accept. Today's hawks, however, continue to ignore perhaps the most obvious question raised by the United States imperial track record: if Washington is unable to bring prosperity, stability, and meaningful democracy to Central America, a region that falls squarely within its own backyard and whose population shares many of the values of the United States, then what are the chances that it will do so in the Middle East?

7

Improving on the Civilizing Mission?: Assumptions of United States Exceptionalism in the Colonization of the Philippines

Michael Adas

Just days after William Howard Taft arrived in the Philippine Islands in early June 1900 to take up his position as the chairman of the five-member commission charged with the task of establishing a civilian government for the newly annexed colony, he wrote to J.G. Schmidlapp, an old friend in Ohio, to assure him that he was settling quite comfortably into his exotic surroundings. Taft found the climate in Manila much more agreeable than he had been led to expect was possible in the tropics. The heat, he estimated, was comparable to Cincinnati during the summer months. He was also heartened by the "strong, healthy-looking" young Americans he encountered in the streets of the capital, which he deemed as robust as any back home. But Taft drew a much larger lesson from the apparent ease of his own acclimation and that of his countrymen to the tropical locale. He concluded that though "it may be that it is the survival of the fittest . . . it is evident than men can live here and be healthy."[1]

Given the centuries-old and persisting assumption that tropical environs were inherently debilitating and unhealthy—if not lethal—for "white" men (and women),[2] Taft's uneasiness about his own ability and that of his countrymen more generally to adjust to life in Manila is unsurprising. What is remarkable is his confidence that he and his fellow Americans could defy the received wisdom and scientific evidence that

had accumulated over centuries regarding the high mortality rates suffered by migrants of European descent domiciled in the tropics. Though
Taft does not explicitly mention the recently published essay on *The
Control of the Tropics* by the English writer Benjamin Kidd,[3] the new head
of the Philippine Commission's sanguine assessment of American adap-
tive capacities clearly contravened Kidd's much-discussed and emphatic
recapitulation of the perils-of-the-tropics themes.

Two years earlier, William Griffis, who was widely considered one of
a handful of American experts on "Orientals," had explicitly dismissed
Kidd's suppositions that Europeans could not live or work in the tropics. Griffi's rather extensive travels in the Far East and South Asia convinced him that the experience of European colonization in tropical
areas like India and the Netherlands Indies provided ample evidence
that Kidd was wrong. Griffis pointed out that Europeans had "for centuries lived not only within the tropics but along the equator," and that
many "of the most brilliant achievements of the Anglo-Saxon are to be
noted in th[ese] region[s]." He correctly identified disease as the main
obstacle to European habitation in the tropics, and—with major recent
advances in tropical medicine clearly in mind—he celebrated the ways
in which "civilized man" had employed the "very resources of the tropics to overcome their deadly blight, malaria and fever." These break-
throughs had made it possible for Anglo-Saxons and other peoples of
European descent to make full use of the vital resources of the tropics,
which the indolent and backward indigenous peoples had been unwilling and unable to exploit properly. Griffis was convinced that Americans would prove every bit as energetic and able in their efforts to
develop the long-neglected resources of the tropics as their European
"kinsmen." The United States' colonization of the Philippines would
demonstrate yet again that

what wonders civilized man, with common sense and a knowledge of
the environment and proper precautions, can achieve and endure. De-

spite the climate and deadly malaria, the venom of insect, reptile and plant, and the malice of evil men, thousands of men show that one can spend the best working years of the average and even long life in the tropics. . . . More than ten millions of white men and their descendants are to-day settled in the tropics, laying the foundations of new and possibly great civilizations.[4]

These early and partial assessments of the meanings of the rather abrupt American commitment to formal colonial rule over overseas peoples, with whom there had been previously only minimal contacts, reflect both the deep ambivalence and considerable anxiety that tempered the emergence of the United States as an avowedly imperialist power with visions of global hegemony. Griffis, and particularly Taft, wrote at a time when the plunge into colonial expansion was marked by diplomatic bungles, the brutal betrayal of Filipino allies, and a vicious war to put down the stubborn Filipino resistance to American measures to assert control over the islands. The devastation and hundreds of thousands of casualties wrought by American efforts to crush the so-called insurgency, and the epidemics that these military operations spread among the human and livestock population of the islands, made a mockery of Rudyard Kipling's celebration of the Americans as the latest of the Anglo-Saxon peoples to take up the "white man's burden." Reports of these disasters continued to fuel the fierce debate raging back home over whether or not the United States should join the ranks of the imperialist powers by annexing the islands.[5] Both Taft and Griffis sought to validate the imperialist enterprise by underscoring the capacity of American soldiers and administrators to thrive and fulfill their civilizing tasks despite environmental constraints that, according to Kidd and other experts, had proved to be a major obstacle to successful European colonization in the tropics. But Griffis acknowledged that the Europeans had also surmounted the perils of disease and climate, and both he and Taft looked to European colonial institutions and policies for precedents to guide the neophyte Americans' approaches at a time when most of their initiatives were making a shambles of the societies they professed to be civilizing.

Griffis and Taft were by no means alone among the American officials and publicists who were attentive to the lessons that the more experienced colonial powers, particularly the British and Dutch, might have to convey with regard to colonial administrative practice. Elihu Root, who in 1899 was appointed head of the War Department that oversaw United States colonization in both the Pacific and Caribbean in these years, made an extensive study of British colonial history after he learned what his new responsibilities would entail. Luke Wright, who succeeded Taft as governor of the Philippines, also viewed British precedents as the most obvious model for United States colonial policy, a view that was shared by many of the commissioners who set that policy in the first years of American rule.[6] Even a decade and a half after the annexation of the islands, prominent officials and American visitors continued to cite the practice of the European colonial powers as justification for colonial projects undertaken by the United States. For example, Charles Elliott, a former secretary of commerce, saw Kipling's famous poem "Kitchener's School" as presaging the United States army's remarkable shift from conquest to elementary education, while Carl Crow stressed the example of America's British "cousins" in India as a key source of inspiration for the impressive public-works projects that had been undertaken in the Philippines. Some officials, including Francis Harrison, who was generally critical of the other colonial powers, saw much to emulate in Dutch efforts to promote commerce (and prosperity), agricultural development, and railways in the Netherlands Indies. Maj. General Leonard Wood, who would later play a dominant role in the administration of the islands, opined that there was much to learn from the Dutch about how to govern the Muslim peoples of Mindanao.[7]

•   •   •

These plaudits for their imperial rivals notwithstanding, most American observers were not only critical of European approaches to colonization in Asia but convinced that their own colonial project was unprecedented in the nature and extent of the process of civilizing that it had set in motion. With rare dissent, the mainly Republican, patrician progressives, who quite consciously formulated policies to remake the islands in America's image, concurred that never before had colonial domination meant anything approaching the process of "altruistic regeneration"[8] that American intervention had set in motion in the Philippines. These sentiments became more pronounced as the passage of time allowed the Americans to gain more experience in colonial governance. But almost from the outset, key policymakers stressed the radical departures from established colonial practice that they had initiated in the years after the annexation of the islands. At times claims of exceptionalism were grounded in misreadings of the colonial history of America's rivals, or in rather blinkered assessments of both the domestic situation in the United States and the nature of colonial society in the Philippines. Luke Wright's contention, for example, that the British had little to teach the inexperienced Americans because their colonial administrations were "purely English" and thus did little to promote the "natives" capacity to govern themselves,[9] betrayed a complete lack of understanding of the principles of colonial rule the British had followed for centuries. High-minded claims by prominent officials—such as Elliott and Harrison, and journalists like Lyons—that Americans were free of the racial arrogance that informed the paternalistic policies of other colonial regimes strike one as ingenuous as best.[10] Not only were segregation and racist thinking pervasive in the metropole society that sent the Americans forth to colonize, but social discrimination akin to that practiced by their European rivals was pervasive in the Philippines, from the obligatory clubs and hill station at Baguio to the day-to-day interaction between American administrators, soldiers, and missionaries and the diverse peoples of the islands.

American observers, either inadvertently or quite deliberately, were apt to misrepresent the policies and underestimate the achievements of their colonizing European rivals. But they came in the first decades of their rule in the Philippines to identify several key aspects of their approach to the civilizing mission that they believed clearly distinguished United States colonialism from its European predecessors. Officials like Taft, Elliott, and Harrison were convinced that these initiatives were not only exceptional, but that they were quite rightly viewed as subversive by European statesmen and colonial administrators. As Harrison argues in the following excerpt from his 1922 retrospective on his years as governor of the Philippines, the threat posed by American departures from established colonial practices was seen to account both for the hostility that was so evident in European responses to United States policies in the Philippines, and for the extent to which colonized peoples throughout Asia looked to the United States as a potential ally in their struggles for liberation.

> The results of our heresy have been far-reaching, and have shaken seriously the colonial offices of Great Britain, of France, and of Holland; they have also brought hope and inspiration to millions of patient brown and yellow men who find in the new ideas of America a promise for the future. The European powers which control the news service of the world did nothing, naturally enough, to spread the new ideas. No mention of the Philippines was allowed to appear in any periodical for distribution in the colonies. . . . Few Englishmen, official or merchants, in Asia, until very recently, would even discuss the Philippines; if they did, it was generally in terms of hatred and scorn for the Filipinos, and ridicule for the fantastic ideas of the Americans.[11]

As Harrison stresses, the American experiment in colonization was seen by United States officials to have critical ramifications beyond the rather confined space of the Philippine islands. After two decades of un-precedented political, social, and economic transformations, he pro-claims, it has become a model for the regeneration of societies throughout Asia, both those colonized by European rivals and those, such as China, disintegrating due to internal upheavals and the incur-sions of the imperialist powers. Harrison goes on to report that Annie Besant had confided to him that she and other Indian nationalist leaders looked to the Philippines for precedents to advance their struggle against the British, and that members of visiting delegations from China "frequently" told him of the inspiration they found in the "honor and unselfishness" of United States policies in the Philippines. Turning to the other side of the imperial divide, Harrison intimates that the British had formulated the 1918 Montagu-Chelmsford reform proposals with the example of America's political concessions to the Filipinos in mind, and he leaves the reader to infer that the Dutch were following the American example in recently extending advisory powers to Javanese notables in the Netherlands Indies.[12] Harrison's sense that the rapid de-velopment of the Philippines under United States rule had made the is-lands a model for the rest of Asia was shared by numerous officials and commentators by the end of the second decade of American control. But none seconded his claims in this regard more expansively than the members of a special mission sent by Congress to report on conditions in the islands in 1921. The commissioners declared:

> The influence of our efforts to establish representative self-government in the Philippines extends far beyond the Philippines. It reaches every part of the Orient where free institutions and representative government are the dreams of the people.[13]

Perhaps even more remarkably, the American conviction that they had turned the Philippines into the showcase of Asia was so firmly held and routinely reiterated that members of the Filipino elite themselves bought enthusiastically into the colonizers' hegemonic rhetoric. In 1917, Gregorio Nieva, the editor of the *Philippine Review,* wrote to David Barrows, who had served as the general superintendent of education in the early 1900s, to ask him to contribute an essay to a special issue on the "great work done by the United States in the Philippines and its far-reaching consequences in the whole Far East." Nieva observed:

> The issue should prove extraordinarily interesting and inspiring not only for the Filipinos themselves but for the whole Orient, particularly for the powers who are still holding colonies in the Far East. For, had the powers acted with the same purpose and sincerity for the promotion of the welfare of the respective dependencies as the United States with regards to the Philippines, the way to the better and more dignified Orient should already have been shortened a great deal.[14]

In part, notions regarding the exceptionalism of American colonialism were grounded in a larger teleology that encompassed the history of the rise of the United States from an oppressed colony in its own right to its newly claimed position as a global power. The leap across the Pacific (and into the Caribbean) at the turn of the century was for pro-annexationists like Teddy Roosevelt, Brooks Adams, and Alfred Thayer Mahan merely an extension of centuries of frontier expansionism. But it was also seen as part of a much greater historical process by which the locus of civilization that had originally resided in China or the "Far East" had, over the millennia, steadily shifted westward to India, the Middle East, and, since the fifteenth century, Western Europe. From this perspective, American colonization in the Philippines represented more than just a sign of America's emergence as the global power or a test of its capacity to turn its domination to constructive ends. As early as the Taft administration (1900–1903), American officials enunciated a rhet-

oric of development and initiated ambitious experiments in the engineering of Filipino society that were seen to set the standards for what
they perceived to be uniquely American approaches to the materially
backward and morally deficient peoples and cultures of the non-
Western, nonindustrial world. Thus, the colonial experiment in the
Philippines proved in many ways decisive in the formulation of the
hitherto inchoate ideology of modernization that informed American
policies toward and interactions with most of the rest of humanity
throughout what Henry Luce would later dub the "American century"
that followed.

Almost from the outset, Americans engaged in the colonial experiment in the Philippines singled out their determination to prepare the
subject peoples of the islands for self-government in the near future as
the critical difference between their approach to the civilizing mission
and those pursued by the other colonial powers. It was this commitment that convinced Luke Wright that for all of their experience in
colonial domination, the British had little to teach the Americans.[15]
William Howard Taft, Wright's predecessor and soon to be president of
the United States, agreed. He charged that despite the "severe criticism"
of the other colonial powers, the Americans' "obligation" to prepare
the Filipinos for self-government was the "chief reason" for retention of
the islands.[16] Two decades later, Francis Harrison, who did more than
any other American official to promote the Filipinization of the colonial administration, concluded that it was the unprecedented American
encouragement of Filipino self-government and independence that had
shocked "the colonial offices of Europe," and led them to conclude that
"Uncle Sam was a rude, hustling fellow who refused to take his appointed seat at the table and join the feast."[17] In contrast to their European rivals, the Americans prided themselves on understanding, in fact
embracing, the logic of guardianship that, as J.A. van Doorn has argued
in a recent study, the Dutch and other European colonizers were dis-

mayed to find profoundly subversive of their efforts to extend their colonial domination indefinitely during the decades of nationalist agitation.[18] Like the European colonizers, Americans were inclined to represent the Filipinos as children who required more mature guardians to instruct them in the progressive ways of modern civilization. But in contrast to their European counterparts, the Americans explicitly acknowledged that if they succeeded in the tasks of modernization, which they conflated with civilizing, the Filipinos would rapidly come of age and insist that they be granted independence befitting their adult status.

As American policymakers conceived of it, self-government for the Philippines was to be modelled upon the liberal democracy that had been nurtured for over a century in the United States itself. President William McKinley's early promises to respect the traditions and customs of the Filipino peoples were explicitly overridden by a determination to inculcate "the great principles of government which have been made the basis of [the American] governmental system."[19] But to succeed, American-style liberal democracy required a constellation of institutions, attitudes, and orientations that American leaders were convinced added up to the very essence of modernity. Their Filipino wards could not sustain liberal democracy, nor even long remain independent, unless the islands were "developed" in this more comprehensive sense. American policymakers and social commentators also conceived of that broader project as exceptional, without precedent, not only in the history of colonization but in the history of cross-cultural interaction between progressive and backward societies. Different observers stressed different aspects of this modernizing mission. But most agreed that it included the introduction into the Philippines of a system of mass education, a capitalist market economy, and an up-to-date public-works infrastructure. American policymakers were aware that other colonizers, particularly the Dutch and the British, had also sought to introduce these improvements into their Asian colonies. But virtually all American observers believed that in the Philippines the United States had pushed these projects far beyond anything their European rivals could imagine. The Americans were able to do this both because they had a more coherent and ambitious development agenda and because self-governance was uniquely their overriding purpose as colonial over-lords.

In establishing a colonial regime in the early 1900s, the succession of Philippine Commissions laid great stress on the scientific nature of their undertakings. Each conducted extensive inquiries, which included lengthy hearings where both cooperative Filipino notables and Americans who were seen to possess special expertise in Philippine affairs were invited to testify. They commissioned special reports on all aspects of colonial administration and Filipino society, from legal and banking reform to sanitation systems and the relative merits of indigenous and immigrant Chinese laborers. But of all of these early projects, the committee appointed by the second (Taft) Commission to investigate the potential of the Benguet region as the site for a "health resort" perhaps best exemplified the aspirations of the neophyte colonizers to proceed in ways that accorded what they conceived to be the most exacting scientific standards. The committee was headed by H.C. Higgins, an engineer who had overseen the construction of the Manila-Dagupan railway. He was assisted by the chief medical inspector of the Eighth Army Corps and an assortment of scientists, including meteorologists and ethnologists. The team provided the Commission with a series of reports, which ran to over one hundred pages of fine print, on everything from average temperatures and humidity and the frequency of tropical storms to the numbers and culture of the Igorrotes who lived in the area. The thoroughness of the scientific procedures followed by the committee and the detailed statistics generated by their sophisticated measuring instruments left the Commission with no hesitation in rec-

ommending the Baguio area as an ideal location for what was to become the main hill station established by the Americans in the Philippines.[20]

Even before such special inquiries had begun in the early 1900s to
compensate for the abysmal ignorance of the Philippines on the part of
the great majority of Americans involved in the colonizing project,
United States officials and publicists routinely dismissed their Spanish
predecessors as hopelessly backward and misguided. The Americans
contrasted themselves as the bearers of modernity with the medieval
Spanish. They pitted their systematic and scientific approaches to colonization against what they believed to be the desultory, haphazard, and
superstition-driven policies pursued by the Spaniards.[21] When American administrators referred approvingly to policies adopted by worthy—that is "modern" European—rivals they often stressed the
scientific dimensions of these measures, even though the meaning of
"scientific" in this context was rarely specified. Francis Harrison's summary of the enlightened initiatives undertaken by the Dutch in Java and
Sumatra, for example, extolled the "thoroughness and scientific accu-
racy" for which he felt the Dutch were deservedly famous. He was particularly impressed by the "marvelous development" of "scientific"
agriculture in the Netherlands Indies, which he traced to government-
sponsored laboratories, which Harrison felt "should be the model for all
other countries."[22]

Charles Elliott criticized his American compatriots for their tendency to assume that their colonial rivals—the British, French, and
Dutch—were less committed to applying scientific methods in their
colonial endeavors. But Elliott went on to affirm what he averred was a
widespread American conviction that in the Philippines, scientific principles had been applied more confidently and comprehensively than in
any European colony.[23] Like Wright, Taft, and other influential policymakers before him, Elliott stressed the Americans' promotion of mass

IMPROVING ON THE CIVILIZING MISSION?

education and self-government as the critical areas where the project of rationalizing Filipino society had been extended far beyond that attempted by any other colonizer. But for Elliott these advances were but facets of America's supreme achievements in the Philippines, and he was eager to frame these with the declaration that "No British, Dutch, German or French colony has made more progress materially than have the Philippines, during the last ten years, or enjoyed a higher degree of order and justice." [24] Elliott, Harrison, and numerous other American observers celebrated what they believed to be the unprecedented economic growth and social improvement that had resulted from United States colonial policies and projects in the Philippines. In their view, these had stimulated a process of development along American lines that was building the vital foundations for Filipino self-government and for the islands to flourish as an independent state, which would be fully integrated into the global market system.

Because few American observers were cognizant of the often pivotal roles that public-works projects and social engineering had come to play in the policies pursued by their European rivals in the latter half of the nineteenth century,[25] they were prone to see infrastructural development and indices of advances in the health and prosperity of the Filipino population as irrefutable evidence of just how exceptional the United States approach to colonialism was. In fact, the construction of railways, bridges, and roads, massive irrigation schemes, increasingly ambitious campaigns to control epidemic disease, and efforts to rationalize colonial bureaucracies had, in the fin de siècle era, become prominent features of British, Dutch, and French imperial systems in Asia.[26] But none of America's European rivals accorded these development measures as dominant a place as they assumed in the Philippines, where in the early 1900s colonialism came to be seen as a grand engineering project. Jacob Shurman, the head of the first Philippine Commission, anticipated this mind-set in attempting to answer a series of questions that he himself had posed as to how the United States could undo centuries of benighted Spanish rule and prepare the Filipinos for self government.

> How are we going to do it? They need roads out there, and their construction is the first necessity when peace is restored to the islands. Not even schools are so important. Then after that should come the schools fashioned after systems which we have in this country [the United States].[27]

Nearly two decades later, Charles Elliott's survey of the key achievements of the first four American administrations in the Philippines reaffirmed Shurman's early priorities and underscored the material development in which each had excelled. Elliott concluded that from Taft onward it was "the accepted theory" that the "colony should be made materially prosperous before much attention was given to educating the people and preparing them for self-government."[28] Like his predecessors and successors, Elliott viewed the "policy of material development" as "much more than the building of public works":

> The markets of the world were waiting for the timber, the sugar, the copra and particularly for the kind of hemp that grows only in the Philippines. Of the one hundred million acres of arable land, less than ten per cent [sic] was productive. The soil was awakened from its sleep of centuries. The cultivation of more land, the cadastral survey necessary to enable titles to be registered, the creation of an agricultural bank from which the small farmers could borrow money at reasonable rates . . . the control of waters and the irrigation of waste land, the opening of mines, the search for much-needed coal, the teaching of scientific agriculture and the use of modern farm machinery, the establishment of a postal savings bank, the introduction of foreign capital, the organization of industry on modern lines, the construction of suitable public buildings,

hospitals and markets, water-works and sewers necessary for the protection of public health and comfort, and the highways and other appliances for communication by post and wire and the transportation of persons and products—all were but the means to an end, the relief of the people of the country from the bondage of poverty in order that they might have a fair opportunity to develop into an independent, self-respecting and self-supporting community." [29]

No modernization theorist of the 1960s articulated America's enduring developmentalist agenda more comprehensively or enthusiastically.

Engineers played vital roles in virtually all sectors of Philippine colonial society. By statute, one member of the three-person boards that made up the highest level of administration in the provinces was an engineer, and, wherever possible, the engineer appointed was director of the board. Civil engineers were in charge of the great majority of the disparate projects, from road and railway construction to sewage systems and mining operations, which Elliott all but equated with America's civilizing mission in the islands. Engineers very often served as the chairmen of the innumerable committees appointed to carry out special inquiries, such as that relating to the hill station at Baguio, which in many ways had inaugurated civil administration in the islands. In tandem with other specialists, engineers played a major role in government efforts to control the epidemics that ravaged the islands in the years after annexation, and in successive campaigns to improve sanitation and health, which became a central feature of American rule. Though none of the governor-generals were engineers by profession, until well into the 1920s all were deeply committed to the development-minded agenda that Elliott had detailed so enthusiastically.

The emergence of what can best be seen as engineers' imperialism in the Philippines owed much to conditions in the United States as well as to the balance between administrative factions in the islands themselves. On both counts, but particularly the latter, American colonizers were in fact quite distinct from their European counterparts in other areas of Asia. The status and remuneration of engineers had improved markedly in all Western, industrial societies in the last decades of the nineteenth century due to their growing professionalization and the relevance of their skills and training to a rapidly proliferating number of tasks created by the second industrial revolution. But by century's end engineers had gained far greater prominence in the United States than anywhere in industrial Europe. In fact, engineers and inventors were in most cases the great heroes of what Mark Twain dubbed the gilded age in the United States. Their exalted, in some quarters mythical, status owed much to a persisting American stress on the *applied* scientific expertise they were seen to possess. It was also due to the growing perception that the engineering skills that had been vital to technological advance and material increase in the United States, and which were valorized as the essence of progress, were also applicable to social reform and planning by both state and corporate agencies, including those involved in America's colonial enterprises.[30]

In the face of the stubborn Filipino resistance and severe setbacks that dominated the first years of intervention in the Philippines, engineering skills were seen to compensate for American ignorance, misguided policies, and downright bewilderment. In this same period, the unprecedented advance of the social sciences—particularly sociology, anthropology, and political science—in the United States impressed both domestic and overseas policymakers with the possibilities of engineering material well-being and social change.[31] This perception was enhanced by the critical roles that engineers played in the military campaigns to put an end to the insurrection, as well as their prominent participation in efforts to control epidemic disease and provide the communications infrastructure essential to American administration of the islands. Equally crucial in this regard was the fact that in the Philippines, in striking contrast to the neighboring colonies of the European imperialist powers, there was no entrenched corps of "Orientalists," whose knowledge of the indigenous cultures could be used to check the influence of the engineers.[32] This meant that it was possible for American policymakers to regard Filipino societies and cultures as tabula rasas, waiting to be transformed by the colonizers' experiments in social engineering.

In the first years after annexation, American ignorance of the history and cultures of the Philippines did little to dispel this mindset and the developmentalist agenda that it appeared to justify. As the special inquiries, censuses, cadastral surveys, and other modes of information gathering initiated by successive Commission governments were compiled into a fairly impressive archive of information on the islands,[33] the tabula rasa trope was sustained by a growing tendency to see the proper study of Filipino societies as a task for ethnographers. This approach was reinforced by the related assumptions that none of the peoples of the islands had produced "high civilizations" comparable to those of Java, India, or Indochina, and that until the arrival of the Spanish, the Filipinos' evolutionary development had stagnated at the level of savagery or at best barbarism. As a result, the critical roles played by Orientalists in the administrations of neighboring European colonies, such as India and the Netherlands Indies, were monopolized in the Philippines,[34] by "experts" like Dean C. Worcester, who built highly touted careers on fieldwork among the "primitive" peoples of the islands.[35]

This propensity to delegate the study of "exotic" non-Western peoples like the Filipinos to the ethnographers was, of course, rooted in earlier approaches to the Indian peoples of the Americas. At times work among the Indians proved useful for those seeking positions or promotions in the Philippine administration. In his aspiration to become superintendent of the Department of Public Instruction, for example,

David Barrows was eager to impress Dean Worcester with the fact that his fieldwork among the Indians of California had done much to prepare him for the tasks he had been assigned in the Philippines.[36] As had been the case in much of the research carried out by Barrows and aspiring ethnologists on the North American Indians, a vision of moral and material backwardness informed the books that Worcester and other specialists wrote about the Filipinos. And like essentializations of the Indians, this vision was popularized in the United States by the prominent place of exhibits devoted to what were explicitly characterized as primitive or savage peoples, such as the Negritos and Igorottes, at the World's Fairs and national expositions that were visited by millions of Americans in the fin de siècle decades.[37]

These impressions of Filipino savagery required, of course, selective representations of the island's peoples that excluded the Western-educated illustrado elite and for all practical purposes the peasants who made up the majority of the population on Luzon and in the Visayans. The illustrados, whom American policymakers were usually careful to distinguish from both peasants and primitives, were seen as products of the limited process of Westernization that had occurred during more than three centuries of Spanish rule. Though American observers at the time and later on were unlikely to acknowledge it, the fact that this highly educated elite was established prior to United States efforts to modernize the islands marked a major difference between the experience of colonization in the Philippines and that in British India, the Netherlands Indies, or French Indochina. It meant for starters that Filipino resistance to American annexation of the islands was very different from that faced by the other European powers in their conquests of Asian and African territories. In brutally crushing the "insurrection," the Americans delayed for decades the emergence of what might have been a viable Filipino nation-state. It is probable that an independent Philippines would have been the beneficiary of a good deal less capital investment, at least from the United States, and it would almost certainly have been more vulnerable to the incursions of other colonial powers, especially Japan. But, given the dependence of the illustrado elite on popular support for the revolt against Spain, and without American backing, nationalist regimes might have been obliged to expand meaningful political participation and more equitably distribute the material gains garnered by a slower pace of development.

In the first decades of the twentieth century, American administrators in the Philippines were a good deal more aggressive than their European counterparts in their efforts to establish collaborative relationships with those members of the Western-educated classes willing to cooperate with the colonial regime. As United States officials were well aware, their most radical departure from established colonial practice was contained in their quite explicit and tirelessly reiterated promises of Filipino self-rule in the foreseeable future. Perhaps even more unsettling for those who sought to maintain Western colonial dominance was the fact that from the first years of civilian government these pledges were fulfilled by the accelerating Filipinization of the administration that peaked in the years when Francis Harrison was governor-general between 1913 and 1921. United States officials increasingly relied on their "compadre" allies among the illustrado elite to govern the islands and control the colonized population in an era when European colonizers elsewhere in Asia were struggling to limit the influence of restive and alarmingly assertive Western-educated professionals and political activists. Also in contrast to their European counterparts in Asian and African colonies during this period, with the exception of Mindanao and the "tribal" enclaves on the other islands, the Americans made few efforts to create or prop up "traditional" elites, such as the princes in India and Java, to counterbalance the growing challenges posed by the politicized Western-educated classes.[38]

The relatively rapid establishment of an elected legislative body, the Philippine Assembly, in 1907, where members of rival Filipino parties made up the overwhelming majority of representatives, and the accelerating Filipinization of the colonial administration at all levels were perceived by American observers as initiatives without precedent in the annals of Western colonial rule. Capturing the self-satisfied sense of successful pioneers that most American officials believed themselves to be, Charles Elliott saw this promotion of Filipino self-government as the predictable outcome of more fundamental differences between American and European approaches to colonization. In contrast to the British, whose position Elliott generalized on the basis of a typically arrogant quote by Lord Cromer asserting that he not the Egyptians knew what was best for them, Elliott claimed that the "impractical and theoretical Americans" were willing to give "the natives themselves . . . a constantly increasing influence in determining their own affairs."[39] This confidence that the Filipinos were capable of taking charge of their own affairs and shaping their own future, Elliott argued, helped to explain the unparalleled American efforts to promote mass education in the islands, which had begun during the conquest when American soldiers set up schools for the children in the towns they occupied, while continuing to fight the students' parents in outlying areas. Elliott judged that "probably nothing exactly like [this] was ever before witnessed," and he concluded that these daring American innovations did much to explain why the "conquered, irritable and excitable [Filipino] people have not thrown a bomb or attempted to murder an American official" in contrast to the political agitation and violent protest that had recently erupted in neighboring colonies ruled by the British, French, and Dutch.[40]

The commitments to mass education and self-rule that American officials, journalists, and travelers so tirelessly celebrated were, of course, manifestations of an underlying objective that was incontestably pushed further in the Philippines than in any European colony. From the first years after the annexation of the islands, America's self-appointed agents of modern civilization, from governor-generals and engineer-supervisors to school teachers and physicians, were committed to the Americanization of the Philippines in the fullest sense of the term. In rejecting the British approach to colonization in 1903, Luke Wright had stressed the colonizers' objective of "grafting . . . American methods on a Malay stock." Two years earlier, William Howard Taft commended two Filipino students who were travelling to the United States to study at the University of California, whom he averred were "good boys, imbued with a proper spirit to learn English, to become educated Engineers and to become good Americans." Though Charles Elliott doubted a decade and a half later that Malays could be made into Anglo-Saxons, he admitted that a widely held goal of early administrations was to "transmute" Filipinos into "Americans of the most approved sort." Another decade later, Nicholas Roosevelt summed up the American colonial project in the islands as an attempt to transform the Philippines into "a sort of glorified Iowa." Roosevelt's imagery mirrored observations made over two decades earlier by a young school teacher, Paul Gilbert, who had gone out as part of the effort to bring mass education to the Filipinos. Gilbert imagined returning to the islands a few years after his time there as a teacher to find

> instead of brown *nipa* shacks, bright-painted American cottages or bungalows among the groves of palm. I shall expect to see the mountain slopes, waving with green hemp-fields, worked by the rejuvenated native. Railroads will penetrate the dark interior, connecting towns and villages now isolated. The country roads will be well graded and macadamized, and bridges will be built across the streams. The cock fight will have given way to institutions more American, and superstition will have vanished with the mediaevalism [sic].[41]

Although they provided education that was European in content and language instruction for increasing numbers of colonized peoples, and sought to build reasonably advanced economic infrastructures, none of the colonial rivals of the United States attempted to Westernize subject societies as fully as the Americans in the Philippines. Even the French, whose doctrine of assimilation permitted Senegalese or Vietnamese natives to aspire to full French citizenship, only extended this opportunity to a tiny minority of the subject peoples in any of their colonies. In addition, by the end of the nineteenth century the French had retreated to a policy of association that further reduced the possibility of the vast majority of colonized peoples becoming French in any meaningful sense.[42]

Despite the fact that the goal of Americanization was unabashedly ethnocentric, it transcended in important ways the racist strictures that dominated European and, in many cases, American thinking on colonial policy in the fin de siècle era. It was premised on the assumption that the Filipinos had the capacity to master American learning and skills, build American institutions, and run an American-style democracy. Those who pushed for Americanization in the Philippines may not always have realized the full implications of their policies, but they anticipated the more proactively antiracist presuppositions of modernization theorists who decades later would confidently predict that all societies would follow the American, or at least Western, path through industrialization to progress, political stability, and prosperity. Traces of this teleology were, of course, embedded in the reform initiatives of European colonial policy makers in the late-nineteenth century from the promoters of the Ethical Policy in the Netherlands Indies to the French planners who viewed the Indochina railway as the key to reconfiguring economic and social exchange over much of mainland Southeast Asia and south China. Decades earlier, reform-minded British administrators had confidently promoted English education in India and envisioned self-government for the subcontinent—albeit in some undefined and distant future. In the process, leaders like William Bentinck, Charles Metcalf and Mountstuart Elphinstone pointedly ignored those who argued that both projects were doomed to failure because the Indians were racially incapable of mastering either. But by the end of the nineteenth century, racist thinking was in the ascendancy in colonial policymaking circles, and despite the spirited objections of individual thinkers and administrators, European regimes from Algeria to Indochina emphasized ways to perpetuate colonial dominance and curtail the growing pressure from subject peoples for development and self-determination.[43]

The aims of development, mass education, and self-government, which were the key ingredients in the policy of Americanization as it was applied to the Philippines, were in and of themselves laudable. But like all such processes, they cannot be adequately evaluated in isolation. Their planning, implementation, and effects on Filipino society need to be contextualized, and their legacy can only be understood in the longer-term perspective of the subsequent history of both the Philippines and the United States. Contextualization and historical perspective suggest that much of what the Americans intended or at least professed their improved vision of the civilizing mission to be was frustrated in significant, perhaps decisive, ways by their determination to remake the Philippines in the image of the United States. This often led them to promote programs, institutions, and approaches that had not only yielded very mixed returns in the United States itself, but were ill-suited to the social and cultural situations into which they were introduced in the Philippines. A full discussion of the misfits and miscues that resulted and their unintended consequences is obviously beyond the scope of this essay. But I would like to suggest in a general way four dimensions of the commitment to Americanization in the guise of material development that proved critical in undermining much of what the colonizers hoped to achieve in the islands. Because that experience and the rhetoric of improvement that it generated so strongly influenced the formulation of modernization ideology—and decades later more nebulous notions of "nation-building"—which dominated American approaches to all non-Western peoples and societies in the mid- and late-twentieth century, their legacy needs to be explored with reference to global processes that extend far beyond colonial outcomes in the Philippines themselves.

Except for several ill-fated and brief interventions in the Caribbean and Mexico, until they forcibly annexed the Philippines between 1898 and the early 1900s, Americans had little knowledge of or interaction with peasants—subsistence-oriented cultivators who grudgingly surrendered the greater part of whatever surplus they produced to local landowners and government tax collectors.[44] In the American experience those engaged in agriculture were farmers—profit- and market-oriented producers who owned the land they worked and the machinery that was essential to their participation in a vital sector of a larger capitalist economy. The American farmer was also idealized as an independent-minded defender of republican institutions and representative democracy. From the first years of colonization, American officials pursued agrarian policies in the Philippines designed for farmers rather than the peasants who made up the great majority of the population of the islands. Despite an early preoccupation with the logistics of redistributing the lands controlled by the friars, or religious order, to landless cultivators, American agrarian initiatives focused overwhelmingly on increasing the production of key commercial crops. The model farms, hybrid plants, and expensive fertilizers by which the Department of Agriculture gauged success had little relevance for most of the Filipino peasants who rarely owned enough land to support themselves and were more concerned with eking out a subsistence living than improving their market productivity. As tenants and sharecroppers on large estates, or wage workers on hemp or sugar plantations, most Filipino cultivators remained lower-level dependents in local and regional pa-tron–client hierarchies that insured the continued economic and politi-cal dominance of the islands' landed and professional elite classes. These elite groups, whom American observers routinely referred to collec-tively as "the illustrados," reaped most of the profits and material re-wards from the increases in agrarian productivity that the Department of Agriculture officials so dutifully recorded.[45]

The propensity of American officials in charge of agrarian develop-ment in the Philippines to draw on domestic precedents in setting colo-nial policy required not only that they persist in regarding peasants as farmers, but that they refuse to heed the cautionary lessons that might have been learned from the severe depressions and social dislocations rampant in the rural United States itself in the last decades of the nine-teenth century.[46] They also showed little interest in the agrarian set-backs and consequent social unrest occurring in neighboring colonies, such as British Burma and the Netherlands Indies, whose colonial ad-ministrators had been grappling with *peasant* societies for centuries.[47] Even if they had been attentive to the lessons that might have been learned from these earlier forays into agrarian policymaking, it is un-likely that American administrators would have altered their approaches in significant ways. A broader American commitment to infrastructural improvements and market expansion was quite consistent with the re-formist Republican tradition, which had dominated turn-of-the-century politics in the United States, in part due to its capacity to extend capitalist prosperity gradually through selective and limited state interventions. But this approach did little to alleviate the worsening sit-uation of the Filipino peasantry or urban working classes. The commer-cial and landed elites were the main beneficiaries of improved transport and port facilities in the Philippines, as well as of increased production for export markets in the United States and elsewhere overseas.

The creation of an agrarian sector that was genuinely dominated by landowning peasant proprietors required a good deal more direct government intervention than even the Democratic administration under Harrison was able to envision, much less enact. Essential measures included the legislation of legal restraints on moneylending practices and land foreclosures, a proliferation of effective credit institutions for smallholder and agricultural laborers, and the establishment of agricultural extension stations oriented to the needs of the mass of cultivators who had little capital to spend on expensive hybrid seeds or chemical fertilizers. Above all, rural prosperity could be achieved only if the American regime undertook a thorough program of land reform and redistribution, which its early and persisting alliance with the landowning illustrado classes made unthinkable. Not only would significant agrarian reform lead to increased nationalist agitation and social unrest, which Congress would deem intolerable and prospective American investors prohibitive, but virtually all American administrators would have judged meaningful regulation of land distribution as an inappropriate intervention on the part of what proported to be a laissez-faire, capitalist administration.[48]

Even the promotion of mass education, which American administrators and most historians of United States imperialism have routinely bracketed with self-government as the most significant departure from accepted colonial practice undertaken in the Philippines,[49] proved much less transformative of Filipino society than policymakers anticipated and most subsequent historians have claimed. Because instruction in the primary grades was increasingly oriented to "practical" training in techniques of handicraft production, schooling at best qualified ordinary Filipino males for positions as skilled laborers. Education above the elementary level, especially at universities and professional schools, was all but monopolized by the children of the landed and professional classes, as it had been during the last decades of Spanish rule and was in all European colonies.[50]

The American conviction that their efforts to provide mass education for women would prove a force for liberation with no parallels in
any previous colonial system bore little relationship to the realities of
women's lives in the Philippines. Beyond the elite classes, education for
Filipino women meant little more than instruction in hygiene, home
"economics," and domestic crafts, such as sewing, weaving and embroi-
dery. Though college degrees, tennis matches, and fast cars may have
been the emblems of the "new women" whom Filipino social commentators found so worrisome,[51] they had little meaning for women
who did not belong to the elite minority. For even a larger proportion
of Filipino women than men, mass education and opportunities to participate in sporting events did little to ameliorate the gender inequities
that had existed at the time of annexation. As was the case in all instances of Western colonization, well-entrenched, indigenous patriarchal systems were bolstered by the patriarchal legal and institutional
arrangements introduced by the colonizers. In the Philippines, as in
British India and the Netherlands Indies, the modernizing project was
oriented overwhelmingly to males in terms of funding, education, professional training, employment, and legal and institutional reform.

For all of the fanfare and self-congratulations, the American variant of
the civilizing mission that was tested in the Philippines had roughly the
same long-term effects as all but the most oppressive European colonial
regimes, which usually meant those in which expatriate settlers played
prominent roles. Independence and self-determination mainly involved
the transfer of political power and supreme social status to indigenous
elite groups who had benefitted the most from Western education and
the social-engineering projects of the last decades of colonial rule.
Modernizing initiatives, particularly those involving new communications and transportation systems, served to link once relatively inacces-
sible areas to an international market system in which the former
imperialist powers of Western Europe, North America, and Japan re-

tained economic hegemony. Fed by a post–World War II boom in tourism and a related acceleration in the commoditization of postcolonial societies, the cultural influence of the West, and later Japan, grew a good deal more pervasive than it had been even at the height of the colonial era. To a much greater extent than many of the former colonial societies against which Americans had once made their claims to exceptionalism, the independent Philippine nation was racked by agrarian protest movements and, to a lesser extent, urban unrest. An undercurrent of millenarian dissidence, fuelled by the American failure to address effectively the oppressive and impoverished state of much of the peasantry, periodically broke into violence directed against the illustrado elite or the dwindling numbers of American overlords. The years of Japanese occupation in the mid-1940s set the stage for the escalation of this hitherto localized and sporadic protest into a major Communist-led revolutionary assault in the decades after the end of the Second World War.[52] And the lessons that were allegedly learned from American support for the repression of the Huk Rebellion gave rise to the contrary mix of development and counterinsurgency theory that has informed United States responses to much of the developing world from Vietnam to the contemporary Middle East.

All of this brings us back to William Howard Taft, the dawn of the American colonial experiment in the Philippines, and the birth of an improved civilizing mission in Asia. Despite his protestations about the fine state of his health and that of the young Americans he encountered in Manila, Taft and his family, who came out to the Philippines in the following year, retreated, like colonials everywhere, to the hill station at Baguio to escape the heat and humidity of the tropical lowlands. Later, ill health, both his own and that of his wife and children, even forced Taft to return to the United States for R & R.[53] And recent research suggests that some of the young Americans were not as robust as they may have appeared to Taft, that many suffered (and some died) from alcoholism, a variety of tropical diseases, depression, and an assortment of mental disorders.[54] Even the much-heralded Baguio road was literally a wash-out, and a precursor of further engineering debacles to come.[55] Tragically, given the scale of human suffering caused by many of the American interventions into postcolonial societies that followed, these setbacks and the larger failings of the American effort to "modernize" the Philippines were largely forgotten or overlooked. What was remembered was the hubris of men like Taft, who were convinced that, defying all prior experience, they could transform colonial domination into a grand development project that would empower and enrich the subjugated peoples.

8

Occupation: A Warning from History

John W. Dower

I

Starting in the fall of 2002, we began to hear that U.S. policymakers were looking into Japan and Germany after World War II as examples or even models of successful military occupations. In the case of Japan, the imagined analogy with Iraq is probably irresistible. Although Japan was nominally occupied by the victorious "Allied powers" from August 1945 until early 1952, the Americans ran the show and tolerated no disagreement. This was Unilateralism with a capital "U"—much as we are seeing in U.S. global policy in general today. And the occupation was a pronounced success. A repressive society became democratic, and Japan—like Germany—has posed no military threat for over half a century.

The problem is that few if any of the ingredients that made this success possible are present—or would be present—in the case of Iraq. The lessons we can draw from the occupation of Japan all become warnings where Iraq is concerned.

It is difficult for most people today to imagine what the situation was

This chapter originally appeared, in slightly different form, as "A Warning from History" in the *Boston Review,* February/March 2003, 6–8, and as "The Other Japanese Occupation" in *The Nation,* July 7, 2003, 11–14.

like in 1945, in the wake of the Second World War. One must remember that Japan had been engaged in aggression in Asia since 1931, when Imperial Army militarists launched a successful takeover of Manchuria. Open war against China began in 1937, and the great and foolhardy "preemptive" strike against Pearl Harbor took place in December 1941—in the context of a Japanese declaration of war against the United States and European powers with colonies in Southeast Asia. Japan's aggression was as open and audacious as that of its Axis allies Germany and Italy.

Just as is the case with Europe and the Soviet Union, we will never have an exact reckoning of the death toll of the war in Asia. China bore the brunt of Japanese aggression. Estimates vary and have tended to become inflated in recent years, but the number of Chinese who died directly or indirectly as a consequence of the war is probably in the neighborhood of fifteen million. In countries like the Dutch East Indies—known today as Indonesia—estimates of fatalities range from one million to several million. In their final frenzy in the Philippines, the emperor's men massacred around one hundred thousand civilians in Manila alone. U.S. battle deaths in the Pacific War also were approximately one hundred thousand. Japan's own war dead numbered around two million servicemen and another one million civilians—roughly four percent of the total population at the time.

This was a charnel house in which the Japanese not only savaged others but were themselves savaged by war and militarism and their own repressive leaders. So, the dream that everyone embraced once Japan had been defeated was of a nation that would never again bring such havoc on its neighbors or, indeed, on its own people. "Demilitarization" became the watchword of the time, and it was argued that this could only be enduring if the country was "democratized" as well, so that irresponsible leaders could not repeat these horrors.

When I say that "everyone" embraced this vision of a demilitarized, democratized Japan, I have in mind not merely the victorious Allied nations but also the Asian peoples who had been so grievously victimized by the Japanese war machine—many of whom remained at war's end colonial subjects of the British, French, Dutch, and Americans. I also have in mind the great majority of the Japanese, who found themselves not only bereaved but also living in a country utterly devastated by a miserable, losing war. Even people who are familiar with the atomic bombings of Hiroshima and Nagasaki that preceded Japan's surrender in August 1945 often are unaware that the U.S. terror-bombing raids that came before them—aimed primarily at destroying civilian morale— had pulverized large portions of sixty-four other major cities. Tokyo, for example, had been mostly reduced to rubble.

It is important to keep all this in mind when we begin to talk about drawing lessons from Japan for application in Iraq in the aftermath of U.S. hostilities. The postwar occupation of Japan possessed a great intangible quality that simply is not present in the U.S. war against Iraq. It enjoyed virtually unquestioned *legitimacy*—moral as well as legal—in the eyes of not merely the victors but all of Japan's Asian neighbors and most Japanese themselves. Japan had been at war for almost fifteen years. It had declared war on the Allied powers in 1941. It had accepted the somewhat vague terms of surrender "unconditionally" less than four years later. The result of the U.S. attack on and occupation of Iraq has had the opposite effect. The United States has found the legitimacy of its actions widely challenged—within Iraq, throughout the Middle East and much of the rest of the world, and even among many of its erstwhile supporters and allies.

II

What made the occupation of Japan a success was two years or so of genuine reformist idealism before U.S. policy became consumed by the Cold War, coupled with a real Japanese embrace of the opportunity to start over. There are moments in history—fleeting occasions of opportunity—when people actually sit down and ask, "What is a good society? How can we bring this about?" Winners in war do not ask this of themselves. Winners tend to say we won, we're good, we're righteous, what we did was just, now it's time to get back to business and build on our strengths. But losers—certainly in the case of Japan—are under more compulsion to ask what went wrong and what they might do to make sure they don't fall into the same disasters again.

American policy toward defeated Japan meshed with this Japanese sense of failure and the necessity of starting over. The Americans may not have been self-critical, but they had definite ideas about what needed to be done to make Japan democratic. Much of this thinking came from liberals and leftists who had been associated with Franklin D. Roosevelt's progressive New Deal policies—policies that were already falling out of favor in Washington before the war ended. One might say that the last great exercise of New Deal idealism was carried out by Americans in defeated Japan. It was this combination of the Americans using their "unconditional" authority to crack open the old authoritarian system and Japanese at all levels seizing this opportunity to make the reforms work that accounts for the success of the occupation.

The reforms that were introduced in the opening year and a half or so of the occupation were quite stunning. They amounted to a sweeping commitment to what we now call "nation-building"—the sort of hands-on commitment that George W. Bush explicitly repudiated in his presidential campaign. The Americans introduced in Japan a major land reform, for example, that essentially took land from rich landlords, eliminated widespread tenancy, and created a class of small rural landowners. The argument for this was that rural oppression had kept the countryside poor, thwarted democracy, constricted the domestic market, and fueled the drive to control overseas markets. We introduced labor laws that guaranteed the right to organize, bargain collectively, and strike, on the grounds that a viable labor movement is essential to any viable democracy. We encouraged the passage of a strong labor-standards law to prevent exploitation of workers, including women and children. We revamped both the content and structure of the educational system. In all this, the input of Japanese bureaucrats and technocrats was essential to implement such reforms, and serious grass roots support was basic to their survival.

One of our major initiatives was to create an entirely new constitution. There were no citizens in Japan in 1945. There was no popular sovereignty. Under the existing constitution, sovereignty was vested in the emperor and all Japanese were his "subjects." So, the Americans drafted—but the Japanese translated, debated, tinkered with, and adopted—a new national charter that remains one of the most progressive constitutions in the world. The emperor became a "symbol" of the state. An extensive range of human and civil rights was guaranteed including an explicit guarantee of gender equality. Belligerency of the state was repudiated. Changing the constitution meant, moreover, that much of the civil code had to be rewritten to conform to these new strictures concerning equality and guaranteed rights. Although the occupation ended in 1952 and there are no restrictions on amending the constitution, not a word of it has been changed.

There will be revisions in the near future, I would predict, primarily to clarify the legal status of Japan's present-day military forces. But it is inconceivable that they will undo the principles of popular sovereignty and extensive guarantee of democracy rights. And, in one way or another, whatever revision takes place, we should expect to see reaffirmation of the fundamental ideals of antimilitarism.

I have no doubt that huge numbers of Iraqis would welcome the end of repression and establishment of a democratic society, but any number of considerations make the situation there very different than it was in Japan. Apart from lacking the moral legitimacy and internal and global support that buttressed its occupation of Japan, the United States is not in the business of nation-building anymore—just look at Afghanistan.

And we certainly are not in the business of promoting radical democratic reform. Even liberal ideals are anathema in the conservative circles that shape U.S. policy today. And beyond this, many of the conditions that contributed to the success of the occupation of Japan are simply absent in Iraq.

III

John Stuart Mill has a wonderful line somewhere to the effect that a country can be laid waste by fire and sword, but in and of itself this really doesn't matter where recovery is concerned. What matters is not so much what is destroyed but rather what human resources survive. Even though Japan had been laid to ruin by the terror-bombing of its cities, what survived was an exceptionally literate populace whose long war effort had, in fact, contributed to great and widespread advances in technological and technocratic skills. At the same time this was an essentially homogeneous populace that had been mobilized behind a common national cause.

The failure and discredit of the cause did not destroy this general sense of collective national purpose. It meant, however, that these great human resources were available to be mobilized to new ends that were more peaceful and progressive. Put simply, one of the reasons the reformist agenda succeeded is that Japan was spared the type of fierce tribal, religious, and political factionalism that exists in countries like Iraq today.

Particularly in the early stages of effecting a smooth surrender, Japan also possessed an unusually flexible—some would say chameleonlike—leader in the person of Emperor Hirohito. The emperor had certainly been the symbol of presurrender militarism, and no innocent bystander to wartime policymaking. He was not, however, a hands-on dictator akin to Hitler or Mussolini—or to Saddam Hussein. Once surrender became unavoidable, the emperor adroitly metamorphosed into a symbol of cooperation with the conquerors. He came quietly, and for reasons of pure expediency the Americans happily whitewashed and welcomed him. He became, as it were, a beacon of continuity in the midst of drastic change. We cannot, of course, imagine anything of the sort taking place in a post-hostilities Iraq.

Much the same sort of continuity took place at the levels of both national and local government. Certain important reforms were introduced at the national level—most notably the abolition of the War (army) and Navy ministries and the breakup and gutting of the once-powerful Home Ministry, which had controlled the police and dictated policies at the level of the prefectures or states. But for all practical purposes the bureaucracy remained intact, top to bottom. And to a far greater extent than anyone really anticipated, bureaucrats and civil servants cooperated in implementing the early reformist agendas. "Democratization" of the structure and content of the educational system, to take but one example, required and received enormous input from bureaucrats and teachers at every level. The skills and education levels of the Iraqi people are substantial, but it is nonetheless difficult to imagine a comparably swift, smooth, and substantial redirection of existing administrative and institutional structures in a post-hostilities Iraq.

We should also keep in mind what defeated Japan did *not* possess. Japan is notoriously poor in natural resources. A desperate quest for control of raw materials as well as markets was one of the major considerations that drove Japanese imperialism and aggression in the first place. That, after all, is why the emperor's men deemed it necessary to invade Southeast Asia and—once that decision had been made—attempted to forestall American retaliation by launching a preemptive strike at the U.S. fleet at Pearl Harbor. In the wake of Japan's shattering defeat, no one ever imagined that it would ever again become a major power; and there were no resources within Japan itself to covet. And so the reformers—Americans and Japanese alike—had a brief breathing space in which to push their ambitious agendas without being hammered by special economic interests. Iraq, of course, with its great oil resources, will not be spared such interference.

IV

The occupation of Japan offers no model whatsoever for any projected occupation of Iraq. On the contrary, it should stand as a warning that we have lurched into war with no idea of what we were really getting into. What is presented as hard-nosed realism by the advocates of a preemptive strike against Iraq is really—what? I have concluded after much thought that our so-called realism is simply a terrible hubris.

But to an historian of the United States and Japan and World War II there are also terrible ironies in these recent developments. Part of the irony is that Americans—certainly Americans in the current administration—have no sense of irony. "September 11" has become our terrible new "Pearl Harbor," and at the very same time we are touting "preemptive strikes" as a moral and practical modus operandi. In the name of curbing weapons of mass destruction we have embarked on a massive program of producing *new* arsenals of mass destruction and have announced that we may resort to first-use of nuclear weapons. We express moral repulsion and horror at the terror-bombing of civilians, and rightly so; and then an endless stream of politicians and pundits explains how this is peculiar to Islamic fundamentalists who do not value human life as we do. But "terror-bombing" has been everyone's game since World War II. This is the term historians routinely use to describe the U.S. bombing campaign against Japan that began with the destruction, in a single air raid, of fourteen square miles of downtown Tokyo in March 1945 and continued through Hiroshima and Nagasaki. There is nothing cultural or religious or unique about this.

There is one "lesson" from my own field of Japanese history that I find increasingly difficult to put out of mind these days, and that concerns the road to war that began in the early 1930s for Japan and only ended in 1945. Until recently, historians used to explain this disaster in terms of Japan's "backwardness" and "semifeudal" nature. The country had all these old warrior traditions. It wasn't a democracy—and, of course, democracies *don't* wage aggressive war. More recent studies, however, cast Japan's road to war in a different and more terrifying light.

Why "terrifying"? First, much recent scholarship suggests that it was the *modern* rather than "backward" aspects of Japanese society and culture that enabled a hawkish leadership to mobilize the country for all-out war. Modern mass communications enabled politicians and ideologues to whip up war sentiment and castigate those who criticized the move to war as traitors. Modern concerns about external markets and resources drove Japan into Manchuria, China, and Southeast Asia. Modern weaponry carried its own technological imperatives. Top-level planners advanced up-to-date theories about mobilizing the entire resources of the country (and surrounding areas) for "total war." Sophisticated phrasemakers pumped out propaganda about defending the homeland and promoting "coexistence and co-prosperity" throughout Asia. Cultures of violence, cultures of militarism, cultures of unquestioning obedience to supreme authority in the face of national crisis—all of this was nurtured by sophisticated organs of propaganda and control. And, in retrospect, none of this seems peculiarly dated or peculiarly "Japanese" today.

The other aspect that is so terrifying to contemplate is that virtually every step of the way, the Japanese leaders who concluded that military solutions had become unavoidable were very smart and very proud of their technical expertise, their special knowledge, their unsentimental "realism" in a threatening world. Many of these planners were, in our own phrase, "the best and the brightest." We have detailed records of their deliberations and planning papers, and most are couched in highly rational terms. Each new escalation, each new extension of the empire was deemed essential to the national interest. And even in retrospect, it is difficult to say at what point this so-called realism crossed the border into madness. But it was, in the end, madness.

V

It is the almost forgotten interlude of Japan as an occupying power in Manchuria and later China, however, that poses the most intriguing analogy to the creation of a new American imperium today. Obviously, there are enormous differences between the two cases. Imperial Japan was not a hyperpower when it launched its campaign of accelerated empire-building in 1931. Its propagandists did not spout the rhetoric of democratization, privatization and free markets that fills the air today. Domestically, Japan operated under the aegis of a real emperor, rather than behind the shield of an imperial presidency.

Still, the points of resonance between the abortive Japanese empire and the burgeoning American one are striking. In both instances, we confront empire-building embedded in a larger agenda of right-wing radicalism. And in each, we find aggressive and essentially unilateral international policies wedded to a sweeping transformation of domestic priorities and practices.

Scholars are only now beginning to appreciate fully how perversely "modern" imperial Japan's mobilization for war and accelerated expansion actually was. Self-styled patriotic renovationists not only seized the initiative in calling for a "new order" abroad and "new structure" at home but also made it clear that these goals were inseparable. Their exhortations were bold and articulate. They did not hesitate to employ subterfuge, intimidation and fait accompli to achieve their ends. They forged potent alliances of corporate, bureaucratic and political interests while vesting unprecedented power in the military. And they mobilized popular support domestically through masterful manipulation of a newly emergent mass media.

In retrospect, we tend to dwell on the hubris and madness of these men. Their short-lived empire is dismissed as little more than a "dream within a dream," to borrow a Japanese phrase, but this is too simple. In their passing moment of devastating triumph, these right-wing radicals not only changed the face of Asia in unanticipated ways but also permanently transformed Japan. And their great concerns, aspirations and accomplishments find eerie echo in much of what we behold in US policy today. Regime change, nation-building, creation of client states, control of strategic resources, defiance of international criticism, mobilization for "total war," clash-of-civilizations rhetoric, winning hearts and minds, combating terror at home as well as abroad—all these were part and parcel of Japan's vainglorious attempt to create a new order of "coexistence and co-prosperity" in Asia.

It is testimony to the peculiar power of the silver screen that Bernardo Bertolucci's 1987 epic *The Last Emperor,* winner of an impressive nine Academy Awards, managed to fascinate moviegoers without restoring the Japanese quest for hegemony on the Asian continent to popular memory. The new stage of empire in Asia began in 1931 when Japan, which had long exercised neocolonial control over Manchuria in collaboration with local warlords, seized the region in the wake of a bogus casus belli. (Elements in Japan's Kwantung Army blew up railway tracks controlled by the Japanese near Mukden and blamed indigenous forces.) The following year, the puppet state of "Manchukuo" was established under the regency of Pu Yi, the "last emperor" of the Manchu dynasty, which ruled China from 1643 until 1912. In 1933 Japan withdrew from the League of Nations in response to condemnation of its defiant unilateralism.

This exercise in what we now euphemistically refer to as regime change was subsequently extended to China south of the Great Wall, where the eruption of all-out war in 1937 left Japan in control of the entire eastern seaboard and a population of some 200 million Chinese. In 1941, bogged down in China and desperate for additional strategic resources, the imperial war machine advanced into the colonial enclaves of Southeast Asia (French Indochina, the Dutch East Indies, America's Philippines colony and Great Britain's Hong Kong, Malaya and Burma). The attack on Pearl Harbor was in today's terminology a pre-emptive strike aimed at delaying America's response to this so-called liberation of Asia.

"Liberation" was the consistent byword of Japan's advances—liberation from warlords, guerrillas, "bandits," and generalized chaos in Manchuria and China proper; liberation from the uncertainty and rapacity of the global capitalist system in the wake of the Great Depression; liberation from the "Red Peril" of Soviet-led international Communism and the "White Peril" of European and American colonialism. In the grandest of ideological formulations, Japanese propagandists evoked the image of a decisive clash between "East" and "West"—manichean hooey as seductive then as it is today.

VI

While the takeover of Manchuria initially produced deep anxiety in Japan, this was soon dispelled by a great wave of patriotic solidarity. ("A hundred million hearts beating as one" was the analogue to today's "united we stand.") Propagandists evoked the same rhetoric of mission and Manifest Destiny that had animated European and U.S. expansionists. They even appropriated the language of America's Monroe Doctrine by defending the seizure of Manchuria as part of creating a new "Monroe sphere in Asia." It was acknowledged that control of Manchuria would guarantee access to strategic raw materials (notably

iron and coal), but the greater objective was, of course, peace and prosperity. The establishment of Manchukuo, it was declared, would bring
about an unprecedented "harmony of the five races" (Japanese, Chinese, Manchus, Mongolians, and Koreans). Beyond this, and of far
greater significance, Manchukuo was envisioned as a perfect pilot project for establishing a political economy consistent with the most basic
ideals of the radical right-wing agenda.

The evocative catchphrase of those heady days was "Manchuria as
ideology," and the ideology embraced was on the surface very different
from that trumpeted by the hard-core ideologues of a new American
empire today. In the wake of the Depression, which had savaged Japan as
it had the rest of the world, the very notion of "free markets" and unrestrained capitalism was, to put it mildly, unpalatable. In this milieu,
Manchukuo was seized upon as an ideal opportunity to introduce a
new model of "state capitalism" or "national socialism."

Even this great difference, however, does not diminish the many
points of similarity between the Japanese and the American cases. As always, the devil is in the details, and the most interesting details concern
the manner in which adoption of a positive policy abroad was accompanied by a sweeping reordering of the domestic political economy. As
in the United States today, governing circles in imperial Japan were rid-
dled with factionalism. Out of these internecine struggles, elements associated with the military emerged as dominant, led by the "Control
Faction" (*Tosei-ha*), associated with General and later Prime Minister
Tojo Hideki.

The Control Faction's name had a dual origin. It implied controlling
other factions, including more hotheaded rightists. More important, it
signaled a dedication to harnessing the economy, and society as a whole,
to the ultimate objective of creating a capacity to wage "total war." The
"total war" concept had captured the imagination of military planners
since World War I. The "Manchurian incident" of 1931 made it possible to put these plans into effect.

Politically, mobilization for total war entailed military domination of domestic as well as international policy. The Ministry of Foreign Affairs—Japan's counterpart to our State Department—was shouldered aside. Economic ministries and agencies became handmaidens to military demands. The Home Ministry—roughly comparable to the Justice Department and the Department of Homeland Security—intensified its role in domestic policing and the suppression of "dangerous thoughts." (The 1930s also witnessed a number of homegrown terrorist incidents in Japan, involving assassinations of prominent figures and, in 1936, a major attempted coup d'état.) The elective Diet or parliament became a rubber stamp. Communists and leftists in great numbers publicly recanted their criticism of the imperial state and declared themselves to be devoted to bringing about "revolution under the brocade banner" of the emperor. The mass media, hamstrung by formal censorship, also practiced self-censorship. Once the war machine had been put in motion, and a "blood debt" to the war dead established, it was inconceivable not to support the emperor's loyal troops.

VII

Economically, mobilization for total war was particularly striking in its modernity—a notion that overturns the once-fashionable argument that backwardness and "feudal legacies" precipitated Japan's drive for control of Asia. The national budget was tilted overwhelmingly toward military-related expenditures. The decade after the seizure of Manchuria witnessed what academics now refer to as Japan's "second industrial revolution," marked by the takeoff of heavy and chemical industries. A massive wave of mergers took place, not only in the industrial and financial sectors but in the mass media as well.

Before the 1930s, the modern Japanese economy was dominated by four huge "zaibatsu," or conglomerate-type business combines (Mitsui, Mitsubishi, Sumitomo, and Yasuda). After the takeover of Manchuria, the "big four" became major suppliers of the military, major beneficiaries of development projects in occupied areas, major actors in the suppression of a nascent labor-union movement, and major contributors to the consolidation of a domestic "dual structure" characterized by increasing disparities of wealth and power.

At the same time, the 1930s also witnessed the emergence of a technologically innovative corporate sector known as the "new zaibatsu" (*shinko zaibatsu*), which was primarily devoted to military contracting and empire-building. Like the big four—and like the cutting-edge U.S. corporations clamoring to get in on the gravy train of today's "war on terror"—these new zaibatsu worked hand in glove with the military and cultivated what we now call crony capitalism. By war's end, the six largest new zaibatsu (Asano, Furukawa, Nissan, Okura, Nomura, and Nakajima) accounted for more than 16 percent of paid-in capital in mining, chemical, and heavy industries, while the share of the big four had increased to more than 32 percent. When all was said and done, "national socialism" proved very hospitable to aggressive privatization.

Within the civilian ministries, the counterpart to the military hawks and innovative new zaibatsu was a loosely linked cadre known as the "new bureaucrats" (*shin kanryo*) or "renovationist bureaucrats" (*kakushin kanryo*)—accomplished technocrats devoted to wedding the new order abroad to new institutional structures at home. Adversaries and factional opponents may have denounced these men as rogue bureaucrats—or rogue capitalists, or rogue military—but the rogues were in the saddle.

Although we speak of a military takeover of Japan in the 1930s, electoral politics and most functions of civil society continued through war into the postwar era. Tojo himself was eased from power, in proper parliamentary manner, in 1944. No one could stop the machine he and his fellow right-wing radicals had set in motion, however, until the war came home, culminating in Hiroshima and Nagasaki. Japan's was a short ride as empires go, but the devastation left in its wake was enormous.

Despite the deepening quagmire of occupation and empire, Japanese leaders and followers alike soldiered on—driven by patriotic ardor and a pitiful fatalism. It was only afterward, in the wake of defeat, that pundits and politicians and ordinary people stepped back to ask: How could we have been so deceived?

We are in a better position to answer this now.

9

Japan and the United States in Re-Imperial Times

Carol Gluck

From a transpacific dialogue with Kang Sangjung and Wada Haruki, November 2001 to January 2003, published as "Nichibei kankei kara no jiritsu" [Towards Autonomy in U.S.-Japan Relations] (Fujiwara Shoten, 2003).

November 2001: Anachronisms All Around

If the world changed after September 11, why do international relations still look much the same? Why do Japan–U.S. relations, in particular, have a depressingly familiar ring to them? With nations as with people, old habits die hard, and while everyone is talking about the need for a global response to global terror, no one seems to know how to go about it.

Coolly seen, much of the multilateral antiterrorist effort so far has emerged as a series of bilateral relations in which allies pledge to stand "shoulder to shoulder" not with one another but with the United States. The photographs of each leader with George W. Bush are like souvenirs of some diplomatic ball, at which heads of state vie with one another to dance with the president. And in the midst of these bilateral pairings left over from the last century, the United States plays its role of world soloist, courted by old friends like Tony Blair and wooing new partners in Pakistan and other not-always-friendly places. These bilateral multilateralists are enough out of sync with the times that they might as well wear period costumes—something from the 1950s perhaps.

The Japanese-American relationship may be the most anachronistic of all. Japanese leaders worry about incurring Gulf War–style criticism if their support of the U.S. action is judged insufficient (though it was the United States that found Japan's $13 billion too little too late while much of Europe commended the Japanese contribution). So after dropping the words "in support of the U.S." from its title, antiterrorist legislation is passed by the Japanese Diet; men and ships will be sent to the Indian Ocean. Japan commits to aid in "rebuilding" Afghanistan after the United States and others finish flattening it (though allied leaders have as yet thought far less about the rebuilding than the flattening).

Even as Japan rushes to aid the United States, American officials and commentators offer pronouncements about what Japan ought to be doing: follow the United States and "show the flag"; or resist the United States and take the pacifist high road. It is Japan's obligation, some say; it is Japan's opportunity, say others.

And what does Japan say? Often what it thinks the United States wants to hear. It's the old Japanese-American tunnel vision, which derives from the asymmetry of power that characterized U.S.-Japan relations throughout the Cold War. Yet we are now not only post–Cold War but post post–Cold War as well. And still Americans speak of Japan in terms reminiscent of decades past. Can anyone imagine an American ambassador to Germany using Howard Baker's words when he congratulated Foreign Minister Tanaka on the passage of the new antiterrorist bill? "The American government understands that Japan is a great sovereign nation," he said, as if it had just figured that out. He added that the United States made no demands and no requests that day, in acknowledgment perhaps that most days that is exactly what the United States was doing.

Some things, of course, have changed over the past twenty years. Prime Minister Koizumi speaks of maintaining independence of action, and in parts of the world Japan is no longer seen as a blind follower of U.S. policy. The Bush administration at least began by taking a deliberately more polite tack in its "demands" and "requests." And despite his more frequent and comfortable mention of Mexico, Canada, Great Britain, and even Russia as the most important U.S. allies, there is no doubt that Bush considers Japan a partner and not a subordinate.

I am not arguing that Japan should "say no" to the United States or "go it alone" in the world. Indeed, as an American I refuse to join the chorus that ends every sentence about Japan with a declaration of what the Japanese ought to do. It is enough to try to get my own country to outgrow its anachronisms of power and to consider, just for a moment, that large parts of the world have a different view both of the "War on Terrorism" and of the reasons for it. No, I am arguing against anachronism on all sides, not only because the current national and binational responses are seriously behind the times but because they are also ineffective and dangerous. The current coalition cannot "win" a war on terrorism without wreaking as much havoc as it prevents.

The twenty-first century world requires a balance not of power but of action: a balance among national, bilateral, regional, and multilateral approaches to create a genuinely international space where global issues like terrorism can be addressed singularly but in common, without dragging in all the accumulated political baggage of the last fifty years. And the first step toward this future is to relinquish the unhelpful habits of the past.

December 2001: Japan in the American Imperium

Having identified Japanese-American tunnel vision as an aspect of the present problem, I have been asked, as an American, to explain how the bilateral syndrome looks from the U.S. side. Resisting the national label, I will try to answer as a historian, beginning with an account of its origins in the early postwar years.

The bilateral syndrome predated the Cold War, originating in "The Great East Asia War," Japan's defeat, and the Allied occupation. Long before the war was won, the United States had undertaken presurrender planning for its postwar objectives in Japan. Disarmament, peace, and democracy were the goals; unlike in Germany, where the Allies themselves ruled, in Japan they would act through the Japanese government in an "indirect occupation." The initial framework for postwar bilateralism was thus established well before the surrender. Despite the obvious disparity of power between the victorious Americans and the defeated Japanese, the illusion—and reality—of joint action in the occupation reforms is part of what John Dower means by "embracing defeat."

Reform was only part of it, however. The United States was also responsible for the early disappearance of Asia from Japan's postwar consciousness—again, before the onset of the Cold War. In the fall of 1945, General Douglas MacArthur decreed that the name of the Great East Asia War be changed to the Pacific War (in the title of the "true history" of the war published in the Asahi newspaper for the re-education of the Japanese public). The Pacific War, from Pearl Harbor to Hiroshima, was of course the war the Americans had fought—the Japanese-American War, in fact. With that name change, the China War all but disappeared: the China War that had been the reason for Pearl Harbor in the first place. And this focus on the 1941–45 war also produced what I call an "amnesia of empire." Gone were Taiwan, Korea, Manchukuo, the South Pacific. Only "Japan" was left, now to become ethnically homogeneous within the home islands. Thus, even before the structures of the Cold War set in, Asia had vanished—or rather, had become a specter—in the Japanese-American view of the postwar world.

The United States cast other powerful shadows across the origins of postwar Japan, not least in its dominance in the occupation and the Cold War alliance, its role in the retention of the emperor system (and, worse, the emperor), and its influence on Japan's postimperial relations with Asia.

First: the United States and the occupation. Everyone knows the mythic story of American generosity and Japanese gratitude in the earliest days of the occupation. This had nothing to do with America's role in Japan's subsequent prosperity, which in the hard years of 1945 and 1946 no one foresaw even on the distant horizon. It was rather that the Americans seemed generous in contrast to what they might have done to their defeated enemy in a total war and to what many Japanese reasonably expected that they would do: level the nation and its people. That the Americans didn't do this was one reason for Japanese "gratitude"; another, of course, was plain relief on the homefront at being released from the hardships of war.

Here one might compare other postwar occupations in which the United States was involved: Germany, Austria, Korea, Okinawa, for example. Bruce Cumings's work on the U.S. occupation of Korea shows what happened to a country which, unlike Japan, did not lose the war and which was liberated from Japanese colonial rule—only to suffer partition, domination, and a bloody proxy Cold War conflict on its soil. In comparison, I suppose one might agree that the Japanese occupation, at least at the beginning, had a more welcome tenor to it.

But these images of a generous United States and a grateful Japan would not have lasted without the Cold War. Indeed, U.S. congressional and public opinion soon began to agitate for closing down the occupation and concluding an early peace treaty, as postwar America rapidly demobilized and turned away from what is now called "nation-building." It is a testament to Americans' vestigial sense of history that today they can take credit—with a straight face—for the "successful occupations" of Japan and Germany and compare them to postwar Afghanistan. The idea that the United States "brought" democracy to Japan is as absurd as it is arrogant. For had it not been for the Soviet threat, the generous Americans would have pulled out of Japan before you could say Coca-Cola, leaving Japan to democratize itself, which is pretty much what it did. As for Japanese gratitude, the political elites, for their part, had no fondness for the occupation's meddling in every aspect of the nation's business and moved quickly after independence to implement their own conservative vision of what Japanese democracy ought to look like.

So we are back to the Cold War, to explain not only the survival of the myth of American generosity and Japanese gratitude but the eventual arrival of prosperity as well. As for the frequently asked "what-if" questions: What if Japan had experienced a genuinely Allied occupation, with major power in the hands of the British, French, Soviets, Chinese, or Australians, or if it had been divided into occupation zones like Germany and Austria? What if there had been no occupation at all— just demobilization, destruction of military matériel, heavy reparations, and nothing else except surveillance of the peace from overseas? One might conjecture that even without an occupation, the Japanese economy would have benefited from U.S. support, as it spread dollars around the globe in order to keep nations on the side of the free world. As it was, the Korean War did the economic trick, finally jump-starting the economic recovery that the occupation had failed to bring about. As a historian, I'm not good at counterfactuals, but it may be worth imagining what direction postwar Japan might have taken had the Americans decamped earlier on. Who would have taken power, what would have happened to the emperor, what kind of postwar measures would have ensued, where would Japan have stood in the Cold War?

There is little doubt that the United States operated not only as a victor but as an imperial power during the nearly seven years of occupation. But it is also true that Japanese and Americans colluded in the postwar project—sometimes contesting, sometimes manipulating one another—and that the myth of U.S. generosity and Japanese gratitude survived because it proved convenient to both sides: the Japanese-American syndrome at work.

Second: the emperor. Japanese progressives have long criticized the ignorance and orientalism of the victorious Americans, which led them to think that without the emperor the Japanese nation would crumble into chaos and Communism. Ironically, it wasn't politicians but Japan experts who first argued for keeping the emperor during the presurrender planning phase: not only Ambassador Grew with his condescending notions about Japan but also the American Quaker Hugh Borton and the British diplomat George Sansom, both of whom were respected historians of Japan. Many Americans, as revealed in the polls—like most Australians, Chinese, and many others—wanted Hirohito punished, if not strung up. And the Americans were indeed preparing to prosecute him. Enter General MacArthur, who was in good part responsible for saving the emperor, not only from trial but also from abdication. From the vantage point of history and what is now known as transitional justice, both actions were surely misguided: Hirohito should at least have stepped down, and many would agree that he should also have been prosecuted.

Considering the emperor's personal reluctance to abdicate—a reluctance clearly expressed in sources made public since his death—it seems probable that only the occupation had the power to decree the end of Hirohito's reign in 1945. It is true that Nanbara Shigeru and Nosaka Sanzō made such proposals, but it is hard to imagine that either of them (or any other Japanese) could have prevailed against the emperor's will to remain in office, especially when combined with the support of those conservatives who benefited from claiming to act "in the name of the emperor." The Americans, however, could certainly have forced abdication, but they did not. So the same emperor who had presided over imperial aggression and war perambulated into the postwar, his military uniform exchanged for a business suit, transformed by the new constitution (written by the Americans) into an allegedly harmless "symbol of the state." Among the consequences of this "symbolic" imperial continuity was the national erasure of war responsibility. For transformation of the emperor from commanding autocrat to peaceable democrat was indeed a symbol: a symbol of evasion of responsibility for the past.

Third: Japan and Asia. Japan's evasion of the past created a memory vacuum where the war in Asia should have been, a hole in consciousness that plagues Japanese relations with China, Korea, and other Asian countries today. And of course the United States also played a major role in turning postwar Japan away from Asia toward the Pacific under the Japanese-American security alliance. Japan's position of "subordinate independence" in the American Cold War imperium has long been characterized by Japanese critics as a colonial relationship. And they have argued that Japan should assert itself in postcolonial terms against the United States. So far, so good. But—not to forget—Japan was also an imperialist power in Asia. And yet for a long time, postwar Japan gave little evidence of any postimperial recognition. For relations with Asia today, Japan's postcolonial critique of the Cold War United States is less important than the lack of postimperial reflection about empire and war in Asia. Thus, even in the realm of anti-American sentiment, the Japanese-American syndrome, which dates to the occupation, impedes Japanese thinking deeply about Asia, in both the past and the present.

January 2002: Habits of History

I have now been asked to explain why the United States continues to behave like a lone superpower, cloaking unilateral action in a veil of coalition and waging an air war on an already devastated Afghanistan.

Once again I resist speaking "as an American" and instead offer some thoughts as a historian. This is because I see the past written all over the actions of the present: the "War on Terrorism" owes everything to the habits of history.

The habits of hegemony, for example, are notably hard to break. Not that the United States had such long practice in world domination. The era of U.S. hegemony—the so-called American century announced by Henry Luce in 1941—was actually short, in fact only half a century, if that. And during the fifty years since World War II, while the United States acted as the "leader of the free world," it continued to harbor the fundamental ambivalence toward the world that had been present since the beginning of its history. Always certain of their exceptionalism, Americans were also always unsure of the best way to pursue their special "destiny." Should they keep themselves separate from the rest of the (less noble) world, or should they intervene in the (less civilized) nations to save them? As Anders Stephanson argues in his *Manifest Destiny: American Expansion and the Empire of Right,* separation prevailed most of the time, until the United States found itself "falling into the world" with the advent of World War I.

During the Cold War, even as the United States threw its massive weight around in the global effort to contain Communism, the attention of ordinary Americans was more often directed inward. Foreign policy, as all U.S. politicians know, does not bring in the votes. This was all the more true after the Cold War ended. The first President Bush "won" the Gulf War and lost the election, and President Clinton, always the politician, kept away from foreign "entanglements" as much as he possibly could, from Bosnia to Somalia to Kosovo. The recent book by David Halberstam entitled *Waging War in a Time of Peace* describes how the United States continued to play hegemon in the 1990s but did so timidly and ineffectively. In places like Rwanda even humanitarian intervention failed and Americans became—to quote Samantha Powers—"Bystanders to Genocide."

These habits of hegemony and ambivalence underlie such striking recent examples of U.S. unilateralism as the abrogation of arms treaties, the refusal to ratify the Kyoto Protocol, and the rejection of the International Criminal Court. In other words, the United States both intervenes in the world and withdraws from it at will, as if it were indeed the lone superpower.

But it isn't. And we do not live in a unipolar world either. The collapse of the Soviet Union did not mean subtracting one from two to get a single remaining superpower, the United States. Global arithmetic doesn't work that way. No nation at present possesses all-encompassing military, economic, political, and ideological dominance of the sort that used to define superpowerdom. The military power of the United States remains vast and lethal (although in a post–star wars era, even the fantasy of a missile shield cannot protect against attacks like that of September 11). Economic power is spread among the rich nations of the North—the tiny group of countries that gathers at the G8 summit—and they are increasingly interdependent not only with one another but with the have-not nations of the South. Political power does not belong to the United States alone, as the widespread international criticism of U.S. policy demonstrates. And ideological power does not reside solely in American versions of individual freedom and market capitalism.

Habits of hegemony are slow to change: think of the time it took for postimperial Britain to adjust. And new world orders are hard to come by. But the world is changing—the International Criminal Court, for example, will be established, with or without the United States—and even the United States will have to move in the direction of multilateralism. The question is whether it will happen soon enough to prevent irreparable damage.

Then there are the habits of the North, which help to explain why the "War on Terrorism" was in the first instance a war on Afghanistan. Although people insist on saying that everything changed on September 11, everything of course did not change. One important thing that did not change was the disparity between the rich and powerful nations of the North and the disadvantaged and unempowered nations of the South. The long legacy of imperialism remains inscribed in North-South relations today.

The terrorist attacks of 9/11 gave the U.S. government its first clearly named enemy since the fall of Communism. Reagan's Evil Empire was replaced with Bush's evil al-Qaeda (and later the Axis of Evil), so that the War on Terrorism provided the justification for military action that had been lacking during Clinton's "timid" wars in the nineties. (The 1991 Gulf War had been justified in more conventional terms of Iraq's invasion of Kuwait prompting the first President Bush to resort to the kind of hollow analogies so favored these days, and to compare Saddam Hussein to Hitler.) The second President Bush used the justification of a new enemy in a new War on Terror to make the war on Afghanistan politically possible at home. September 11 overwhelmed the inward orientation of American voters and made them leap to intervention—in this case understood as defense and retaliation—rather than separation from military engagement and its risks.

Americans expressed overwhelming support for the war on Afghanistan in precisely these terms. It was a War on Terrorism, not on Islam, and everyone, including the government, made that clear from the beginning. And it wasn't a "clash of civilizations" either. Nor does one have to rely on racism to explain why it was easier to go to war against Afghanistan than it might have been against Russia, if bin Laden had happened to be hiding in a cave in the Ural Mountains. It was as much geopolitics and the structural disparity of power between the developed and developing countries that produced these habits of the North—or in earlier terms, the habits of the West.

The same disparity had kept the Cold War cold between the United States and the Soviet Union while they engaged in proxy hot wars in Korea, Vietnam, and all over the Third World, including Afghanistan.

(Long before the Soviets invaded and the Americans armed the mujahideen in the 1980s, I remember seeing the Soviets and Americans fight it out in Afghanistan using foreign "aid" to build airports in 1963. Even a naïve young hitchhiker like me understood how little either superpower cared for Afghanistan or its people.) The same disparity of power makes Africa all but invisible to the so-called advanced industrial countries. Indeed, I doubt that Americans would be nearly as concerned with the fate of Sudan or Somalia, should the War on Terrorism have occurred in those countries, than they seem to be with the future of post-Taliban Afghanistan. Prejudice, civilizational arrogance, and racism are part of the picture, with inequities of power as the overall frame.

And not to forget habits of the nation, which are perhaps the most deeply ingrained of all. The simplest answer to the question of what ordinary Americans think about the war is that they think their country was attacked. The terrorism of September 11 was almost instantly packaged as a national calamity (perhaps somewhat less in New York, where for a while human beings rather than flags held the center of attention). On TV, banners announcing "Attack on the World Trade Center" soon gave way to those pronouncing "Attack on America." The inapt references to Pearl Harbor were immediate—within thirty minutes—and they came from everyone from movie stars to Henry Kissinger. Then came the rhetoric of resolve, the patriotism, the flags—endless, countless flags—and the narrative of "A Nation Challenged," the title of the *New York Times* special daily section on the war and terrorism.

The nationalizing of global terrorism was itself a global phenomenon. Most countries saw the events in national terms; Japan is but one example. The fact is that, despite the forces of globalization, we live in a world of nation-states. And nation-states operate in terms of national interest, national defense, and national power. Thus the coalition that the U.S. government sought to form in the days after the attacks was a product of a series of bilateral negotiations between two leaders looking after the interests of their respective nations. This was old-fashioned diplomacy and certainly not the way to combat collectively and cooperatively the network of global terrorism.

Recent polls of U.S. public opinion show, however, that while 91 percent of Americans support military action in Afghanistan, 95 percent also believe that terrorism must be combated "through the effort of many countries working together." Eighty-four percent regard the support of the United Nations as essential, and half think that if Osama bin Laden is captured, he should be tried in an international criminal tribunal—clearly not the views of the Bush administration. Support for non-military measures against terrorism, such as cutting financial sources, improving intelligence, and strengthening international law is as strong as support for military force. The concern about civilian casualties is also clear in the opinion polls. George Kennan's warning about "commitment to massive civilian destruction" belongs to an earlier Cold War era. Of course, most Americans don't know the extent of the casualties in Kabul and Kandahar, just as they didn't find out about the Iraqi civilian deaths in the 1991 Gulf War until after the conflict had ended. It is possible that the current national consensus—and flag waving—may begin to fade as events unfold—or so one hopes. Not that the habits of the nation will disappear, but Americans will perhaps begin to dispute among themselves where their true "national interest" lies. If their answer is "in multilateral cooperation," it might help change the tone of the conflict.

I would add one more aspect to the habitual mix: the habits of critique. By that, I mean that it is easy enough for critics like ourselves to see the human and social carnage wrought by the current "War on Terrorism." It is easy as a historian to spot the habits of hegemony, the habits of the North, and the habits of the nation at work in the present situation. But criticism isn't enough; we need to change things, to work for the things we say we believe in. For me that means such things as supporting the International Criminal Court to try terrorists for crimes against humanity; it means fighting what I think of as "advanced-country nationalism," which afflicts both Japan and the United States; it means trying to promote the sort of global interactions that help the nations of the South, not just of the North. If we don't break our own habits of critique, we are, as they say, part of the problem, not the solution—and that means part of the past, not of the future.

January 2002: Grand Causes and Concrete Change

To the question of the nature of the United States as an imperial state (but still a nation-state), this is nothing new for the United States, whose imperial actions long preceded the Cold War and even the existence of the Soviet Union. At the same time, by the end of the twentieth-century empires of the old sort were in decline. Or, to quote Hardt and Negri, empire has not disappeared; it just works differently now, through "network power" in a global space of imperial sovereignty. Overreaching military power and force of habit make the United States a major actor in this global space, although its recent actions seem more in tune with the old hegemony than with the new network power.

What real choices can one then offer in the present real context? The lessons of the past are not encouraging. Americans learned little from the Korean War except how to forget their role in it. From the Vietnam War, which they do indeed remember, they learned skewed lessons: either avoid any military involvement or intervene in the form of surgical strikes that cost enemy, but not American, lives, as in the 1991 Gulf War. In my view, neither Japan nor the United States has sufficiently confronted the suffering caused by imperial Japan's Great East Asia War and imperial America's "cold" wars in Korea, Vietnam, and other places. But the point now is how to keep from causing new suffering in the name of antiterrorism.

One thing we might learn from the past in the present context is to avoid "Grand Causes," such as the Great East Asia "co-prosperity sphere" or saving the world from Communism—or the current War on Terrorism. Better perhaps to argue the case against bombing Afghanistan (and Iraq, and who knows where else) with the American public on the basis not of the Great Cause of combating global terrorism but rather of the countless outcomes in loss of human lives and suffering. As long as the government and the public see military action in terms of a crusade against evil, the hope for better choices remains slim indeed.

The propensity of people to see—and treat—the world in black-and-white terms seems irresistible. If the present Grand Cause of antiterror were to become analogous to the past Grand Cause of anti-Communism, then all manner of unjustifiable actions could be justified in its pursuit. That is why I am arguing against such "Big Ideas," which so easily arouse patriotism at home and bullying abroad. It would be better, I think, to face each issue on its own terms, from dropping bombs in faraway places to curtailing civil rights at home, not as part of a blanket injunction to "win the war against terrorism."

In regard to the question about the United States failing to meet the challenge of its multicultural society, I agree that Americans continually betray the best in their own ideals. But I still think it's possible that the multiethnicity of the United States is a potential ally in combating bad Big Ideas like the "clash of civilizations." Consider the principled activism by—and on behalf of—Arab Americans and other resident Muslims over the past several months. This public discourse expressly rejects the notion of a clash of civilizations or of religions, making it harder for those who prefer such blanket ideologies to say so out loud. True, this has not stopped the harassment, detention, and other violations of civil rights of many citizens. But Arab-American groups and others who have frequently referred to the wartime internment of Japanese Americans as a lesson to be learned from the past have also insisted on the diversity of Islamic regimes and peoples, against the rhetoric of all-al-Qaeda-all-over-the-Muslim-world. In short, the multiplicity of hyphenated Americans may help to steer U.S. foreign policy away from ideological absolutism both at home and abroad. The social premise at least is principled, however breached it is in practice.

How to live together, honorably, in a world of differences is no easy challenge. As I write this, the World Economic Forum, once of Davos, Switzerland, is now underway in Manhattan, while the World Social Forum, the "anti-Davos," is meeting in Porto Alegre, Brazil. The WEF gathers its 2,500 participants largely from the rich, powerful, globalizing North. The WSF, with some 14,000 delegates, symbolizes the poor, unempowered South. It stands for the countries and classes that are subject to—rather than the subjects of—the forces of globalization. The WEF and the WSF are both working, each in its own very different way, in the terrain of an emerging global civil society that seeks nonviolent transnational solutions and believes, in the words of the theme of this year's WSF, that "another world is possible."

So, do we need a Grand Idea to get there? I appreciate the point that without some way to transcend our differences we are doomed to reenact the hostilities toward others that seem to lodge so deeply in our political unconscious. But I still think that Grand Ideas are not the answer, since they function so often as ideological covers that justify those same hostilities toward peoples or cultures that are different from our own. I am happy to live in a "nontopian" age, precisely because it lacks any large utopian conception of what the future ought to look like. And I reject catchall categories like civilization, which have already caused so much imperialist mischief. If one must think big, then I prefer Amartya Sen in his encouraging "development as freedom" to Samuel Huntington and his divisive "the West and the rest."

I propose instead smaller moves to establish what I think of as common ground among peoples, groups, nations, and beliefs. Common ground means recognizing the existence of commonalities, but in partial, not totalizing, form. Common ground means leaving space for difference—like multiple intersecting circles in which only the overlapping sections are common while the rest of each circle retains its distinctive character. For example, I think that the evolving discourse of transnational human rights, or the newer term, "human security," reveals the possibility of building, brick by brick, straw by straw, an edifice on common ground. Almost everyone can agree on the right not to be tortured or the right not to be starved without having to insist on some allegedly universal value—which is seldom universal anyway, but rather the extension of one particularity over the particularities of others. This kind of common ground seeks the fundamental rather than the transcendental and can only be achieved in incremental steps that do not trample the differences of others.

I would argue that this is also probably the only way to accommodate the diversity in the history and memory of the United States, a question that has often recurred in this transpacific conversation. The melting pot of a hundred years ago was in fact a smelting pot which insisted that every immigrant become 100 percent American. This image has given way over the past several decades to the so-called salad bowl, which metaphorically evokes a society composed of many different ingredients that are not melted down but mixed together, each retaining its taste and color. The question then becomes how to bind the salad together without sacrificing ethnic identity to national unity and vice versa.

Again, I think the answer is common ground, which is in any case the sole basis for democratic politics in a pluralistic society. And it is also the basis for a fuller public memory that incorporates the historical experiences of Native Americans, African Americans, Vietnamese Americans, and the rest into a more capacious national history. At this point the struggle continues, but with some small success. Proof of this success is found in the "history wars" of the mid-1990s, when patriotic conservatives were enraged that the new history standards for the schools included so many "women and minorities" instead of the usual big-name military and political heroes.

The new inclusiveness does not mean that racism has disappeared in the United States—far from it—but national history at least now has a different "face" to it. The awful saying, mentioned earlier in our conversation, "the only good Indian is a dead Indian" was spoken in Congress already in 1868 and had a long career both in public speech and in the movies. But no longer. Similarly the marine who testified before Congress in the War Crimes Hearings in 1971 after the My Lai massacre in Vietnam and (actually) said that "the only good gook was a dead gook" now belongs, thankfully, to another era. Ethnic epithets and racial slurs have a long history in the United States, but over time, and with great effort, the worst of them can be gradually excluded from the vocabulary of civil discourse. That is the meaning of the current campaign against "hate speech," which is kept perennially busy by successive waves of intolerance.

I agree that these domestic developments are not necessarily reflected in U.S. foreign policy. But I don't much sympathize with Japanese conservatives who complain of American racism against Japan today, whether in international relations or in the movies. This is an easy shot from Japanese pot to American kettle that misses the greater global bigotries. I am more troubled, as I said, by the habits of the North. Somali-Americans have recently protested the depiction of the people in their home country as "savages" in the war film *Black Hawk Down,* which seems to them to perpetuate the old racist attitudes toward Africa. In this sense, the legacy of John Wayne lingers on. To me racism is less an issue between Japan and the United States than it is a transnational challenge to both nations to combat racism in their own countries and around the world. To see racism in bilateral terms is Japanese-American tunnel vision at work.

The only way for Japan to gain what we are here calling "autonomy" from the U.S.-Japan relationship is to stop viewing the world in terms of that relationship. It doesn't matter after all whether one argues for the U.S.-Japan alliance or against it, as long as the conversation takes place in the tunnel, there is small hope of escape.

January 2003: Accidents of History

A year has passed since we began this discussion on the past and future of US-Japan relations. From my point of view, it was not a good year. Now I am asked to comment on events in the United States in the months after 9/11 and the war in Afghanistan, once again as a historian and, I assume, as an American. Right now I find both roles difficult to manage, since neither offers much help in understanding or arresting the avowedly unilateral movement of the Bush regime toward "pre-emptive" war in Iraq. What constellation of past habits and present predilections drove the United States to this position—what is the history here? And what combination of arrogance and ignorance impelled the American public to support the president's actions? What is the meaning of "America" in these times?

There was no shortage of analytic comment seeking to explain the history of "George Bush and the World" and "the Bush Doctrine." The popular press and intellectual journals were filled with it, both for the policy and against it. Some, like the progressive historian Walter LaFeber, took an extremely long view, arguing that the Bush Doctrine had almost 400 years of history behind it. He suggested that the standard formula for U.S. foreign policy was always "American exceptionalism plus U.S. power equals efficient unilateralism." He traced the exceptionalism back to the seventeenth-century evocation of America as a city on a hill, stressing the power wielded in the nineteenth century to dominate the western hemisphere, and then, in the twentieth century, the world; and he lamented the triumph of unilateralism in the wake of

September 11. The United States had become "a nation so strong that others could not check it, and so self-righteous that it could not check itself." [1]

Less despairing critics made similar comments about the long history of American isolationism and unilateralism as "ideological twins" that prevented "a more inclusive exceptionalism" from taking hold. Bush's National Security Advisor, Condoleeza Rice, came into office already arguing that national interest superseded "the interest of an illusory international community." [2] With that depressing pedigree for the president's foreign policy, it is no surprise that so many commentators mentioned Woodrow Wilson, a president famous for carrying the banner of American exceptionalism and moralism abroad. Some compared Bush to Wilson and criticized him for similarly domineering impulses, while others pointed out that at least Wilson thought the United States had a mission to do something in the world's interest rather than only in its own.

Medium-term historical explanations focused on the Cold War and suggested that what I've called the "habits of hegemony" were formed in the bipolar world order and had survived, as is, into a unipolar age. Now that the United States was a "hyperpower," the sole remaining "imperial nation" was free to pursue its interests any way it liked without the constraint previously provided by the Soviet Union. While critics decried this perpetuation of Cold War arrogance, Bush supporters employed Cold War precedents for their own purposes. They pointed out, for example, that Kennedy had considered "preemptive" action in the Cuban Missile Crisis forty years ago. Those who were there with Kennedy in 1962 countered by saying that his Cold War brinkmanship was intended precisely to *avoid* taking such action. In any case, I agree with those who thought that the Cuban Missile Crisis was an irrelevant example and that it would make more sense to look at the lessons that the United States failed to learn from the Iranian revolution of 1978–79. [3] At that time the

United States saw the revolution primarily as a challenge to its own power in the Middle East, and pursued a policy which unleashed consequences that still reverberate in the region. Just imagine the consequences of an American war on Iraq today.

The Cold War, of course, is over (in most places, though not everywhere, not, for example in Northeast Asia). For that reason another set of historical explanations adopted a shorter view, arguing that U.S. policy turned a corner after September 11, when it departed from the past and articulated a new post–Cold War "grand strategy." The usual text for this reading was the most recent National Security Strategy published in September 2002, which enunciated the doctrine of "preemptive actions" to make the world safe from terrorists and tyrants. These malevolent twins were presented as the main threats to the "forces of freedom," which won the Cold War and left the United States with "unprecedented—and unequaled—strength and influence in the world." The goal was now to build and maintain American military strength "beyond challenge." The rhetoric was bald and bold, but the statements had been heard often before in the years since the collapse of the Soviet Union. The document also reiterated the importance of international cooperation and coalitions using the practiced language of Gulf War and G-8 politics. What did seem new, however, was the overt statement that the United States "will not hesitate to act alone, if necessary, to exercise our right of self-defense." This essentially meant abandoning the rules of the international order that the United States helped to establish in the decades after World War II. It also signified the unilateral exercise of military power. And what was preemptive attack for the sake of self-defense but an act of aggressive war? It sounds a lot like Pearl Harbor, doesn't it?

Such were the views—long, medium, and short-term—of the history that led to the United States declaring that it would wage war on Iraq, alone if necessary, but necessary even if alone. All commentators seemed to suggest that the outcome was inevitable, as if no other policy were possible for a United States propelled by the force of its powerful past. But when one stops to think about it, much of what happened in the past two years was in fact accidental. The 2000 presidential election was so close that there could easily have been not a Bush but a Gore Doctrine, which, whatever its flaws, would not have been led by the aging trio of conservative hawks, Rumsfeld, Cheney, and Wolfowitz. Their plans for ousting Saddam Hussein had been on the table for a decade and would likely have remained there gathering Republican dust instead of being applied, unreconstructed, in the name of the new War on Terrorism. Once Bush came to power, these same people and others embarked immediately on a unilateral foreign policy of missile shields, treaty-breaking, and the targeting of rogue states. Still, without the great accident of September 11—which could just as easily have occurred one year earlier, before Bush was elected—Republican unilateralists would not have been able to play the terrorism card to make war on Iraq.

Historians like the word "contingency" because it suggests that nothing is inevitable and everything is complicated by factors that cannot be drawn in a straight line from the past. The "habits of history," in short, are not all-determining, and it is nowhere written that the United States had no recourse but to destroy the fabric of international cooperation, exacerbate the turmoil in the Middle East, and go it alone over the cliff into the abyss of preemptive war. So if one believes, as I do, that Bush was an accident and that September 11 did not in fact "change everything," it ought to be possible to divert these particular contingencies to another, more desirable course. At this point it is likely that only two forces could have such an effect: the "international community" so disdained by Condoleezza Rice, and the American people, who vote politicians in and out of office.

Here is where arrogance and ignorance played a role. Would U.S. allies like Germany, whose leaders took a strong position against war in Iraq during their election campaign, hold the line after those leaders were re-elected? And if they did, would the United States in its renewed arrogance pay any heed? Would the UN respond forcefully if the United States ignored the purport of its resolutions and attacked Baghdad "preemptively"? And if it did, would the Bush administration care? One member of the administration had already pronounced that "there is no such thing as the United Nations," only a world in which the United States was "the only real power left." Other nations would have to speak in firm and booming voices to counter the arrogance of such grandiloquence.

And what about Japan? Would Japan take a stand, or would it employ what has been called its "double hedge." In this view Japan continued to use the United States as a hedge against security threats while it established ties with other countries in Asia and the Middle East as a hedge against threats to its economic interests.[4] One would think that if there were ever a moment for Japan to break out of the bilateral syndrome, this might be it. Criticism of a U.S. war on Iraq, after all, rather than isolating Japan would put it in company with much of the rest of the world. Such a move would not seem to require extraordinary courage or vision.

Consider the related case of North Korea. My colleagues in this conversation have both underlined the historical significance of the Japan–North Korea summit in September 2002. Wada Haruki called it an epoch-making event because, for once, Japan had "moved in advance of America."[5] And Kang Sangjung stressed that the meeting was a "decisive step forward in Japanese diplomacy," a move away from the "follow-the-USA" line of the postwar decades.[6] I think so, too, but I also think that the real test is still to come. The Pyongyang Declaration was signed by Prime Minister Koizumi and Chairman Kim on the same day, September 17, that the National Security Strategy was published in the

United States. At that point the nuclear "bombshell" had not yet been made public, though it was known by the U.S. and Japanese governments. But once North Korea's continued development of WMD (now fashionable acronym for weapons of mass destruction) was out in the open, it was clear that the United States intended to treat the East Asian member of the "Axis of Evil" quite differently from the way it would its fellow "rogue state" Iraq. At that point the opportunity expanded for Japan to play a leading rather than a following role, not only in Northeast Asia but also in the debate over the U.S. actions in the Middle East. American arrogance might mean that the Japanese stance would be ignored, but it still seems to me too easy to blame the United States for Japan's reluctance to step forward and take a stand.

Nor is it fair, however, to expect the rest of the world to curb the arrogance of American hyperpower; that is the responsibility of the American people. And as I said earlier in our exchange, for me the most discouraging part of this past year was the unwillingness of Americans to stand up to their government. Although some polls in October 2002, continued to show that less than a quarter of the population favored acting against Iraq without UN support, that position was scarcely reflected either in the Democratic opposition or in general public opinion. Yes, there were speeches, marches, and dissenting voices throughout, but nothing threatening enough to dissuade Bush from his aggressive moralism. And this was an election year, when such voices might have had a greater effect than usual.

I am puzzled by what I think of as the "suffocation of consensus" that continues to afflict the United States a year after September 11. It was somewhat easier to understand this unanimity in the early weeks after the attack, when people were shocked into patriotism. I remember writing in our discussion here last year that the unnaturally total consensus was bound to break, if not on the occasion of war in Afghanistan, then with the move toward war against Iraq. But I was wrong; the con-

sensus hasn't broken even yet, at least in the polls and among the powers
that be—the only sources of public opinion that matter to political candidates. And while it is true that the shock of September 11 continued
to operate to unite people in the determination to fight terrorism, the
easy elision of terrorism and tyranny that appeared in the National Security Strategy document seemed to have been absorbed by the mind
politic almost without thinking. I find this seemingly reflexive predis-
position to preemptive war both dangerous and frightening.

To some degree it is as much a product of ignorance as arrogance: the
ignorance of Americans about Iraq, about the Middle East, about the
world. The media dutifully reported that the Bush administration had
made no convincing link between al-Qaeda and Saddam Hussein; commentators acknowledged that "regime change" in Iraq would not in itself bring stability to that country or peace to the Middle East; and many
pointed out that whatever anti-American animus already exists in Muslim societies would only be intensified by a unilateral war, preemptive
or otherwise. And yet the majority of Americans paid little attention,
and the suffocation of consensus persisted. Perhaps it was the potent
combination of "homeland" emotion and ignorance of the outside
world that revived the ideological twins of isolationism and unilateralism, so unsuited to the times in which we live.

Whatever happens now—whether the United States wages preemptive war against Iraq or withdraws from the brink—I stand by my earlier
statement that, all appearances to the contrary, the United States is not
quite the lone superpower that its present government thinks it is.
Joseph Nye makes a similar point in his book, *The Paradox of American
Power: Why the World's Only Superpower Can't Go It Alone* (2002). The
United States can't go it alone because its vast military power cannot
keep the world at bay, a lesson that September 11 should have brought
home. The more imperial its actions, the greater its troubles and the
more havoc wrought on others. Its soft-power strengths would be
squandered and the meaning of America despoiled.

I hope this won't happen. But the only way to avoid it is for Americans to put the brakes on unilateralism by voting the unilateralists out of office. And the only way to undercut the blinkered, inward-looking patriotism that supports the current unilateralism is to look beyond the confines of the nation to convey the consequences of this latest imperial campaign, both for the United States and for the world. The tendency, in Japan as in the United States, is always to think that whatever it is, it is "all about us," when in fact it is "all about the world," not least its poor and unempowered portions. In this light, rethinking Japanese-American relations is an essential but small part of what's to be done to make the world a better place, more interconnected, more multiple, and less vulnerable to the power of imperial America and wayward accidents of history.

THE FUTURE

10

Onward, Liberal Soldiers?
The Crusading Logic of Bush's Grand Strategy
and What Is Wrong with It

Edward Rhodes

To its credit, the Bush administration has made its foreign policy conception quite clear. In his June 1, 2002, address at West Point, President George W. Bush laid out his administration's conceptual framework for dealing with the post–September 11 world.[1] This conceptual framework was fleshed out in greater detail in the administration's National Security Strategy issued three months later.[2] These are documents that Americans, as citizens of a democracy, should read and ponder with care.

Whether or not one embraces its logic and conclusions, the West Point address must be acknowledged as a masterpiece. It offers the American people a brilliantly lucid and immensely powerful account of the Bush administration's vision of America and America's role in the world. The speech evokes American values, argues the universality of human liberty, and attacks what it describes as the twin dangers of tyrants and terrorism. It rejects the murkiness of moral relativism, distinguishes boldly between good and evil, and unabashedly and unhesitatingly aligns America on the side of good.

America, the president makes clear, has a global duty. Both to protect itself and to be true to its higher calling, America must shoulder the responsibility of constructing a global peace, which can be built only on the foundation of individual human liberty and free societies. The might and will of the United States must be mustered and employed not simply to maintain a balance of power that holds aggressors in check but to create "a balance of power"—or, more accurately, an imbalance of power—"that favors human freedom."[3]

At West Point the president thus made clear his faith that a new world order based on liberalism's cherished values is both necessary and possible. This new liberal order will not construct itself, however. American power will be key in building it. Indeed, more specifically, American *military* power will be key. Order—even a liberal order based on human liberty and on consent—ultimately requires the exercise of power, and in this case the power will need to be America's military might. Addressing the nation's newly commissioned military officers, the president was blunt about the purposes to which American military and political power would be put.

> Wherever we carry it, the American flag will stand not only for our power, but for freedom. Our nation's cause has always been larger than our nation's defense. We fight, as we always fight, for a just peace—a peace that favors human liberty. We will defend the peace against threats from terrorists and tyrants. . . . And we will extend the peace by encouraging free and open societies on every continent. Building this just peace is America's opportunity, and America's duty. From this day forward, it is your [that is, the newly commissioned officers'] challenge as well, and we will meet this challenge together.[4]

As a number of observers have noted,[5] this is Wilsonianism with a vengeance: the objective of American foreign policy, President Bush makes clear, is nothing less than a transformation of world politics, domestic as well as international, using American power—military as well as economic and political—to build liberal societies and polities. We are, President Bush suggests, at a great watershed in human history. We find ourselves at a turning point like the one at the end of the Thirty Years

War, when, from the nightmare of uncontrolled warring, pillage, rapine, and disease, emerged a new political order based on sovereign states able to control and limit violence. Today, in the wake of a century of extraordinary violence between these sovereign states—including a First World War that pitted liberal democracy against authoritarianism, a Second World War that pitted it against fascism and militarism, and a Cold War that pitted it against Communism—new political institutions and a new political order can and must be created. "We have," the president notes, "our best chance since the rise of the nation-state in the seventeenth century to build a world where the great powers compete in peace instead of prepare for war."[6]

We are, the president suggests without using the term, at a millennial moment. We are poised on the brink of some sort of end of history, or at least on the brink of the beginning of an end of history. With American leadership, it is possible to enter into this new world in which humanity achieves, or re-achieves, its natural state. "The United States will use this moment of opportunity to extend the benefits of freedom across the globe," the president declares.[7] "Freedom," he goes on to proclaim,

> is the non-negotiable demand of human dignity; the birthright of every person—in every civilization. Throughout history, freedom has been threatened by war and terror; it has been challenged by the clashing of wills of powerful states and the evil designs of tyrants; and it has been tested by widespread poverty and disease. Today, humanity holds in its hands the opportunity to further freedom's triumph over all these foes. The United States welcomes our responsibility to lead in this great mission.[8]

Although President Bush denies harboring either "utopian" or "imperial" ambitions ("America has," he assures the American people and the world in words comfortingly reminiscent of the founding fathers, "no empire to extend or utopia to establish. We wish for others only what we wish for ourselves—safety from violence, the rewards of liberty, and the hope for a better life"⁹), he embraces the view that, under American guidance, a world free from violence and strife is indeed possible. "Competition between great nations is inevitable," the president notes, "but armed conflict in our world is not."¹⁰

How is America to achieve this utopian goal? (For surely, despite the president's demurral, it is not unreasonable to call freeing the world from armed conflict a utopian goal.) Again, to his credit, the president is perfectly clear. The achievement of a peaceful, liberal world order requires not simply American power, and not simply American military power, but a global American military hegemony. At West Point he declared: "America has, and intends to keep, military strengths beyond challenge— thereby making the destabilizing arms races of other eras pointless, and limiting rivalries to trade and other pursuits of peace."¹¹ It is America's *unchallengeable* military power that provides the aegis under which peace and freedom can be built. The new world order is possible because America's global military power allows it to dictate the rules of international discourse and the means by which political actors can adjudicate their differences. Appeals to force by "sovereign" states or other political actors will be bootless. Indeed, American military supremacy will be so manifest that even the thought of challenging it (and the American-imposed order constructed atop it) will be seen as implausible.

The National Security Strategy returns to this theme of America's military hegemony, developing it more fully and explicitly. "It is time," the president announced,

to reaffirm the essential role of American military strength. We must build and maintain our defenses beyond challenge . . . We know from history that deterrence can fail; and we know from experience that some enemies cannot be deterred. The United States must and will maintain the capability to defeat any attempt by an enemy—whether a state or a nonstate actor—to impose its will on the United States, our allies, or our friends. We will maintain the forces sufficient to support our obligations, and to defend freedom [NB: "freedom," not "our freedom" or "American freedom"]. Our forces will be strong enough to dissuade potential adversaries from pursuing a military build up in hopes of surpassing, or equaling, the power of the United States.[12]

Three extraordinary features in the Bush administration's conception of American military hegemony and of how this military hegemony can be translated into the achievement of political goals deserve to be underscored. The first is that American military power will have to be used aggressively, not passively. The "best defense is a good offense,"[13] the National Security Strategy notes. America's military is not a protective shell but a fist. This fist will be used to strike down freedom's foes. More to the point, it will be used proactively, not simply reactively. Though the ultimate political goal, of course, is the *defense* of humanity's natural right to freedom, the United States will not hesitate to act in a militarily offensive fashion, striking enemies before they can endanger the United States, the free world, or the American interest in a liberal world order. As the president explains,

> Given the goals of rogue states and terrorists, the United States can no longer solely rely on a reactive posture as we have in the past. The inability to deter a potential attacker, the immediacy of today's threats, and the magnitude of potential harm that could be caused by our adversaries' choice of weapons, do not permit that option. We cannot let our enemies strike first . . . The United States has long maintained the option of preemptive actions to counter a sufficient threat to our national security. The greater the threat, the greater is the risk of inaction—and the more compelling the case for taking anticipatory action to defend ourselves, even if uncertainty remains as to the time and place of the enemy's attack.[14]

In fact, the United States will not hesitate to strike even before enemies are *able* to endanger us: "In an age where the enemies of civilization openly and actively seek the world's most destructive technologies, the United States cannot remain idle while dangers gather." [15]

Second, the National Security Strategy makes plain that the liberal order the United States aims to create will, ultimately, rest on *American* military hegemony, not on the combined will and might of the liberal world. American military power, not that of a global liberal coalition, is what will guarantee peace, security, and human freedom around the world. Consensus is desirable, but it is not necessary. Because the global liberal order is essential not only to the world's safety but to America's safety, America's sovereign responsibilities supersede its commitment to international institutions. "While the United States will constantly strive to enlist the support of the international community, we will not hesitate to act alone, if necessary, to exercise our right of self-defense." [16]

Third, the National Security Strategy makes clear that the Bush administration proposes to use American military hegemony not simply aggressively and unilaterally, but globally. In the Bush administration's thinking, a global house divided against itself cannot stand. A world order cannot endure permanently half illiberal and half free. The imperative to spread liberalism's freedom throughout humanity's global home rests not simply on the fact that freedom is every human's right. It rests also on the fact that the absence of freedom, even in places as remote as Afghanistan, poses a danger to the rest of humanity. For this reason, American military forces will be deployed globally—not simply in the industrialized, liberal world of North America, Europe, and Northeast Asia. During the Cold War, American military presence helped provide security and encourage liberal development in the free world. Now it will do the same for the whole world. As the National Security Strategy explains,

The unparalleled strength of the United States armed forces, and their forward presence, have maintained the peace in some of the world's most strategically vital regions. However, the threats and enemies we must confront have changed, and so must our forces . . . To contend with uncertainty and to meet the many security challenges we face, the United States will require bases and stations within and beyond Western Europe and Northeast Asia, as well as temporary access arrangements for the long-distance deployment of U.S. forces.[17]

U.S. military forces must be prepared to go anywhere, any time.

Before the war in Afghanistan, that area was low on the list of major planning contingencies. Yet, in a very short time, we had to operate across the length and breadth of that remote nation, using every branch of the armed forces. We must prepare for more such deployments.[18]

Particular words are, of course, emotionally and politically charged. It does not, however, seem unreasonable to describe a policy that proposes to use military supremacy aggressively, unilaterally, and universally in order to establish a particular form of governance as "imperial." One must, obviously, quickly add the additional adjective "liberal": the Bush administration's grand strategy may be imperial, but it aims at creating liberal, rather than autocratic or totalitarian, governance wherever the American military Pax reaches. The tension between these two adjectives, "imperial" and "liberal," lies at the very heart of the Bush administration's foreign policy, though it is nowhere addressed.

The National Security Strategy makes clear that the new world order will be constructed not only under the beneficial umbrella of America's global military dominance but on the basis of America's blueprint and on the basis of its conceptions of universal values and of order. There is a single truth, and it is America's. Alternative models of social order and political governance are not only morally wrong but are also an impractical basis for moving forward. "Some worry," the president mused in his West Point address, that it is somehow undiplomatic or impolite to speak the language of right and wrong. I disagree. Moral truth is the same in every culture, in every time, and in every place. . . . There can be no neutrality between justice and cruelty, between the innocent and the guilty. We are in a conflict between good and evil, and America will call evil by its name. By confronting evil and lawless regimes, we do not create a problem, we reveal a problem. And we will lead the world in opposing it.

The twentieth century ended with a single surviving model of human progress, based on nonnegotiable demands of human dignity, the rule of law, limits on the power of the state, respect for women and private property and free speech and equal justice and religious tolerance. . . . When it comes to the common rights and needs of men and women, there is no clash of civilizations. The requirements of freedom apply fully to Africa and Latin America and the entire Islamic world. The peoples of the Islamic nations want and deserve the same freedoms and opportunities as people in every nation. And their governments should listen to them.[19]

Though his language is undiplomatically blunt, its utter self-confidence unattractively arrogant, and its global sweep troubling, there is much here with which most Americans can probably agree. Peace is a praiseworthy goal. Freedom and human rights are good. These are, in the end, achievable. The world is not, as Realists would have it, one in which international life is inevitably nasty, brutish, and short, ruled by power rather than justice. For most Americans, who like the president prefer to look at the world through liberal lenses, his message here is somehow familiar and comforting.

Indeed, in two important ways the president taps into the deep liberal vein running through American history and the American psyche. In the first place, he appeals to American beliefs that there is, and always has been, something special about America's role in the world. For America, interests and values are not in tension: what is good for America is also good for the world, and making the world safe for America will make the world a better place. Second, he appeals to Americans' liberal faith in progress. "The U.S. national security strategy," he assures the American people, "will be based on a distinctly American internationalism that reflects the union of our values and our national interests. The aim of this strategy is to help make the world not just safer but better. Our goals on the path to progress are clear: political and economic freedom, peaceful relations with other states, and respect for human dignity." [20]

The Great Crusade

Like Wilson before him, President Bush is willing to enter into a covenant with power to achieve these liberal goals. For this president as for Wilson, America's power and America's mission have met. America's hour has come. It has within its grasp the power needed to transform the world, to fulfill its destiny. "This is," the president notes, "a time of opportunity for America. We will work to translate this moment of influence into decades of peace, prosperity, and liberty." [21]

What is perhaps most striking about the grand strategy outlined by the president is that it is conceived in terms of a moral imperative. "Responsibility" and "obligation" figure alongside "opportunity" in justifying the choices the president proposes that America make. At this historic watershed, when the "great struggle" that arrayed "destructive totalitarian visions versus freedom and equality" is over, and "the militant visions of class, nation, and race which promised utopia and delivered misery have been defeated and discredited," [22] America's power imposes on it a moral duty. America's strategic choices at this juncture are dictated by this calling. The prose is magnificent in its stark clarity and its avoidance of moral or political ambiguity: "The United States possesses unprecedented—and unequaled—strength and influence in the world. Sustained by faith in the principles of liberty, and the value of a free society, this position comes with unparalleled responsibilities, obligations, and opportunity. The great strength of this nation must be used to promote a balance of power that favors freedom." [23]

The particular interpretation of the liberal religion that the president embraces is thus a crusading one. The moral duty to defend and extend liberalism knows no borders. Sovereignty offers no shield or excuse. Societies and states are not free to eschew liberalism. Indeed, societies and states have a moral *duty* not only to embrace liberalism themselves but to impose liberalism on their neighbors. Since the "values of freedom are right and true for every person, in every society," it follows (the president argues) that "the duty of protecting these values against their enemies is the common calling of freedom-loving people across the globe and across the ages." [24]

This crusading impulse is front and center in the grand strategy outlined by the Bush administration.

> In pursuit of our goals, our first imperative is to clarify what we stand for: the United States must defend liberty and justice because these principles are right and true for all people everywhere. No nation owns these aspirations, *and no nation is exempt from them.* . . . Embodying lessons from our past and *using the opportunity we have today, the national security strategy must start from these core beliefs and look outward for possibilities to expand liberty.*[25]

There is no neutrality or halfway position in this global crusade against liberalism's foes. While American-led, this is a crusade in which all must join.

> In building a balance of power that favors freedom, the United States is guided by the conviction that all nations have important responsibilities. Nations that enjoy freedom must actively fight terror. Nations that de-

pend on international stability must help prevent the spread of weapons
of mass destruction.[26]

The liberal religious faith the president embraces is also a crusading
one in terms of its willingness to take up the sword. Between liberalism
and its enemies—terrorists and tyrants—there is a state of war. While
peace will exist within the liberal world and violence is prohibited between members of the liberal faith toward the world outside—that is,
toward the unbelievers who have not embraced liberalism—there exists
a state of war. This war must be waged aggressively. It must be brought
to the enemy. The final peace will come only when the enemies of liberalism have been destroyed and liberalism's sway is global. This struggle
is inevitable.

> We will defend the peace by fighting terrorists and tyrants. . . . To defeat
> this threat we must make use of every tool in our arsenal—military
> power, better homeland defenses, law enforcement, intelligence, and vig-
> orous efforts to cut off terrorist financing. The war against terrorists of
> global reach is a global enterprise of uncertain duration. . . . We cannot
> defend America and our friends by hoping for the best. So we must be
> prepared to defeat our enemies' plans, using the best intelligence and
> proceeding with deliberation. History will judge harshly those who saw
> this coming danger but failed to act. In the new world we have entered,
> the only path to peace and security is the path of action.[27]

Thus, reversing the positions he took in his 2000 election campaign,[28] the president makes both a moral case and a prudential one for
aggressive, preventive American military action to destroy tyrants and
terrorism around the world, arguing not only against any inward turn
toward isolationism but against a continuation of Cold War–era policies
of containment and deterrence that would compromise with, rather
than rid the world of, these evils. In his West Point address the president

strongly implied that in the changed world of the new century, policies
of containment and deterrence had reached a dead end.

> For much of the last century, America's defense relied on the Cold War
> doctrines of deterrence and containment. In some cases, those strategies
> still apply. But new threats also require new thinking. Deterrence—the
> promise of massive retaliation against nations—means nothing against
> shadowy terrorist networks with no nation or citizens to defend. Con-
> tainment is not possible when unbalanced dictators with weapons of
> mass destruction can deliver those weapons on missiles or secretly pro-
> vide them to terrorist allies.[29]

A Dissent

This call to the American people is emotionally powerful. It rests, however, on a deeply troubling vision of America and America's role in the
world. Worse, the strategy that flows from this vision is profoundly
flawed. The road it charts leads only to tragedy, both for the world and
for America.

As a practical matter, the vision woefully misunderstands the power
that would be required to do what it proclaims it is America's mission to
do. Ridding the world of tyrants and terrorists is not simply a matter of
surgical air strikes and guided munitions, of eliminating particular leaders and destroying particular facilities, of employing superior technology and military science. Ridding the world of tyrants and terrorists is a
matter of transforming lives and societies around the world. It is a
process inseparable from great, long-term, historical developments in
culture and economics. Strike down one tyrant or one terrorist and another will grow in his place, unless the environmental niche that allows
them to flourish is altered.

But this is only part—and the least fundamental part—of the misunderstanding. Building a peaceful, liberal world order is not simply a matter of ridding the world of all tyrants and terrorists. Liberalism is not simply the absence of illiberal or antiliberal institutions, like tyranny and terrorism. Nor even is liberalism simply the existence of particular democratic and free-market institutions. Liberalism is a philosophy, a set of beliefs. These beliefs—about how individuals should structure their relationships with each other and organize themselves to deal with collective problems, about the "right" way to live in society—do imply particular behaviors and the development of particular institutions. But ultimately liberalism is a set of beliefs that individuals and societies embrace. For a liberal order to function, for liberal institutions to take root, to grow, and to bear fruit, individuals and societies must believe in the "rightness" of liberalism. Acceptance of the gospel of liberalism, and maintaining the vigor of this gospel in communities that have already accepted it, is in the final analysis an internal matter within each individual and each society. It happens—or fails to happen—not because a hegemon wills it, but because of organic developments within human consciousness and societal operations, developments that render liberalism's assumptions plausible and give evidence that its norms will yield the benefits claimed.[30]

Building a new world order is thus truly a millennial task, one that exceeds even America's enormous power. A liberal world free from tyranny and terror may—and hopefully will—come, but it will not come soon, nor will it come as an act of American will. Governance based on consent rather than on force, amity between peoples, and the rule of reason and law cannot be meaningfully imposed or long sustained at gunpoint.

This is not an idealistic or naïve call for pacifism. In the violent, imperfect world that exists today, America may need to act—indeed, even to use violence—to protect its own people and others who depend on it. This regrettable need to employ power for self-defense should not, though, be confused with a divine calling to do with power what cannot be done with power. Power's ability to change behavior is well documented. No tyrant, terrorist, or torturer doubts it. Power's ability to change beliefs, though, is far more limited, more indirect, and more slowly operating.

Certainly any American leader more well-read in history than Bush would have reason to doubt the efficacy of American power in creating liberal societies. America's experience has not been one to give cause for much optimism. Admittedly, the seriousness of the effort has waxed and waned, and American interest in building liberal institutions has always been uncomfortably entangled with a pursuit of profits, but the history of American intervention in the Caribbean basin over the last century is instructive. The magnitude of American power—economic, military, and political—defies adjectives. And yet, despite the overwhelming American presence and despite repeated interventions, with how much certainty and confidence is the term "liberal" even today applied to states and societies such as Guatemala, Honduras, and Haiti? What should give pause is not simply that American power has been greater in the Caribbean basin than it is likely ever to be in the Middle East, Central Asia, or Africa, and that America has had a century to inculcate liberalism; America has also better understood the Caribbean basin than it understands the faraway nations it now proposes to bring into the liberal fold, has had the capacity to co-opt effectively the national elites, and has been dealing with societies already profoundly exposed to the liberal tradition. What reason is there to suspect that America will do better in Afghanistan than it has in Haiti?

The two often-touted examples of American success—Germany and Japan—are of course the exceptions that prove the rule. Unfortunately for the Bush administration, the rule is that liberalism develops organically within a society, not that it can be imposed from outside or above. Both Germany and Japan had developed functioning liberal political systems in the 1920s. These succumbed to fascism and militarism in the 1930s, but the American task in the 1940s and 1950s was to restore, not to create, liberalism.

Ultimately, however, the problem with the Bush administration's grand strategy is not simply that we are further from the millennium than we would like to believe, or that our power to bring it about is less than we would hope. The problem is that the strategy the administration has embraced for achieving the millennium is fundamentally wrong.

Stripped to its essentials, what the Bush administration envisions is an informal global American empire. It is possible to share with the Bush administration a profound and deeply held belief that America's liberal Western democratic values and institutions are more conducive to human happiness and well-being than any alternative and yet still doubt the wisdom of this grand strategy.

It is, in other words, not the liberal faith that I suggest needs questioning, but the crusading imperative peculiar to particular liberal denominations, like those of Presidents Bush and Wilson. For these denominations, living life as an example to others, and even proselytizing, is not sufficient. The triumph of liberalism requires an act of power. In the Bush administration's conception, a liberal world order can be imposed from above or from outside.

The alternative view, of course, is that values and institutions need to develop organically within cultures. Attempts to impose these by imperial diktat are doomed not only to failure but to tragedy.

As I argue below, crusading efforts lead to failure and tragedy for four reasons. In the first place, they misunderstand the nature of liberalism and therefore misdiagnose what most threatens it. Second, efforts to impose liberalism from above or outside in themselves undermine or even destroy the international community that is the fruit of liberalism. A liberal hegemon that imposes its will on others through force of arms sacrifices its own legitimacy and undercuts the legitimacy of the liberal order it has sought to advance. Third, however noble the objective for which it is undertaken, an imperial mission threatens the liberal democracy of a republic that chooses to pursue this path. Fourth, the imperial pursuit of a liberal world order presumes a moral clarity that is in fact lacking.

Liberalism's Real War

Ultimately, the Bush administration's understanding of liberalism and of humanity's troubled love affair with it is profoundly flawed. This leads to an underestimation of the difficulties of living the liberal life and to a misunderstanding of what most threatens liberal societies.

The Bush administration refuses to acknowledge the possibility that individuals who are free to choose may not choose what we believe is best for them—or indeed what, by some sort of objective measure (if such a thing is conceivable), is in fact best for them. The phrasing used by the president in the National Security Strategy is revealing: we will use our strength, he says, to create "conditions in which all nations and all societies *can choose for themselves the rewards and challenges of political and economic liberty.*"[31] They are free to choose, but only to choose liberalism. There is, in fact, no choice here whatsoever. By denying the possibility that tastes (or even nutritional needs) may vary across societies, or seasons, or ages of life, crusading liberals blind themselves to the possibility that a menu that offers global diners a single choice is a dictation, not a liberation. Though the implicit comparison is not entirely fair (for liberalism is unlikely to yield the enormity of human suffering and degradation produced by so many totalitarian systems), this is a ballot from which all the inferior candidates have already been removed. For the Bush administration, there is no logical inconsistency between freedom and the requirement that the liberal option be selected, since it is inconceivable that anyone, given an opportunity to choose freely, would choose any other option.

In this view, the only obstacles to a liberal world—a world of maximal human liberty, of rule by law, of mutually beneficial cooperation between individuals and societies, and of peace—are those imposed by anachronistic political institutions, by exploitative, self-serving tyrants, and by a handful of deluded, violent individuals. Remove these—that is, remove the tyranny of kings (Wilson's achievement in his war to make the world safe for democracy), remove the tyranny of totalitarian states (the great accomplishment of World War II and the Cold War), remove the tyranny of kleptocratic or brutal dictators (the first of Bush's challenges today), and remove criminal and terroristic elements in political life (the second of Bush's challenges today)—and liberal values and institutions will inevitably triumph. Freed from the chains of tyrants and from the fear of terrorists, the triumph of the human (that is, liberal) will is assured.

This view does not entertain the possibility that the human heart is divided, that the human eye suffers from myopia, or that the human mind is capable of passion and irrationality. This view does not allow the possibility that, even while loving freedom, humans may be motivated by other desires as well—some as healthy as the desire for food and comfort and to guarantee as absolutely as possible the well-being of loved ones or kin, some as dark as a desire to dominate or to savor the pain of others. It does not acknowledge that humans sometimes sacrifice the long-run good for short-term gratification, that they sometimes fail to see that observing the Golden Rule in the short run is (usually?) beneficial in the end. It does not admit the possibility that humans can be moved by anger, vengeance, or pique, or that they are susceptible to demagoguery.

In other words, it fails to recognize that the threat to liberal values and liberal institutions lies within us as well as outside of us. It is not simply illiberal institutions and illiberal individuals that threaten freedom, peace, and cooperation. What endangers liberalism is also the weakness or incompleteness of our own liberal faith and, consequently, our own capacity to adopt illiberal institutions and behavioral patterns.

This failure to see the threat within may well be rooted in American liberalism's tendency toward a belief in both transcendent human rationality and progress. Liberal institutions are conceived of as an end state: once achieved they are assumed secure. Progress is a one-way street. Having reached liberalism, we are secure.

An alternative conception, one that understands liberalism as a particular world view that is then expressed as a way of life—that is, a conception of liberalism that acknowledges the daily struggle to live according to liberalism's rules and precepts, to repress the other desires of our hearts, to view our predicament in long-term perspective and eschew short-term solutions and gratification, to rein in our passions, and to judge wisely and avoid the lures of demagogues—is a more troubling one that threatens both our ego and our mental peace. But surely this alternative conception is a more realistic understanding of liberalism.

Of course, perhaps the president is right. Perhaps the superiority of liberalism (or, even more narrowly, American-style liberalism) is evident to all, except tyrants and terrorists whom we can kill or otherwise remove from the political stage. Perhaps we have indeed reached, or are about to reach, an end of history. This would mean that what is evident to the president, to me, and to most Americans is in fact evident to all people in all societies—that "these values of freedom are right and true for every person, in every society"[32]—and that we are all willing and able to adjust our behavior to comport with this understanding of what constitutes the good life.

Neither a critical reading of history nor an even cursory glance at recent newspapers offers much reason for optimism on this score, however. Liberalism may indeed be the best way to organize our lives, societies, and polities. There are, however, a lot of deluded individuals, societies, and political actors today—as there have always been in the past. One does not have to look to the Muslim world, to the failed states and kleptocracies spotting the map of sub-Saharan Africa, to Confucian societies, to the world's largest democracy, India, or to certain post-Communist states like Serbia to find doubts about liberalism. Even in societies where liberal values and institutions are deeply entrenched one finds challenges. In Western Europe there exist right-wing populist political parties that, while arguably still within the liberal tradition, embrace platforms whose strident nationalism (and in some cases racism, anti-Semitism, anti-Islamism, and xenophobia) balances their commitment to liberalism. The power of fascism and Communism may have been broken, but for the alienated, the lure remains.

Indeed, even in America there have always been voices arguing against liberal institutions and liberal values, voices suggesting either that these values are undesirable or that in some times and under some circumstances they need to be sacrificed or limited in order to achieve other equally important values. These voices have sometimes been influential. The United States lived with slavery for its first three generations. It denied women the right to vote until well into the twentieth century. It was home to the Ku Klux Klan. It restricted civil rights for a century after the Civil War. It long accepted racially or ethnically based immigration restrictions. It tolerated McCarthyism. Such a list is not meant as an indictment of America. It is meant only to remind us that even a polity based on Jefferson's stirring Declaration of Independence and incorporating the Bill of Rights in its fundamental constitution is capable of illiberal thought and action.

This warning of the danger that lies within our own selves and within our own society in no way denies that there is a threat to peace and freedom from foreign tyrants and terrorists. It does, however, underscore that tyrants and terrorists are not the *only* threat to liberalism.

While quantifying such things is impossible, one might even be tempted to argue that tyrants and terrorists represent by far the smaller threat. For a superpower (or, perhaps more accurately, a hyperpower as French critics put it) like the United States, surely there are reasons to suspect that external threats generated by the world's weak and dispossessed will pose less of a challenge than the internal ones posed by an unchecked growth of governmental power, by the breakdown of the family and other vital societal institutions, by alienation from the land and from production, or by racism, sexism, and xenophobia. Yes, some sort of protection against external threats is necessary—whether this is accomplished through preventive war, reactive war, passive defenses, deterrence, negotiation, or appeasement. But to focus solely on external dangers (and opportunities) is to run the risk of losing the real war. Given human nature, the struggle to build and maintain liberalism at home is a never-ending one.

The Costs of Liberal Imperialism

The problem with the grand strategy embraced by the Bush administration, however, is not simply that it focuses exclusively on only one (and probably the lesser) of the threats to liberalism. The problem is that even in terms of the threat it has identified, the strategy is self-defeating. The strategy is aimed at creating international peace and individual freedom. In fact, it jeopardizes both.

The effort to create a global, liberal empire is already bringing us into conflict with our friends around the world—with those who share the very values that we seek to advance and spread. This is hardly surprising. The growing fissure between the United States and its allies is, in fact, what most Realists would predict. As Realists observe, there is a tendency for power to balance power. Efforts to create an empire—any sort of empire—are expected to encourage an offsetting reaction. The harder a sovereign fights to expand its dominion and influence, the larger and stronger will be the coalition that forms against it. The pursuit of empire thus tends to be self-defeating.

Ironically, however, America's crusade to build a global *liberal* empire may be particularly self-defeating. Every appeal to power, every military success, every tyrant overthrown by outside overt or covert force, every terrorist killed, and every terrorist lair destroyed, is simultaneously a blow against the enemies of liberalism and a blow against the liberal norms that are being advanced or defended. It may have been necessary to bomb Afghanistan, funnel decisive aid to the rebels fighting the central government, intervene on a massive scale in the nation's political, economic, and social life, and rearrange the nation's domestic politics to ensure the Taliban is kept from power. It may, on balance, have been wise to target al-Qaeda leaders in the Yemeni desert for assassination (or, if one views them as military rather than political leaders and cavils at the term "assassination," for "elimination") in a high-tech hit delivered from an unmanned drone loitering overhead. It may have been the course of wisdom to invade Iraq and, at American gunpoint, install a new and hopefully different government. In each case, analysts can balance, and policymakers debate, the costs and benefits. Perhaps the benefits outweigh the costs. But it should be clear that the costs are real.

In the end, for the liberal order to be secure and stable, freedom and peace must rest on widespread acknowledgment of the rule of law rather than the rule of power. A liberal order depends on general acceptance that governance needs to rest on consent, not imposition. Every act of violence, every government or law imposed from outside or without consent from above, is a violation of the norms of liberalism, and each violation weakens the liberal edifice that is being constructed.

The harm is twofold. In the first place, it undercuts efforts to transform illiberal regimes and societies into liberal ones. To preach the right of nations to determine their own destinies and to rule themselves free from arbitrary authority, and at the same time to dictate these nations' choice of political constitution, government, and domestic policies is, at a minimum, to risk the charge of hypocrisy. There may be reasons why the possession of weapons of mass destruction by Iraq or North Korea is, in the end, unacceptable and why the United States and its liberal allies need to destroy these arsenals and, perhaps, to overthrow the regimes that chose to build them. But no one should be surprised if one of the lessons drawn from this is that, in the end, the strong do what they will and the weak submit as they must—hardly a lesson that provides a good foundation for the spread of liberal values and institutions.

In the second place, a politico-military crusade to construct a liberal empire is likely to undermine existing liberal international institutions. Liberal institutions are being asked to act in ways that are fundamentally at odds with their own character and values. Again, it may on balance be the course of wisdom to undertake a preventive war against Iraq. But surely it is unreasonable to expect NATO (or the larger community of liberal states) to embrace without dissent or extensive soul-searching an explicitly aggressive war against an opponent that has not undertaken any act of war and that is clearly inferior in power, with the goal of imposing a new government. These are the sorts of activities that liberalism opposes, not embraces, and that liberal institutions are designed to prevent, not facilitate.

It is thus hardly surprising that the Bush administration's crusade has been widely criticized across the liberal world; that states like Germany, which for their own historical reasons are particularly sensitive to concerns about behaving in an illiberal fashion, have been especially firm in opposition; and that liberal international institutions have bent only with reluctance to serve this crusade. Indeed, this reluctance to go a-crusading should be taken as a sign of the general health of liberal values and liberal institutions.

Unfortunately, this tension within the liberal world risks splitting it and weakening or destroying the institutions that have been so painstakingly developed over the last half century and longer. One cannot live or travel in Europe at the present time without being impressed not only by the breadth and depth of the disillusionment over American policy but by the rate at which the decay in Atlantic relations is accelerating. Where doubts about the Atlantic bond and where words of anti-Americanism were never heard, they are already commonplace. The American government's explicit willingness, expressed in both word and deed, to part company with liberal institutions, to ignore the international liberal consensus, and to act unilaterally serves to exacerbate this more fundamental problem. How long, given these trends, international liberal institutions will continue to function is unclear. One should not be overly pessimistic. Surely they will last for years, and perhaps for decades. Unlike the open-ended crusade against tyrants and terrorism, however, they do not have the potential to last forever. In the end, either the crusade or the institutions will probably have to be sacrificed.

The fraying and unraveling of the laboriously woven fabric of international institutions is only one of the prices the United States will have to pay for this crusade, though. The cost at home will be dearer still. Indeed, the real tragedy for America is likely to be that the pursuit of liberal imperium conflicts with its own *republican* values. A liberal democratic republic may pursue imperial dominance, but in gaining the whole world, it loses its own soul.

The United States has found its previous forays into imperialism deeply divisive. In the past it has, wisely, drawn back, leaving scars that with time healed. Past forays, however, were generally limited in scope—for example, in the Philippines after the Spanish American War. After World War I, America rejected Wilson's crusade. After World War II, the United States worked to rebuild liberal democracy where depression and war had overthrown it or cast it into doubt, but compromised and engaged with nonliberal forces across the wide reaches of the globe. But it is worth recalling that even the limited wars it did fight—in Korea and Vietnam—and the limited covert efforts it undertook were difficult for the republic to accommodate.

What the president now proposes is something of an altogether greater magnitude. Its consequences for the American polity are frightening to contemplate.

Gray Is a Color Too

Finally, as a moral matter, the neat distinctions between good and evil that the Bush administration draws so facilely are, in the real world, impossible to make. We cannot evade the need for careful moral judgment by declaring that tyrants and terrorism are, per se, bad: however true, this does not mean that all policies to rid the world of tyrants and terrorism are morally acceptable. Nor does it mean that an absence of democratic institutions or the threat of indiscriminate violence is in every case morally intolerable.

We can, for example, condemn, as the president did at West Point, the evil of killing or threatening to kill innocent civilians and still, as the United States did for forty or more years, base our security policy on a threat to kill hundreds of millions of innocent Russians, Chinese, and Eastern Europeans in retaliation for acts of aggression committed by their unaccountable, totalitarian governments. We can condemn Joseph Stalin as a brutal and ruthless dictator and still make common cause with him against Nazi Germany and decline to start World War III to free the Soviet Union from his grip.

Life, like foreign policy, is all about living with moral tensions and making troubling moral tradeoffs. It compels us, at times, to compromise with evil because the act of destroying that evil would itself require a covenant with evil, yielding in the end an even more evil outcome. In our opposition to terrorists and tyrants we must bear in mind not only the harm our actions might do to the innocent but the danger that in this struggle against evil we will become, in some small measure, precisely what we abhor.

This truth may be either emotionally nor rhetorically satisfying. It does not provoke the same chest-swelling reactions that President Bush's West Point speech triggers. But even in pursuit of a righteous cause such as human liberty, there is danger that the harm done will exceed the good produced.

If a crusade to rid the world of tyrants and terrorists is unlikely to result in the millennial moment the president seeks, if it overlooks the greater danger to freedom and peace that lurks within our own breasts, if it endangers the world's liberal institutions and the stability of our own liberal democratic republic, and if it leaves not moral clarity but continued moral ambiguity, what, then, is to be done? If one shares the president's enunciated goal of human freedom and international peace, is there an alternative path that is more likely to bring us to this destination?

Making his case for the new crusade, this president has suggested that "in the new world we have entered, the only path to peace and security is the path of action."[33] Seventy-nine years earlier, a notoriously more thoughtful, or at least more intellectual, American statesman reached a different conclusion about the pathway to peace. Advocating a policy of trying to develop true amity with other nations, and of encouraging the accretion of liberal institutions that would permit the resolution of disputes without a resort to force and before violent passions became inflamed, Secretary of State Charles Evans Hughes mused that "the pathway of peace is the longest and most beset with obstacles the human race has to tread; the goal may be distant, but we must press on."[34]

There is no millennium at hand. There is no quick fix or single, easy answer. Freedom and peace are possible, but they are not achieved once and for all time, and they are not achieved through a crusade. They are achieved through the daily, often frustrating, and sometimes unrewarding process of compromise, negotiation, and self-restraint. War and violations of freedom are not tumors that can be surgically removed. They are recurring inflammations, the consequence of weaknesses inherent in human nature, that can at times be prevented through forethought and that can at other times be treated. A wise policy aims to strengthen the global body politic to reduce its susceptibility—and our own susceptibility—to these inflammations. But the process of human and societal development is neither rapid nor linear, and it resists efforts to rush it or force it in particular directions. Such an understanding does not condone evil or engage in some sort of confused moral relativism that equates repression with freedom or violence with peace; nor does it deny that violence at times must be countered with violence. It does, however, recognize that amity and peaceful relations between peoples cannot in the end be imposed at gunpoint, and that freedom imposed by imperial diktat is not freedom at all.

11

A Most Interesting Empire

Anders Stephanson

The United States is today the world's largest transoceanic empire. In-numerable islands under the American flag dot the Pacific and the Caribbean, the biggest and most notable being Puerto Rico. This is a colonial empire in the most conventional sense: far-flung territories and populations are held under the control of the center in a state of formal inferiority.[1] Beyond the normal purview of U.S. politics, these old-style imperial possessions are rarely discussed or even acknowledged, set aside if not wholly forgotten. The centenary of "the Spanish-American War" in which many of them were acquired, occasioned only sporadic inter-est.[2] The recent internments, illegal by international law, at Guantá-namo Bay in Cuba served as a brief reminder, but chiefly in terms of legal peculiarities. The overwhelming reality of imperial power in the insular possessions, then, is mirrored inversely in the insularity of the imperial power itself.

In a range of other domains, however, there has been a strong resur-gence of interest in the idea of empire and in thinking about the United States *generally* as an empire. The immediate reason is not hard to detect: empire was and is a readily available way of conceiving the geopolitical situation after the implosion in 1991 of the Soviet Union, which left the United States, in a phrase endlessly repeated, as "the only superpower." Whether one chose to characterize empire as the immanent form of globalized capitalism or, more traditionally, as a form of U.S. domination (and indeed whether one found that domination congenial), the term was doubtless beginning to enjoy renewed currency from the 1990s onward. The U.S. thrust to global power in the wake of September 11 amplified massively these imperial reverberations. Still, it is well to recall that there was growing investigation of empire even before the 1990s. Some of it can be traced, academically, to the confluence of cultural studies and its emergent postcolonial cousin, though "empire" here was less the concept of the exercise than its site, so to speak. Relatedly, if less visibly, there was also growing concern with ancient and peripheral empires in certain subfields within the social sciences. Indeed, the Soviet collapse itself (when not taken simply as irrefutable evidence for the perversity of socialism) could be conceived in part as a problem of imperial disintegration.[3]

If the term fills certain needs, then it is far from clear what it actually explains. When it comes to the United States, its usage is often descriptive and metaphorical. There is a sense, for example, that somehow the aggregate discrepancies between the superpower and "the rest" must amount to something imperial. One is reminded of earlier tendencies in the historiography where the United States is almost but not quite an empire: a way of life perhaps, marked by a will to expansion, or, alternatively, protection and assistance at the eager invitation of potential recipient countries.[4] The more typical procedure, explicit or not, is to create a model of sorts, centered on domination or inequalities of power, and then to measure the extent to which any given relation, situation, or structure can be said to qualify. Lurking in the background is often some abstracted version of ancient Rome; but the historical reference is less important than the method of modelling itself, which allows for comparison of social formations and types of rule across time and space. The procedure can yield interesting results: the rich, comparative tradition of historical sociology is eloquent proof.[5] Yet the conceptual difficulties are undeniable. The Marxist tradition has wrestled mightily with them. Unlike, say, "capitalism," empire is a transhistorical category which can be applied, without much discrimination, in vastly different periods and places. Unlike, say, "mode of production," it is a transhistorical category that permits little room for qualitative historical change. Lenin, famously, tried to historicize and theorize the concept by turning it (as "imperialism") into a particular and final stage in the development of capitalism, a ripened, potentially stagnant and reactionary form dominated by monopoly. His rendition, composed in the midst of World War I to grasp the nature of that cataclysmic event and the antecedent frenzy of imperial expansion, turned out to be wrong in almost every respect. In canonized form, it was to exert a stifling effect on Marxist theory forever after.[6]

All description (or facticity) is of course in some sense theory-laden, but inscription in an implicit conceptual frame does not make "empire" into to a real concept. Still, the term can be used to advantage. First, description is not necessarily bad. "Empire" actually exists as it were. That the United States does indeed possess a colonial empire overseas, whose aquatic area equals that of the lower forty-eight states, may be a descriptive proposition; but it is also an interesting fact that demands exploration and explanation. Empire on that view signifies nothing but a legal and political form, and sometimes, with all the proper caveats, it is illuminating to describe a system as an empire. What is particularly interesting about the U.S. variety is the obvious anomaly: persisting, formal inferiority within a liberal framework, an official anti-colonialism that both recognizes and manages not to recognize the colonial fact. Second, since September 11, one might well raise the question, the eternally returning question, whether the United States was or is indeed sensibly described as an empire, above and beyond its undeniable colonial appendages. In what sense may the bid for supremacy amount to an imperial structure, either in terms of intent or results? Third, the historical uses of empire are always unavoidably ideological, symbolically significant acts that can sometimes tell us about something else. In the United States it has been used authoritatively and favorably as self-description in two periods, first intermittently in the late eighteenth century and nineteenth century before the Civil War, and then in the "imperial" moment around the turn of the century. With the conflagration of 1914 and the concomitant crisis of the Eurocentered ideology of civilization, empire became on the whole a term of opprobrium. After the Second World War, it appears either as radical critique of United States in the world or, in the rhetoric of officialdom, as a designation for Soviet domination. Only in the 1990s, then, can one detect signs of renascent, unabashed neoimperialism, the kind of ideology of beneficent domination by a single power or civilization that marked the conjuncture of a century ago. These shifts reveal something about how the United States has understood itself in the world. In that ideological context, there is a fourth approach, a more specific one centered on Otto Hintze's notion of a "world empire," an empire such as Rome, whose self-constitutive feature is that it can have no equal in the world, that it understands its compass as identical with the world that "really" counts, as opposed to the actual one.[7] The messianic character of the United States, an overdeterminant ideological form that is anything but nebulous, is conducive to such notions. At this nexus between messianism (what often passes under the rubric "American exceptionalism") and empire lies a crack of considerable analytical interest.

These are vast issues. In this essay, I will explore in what sense Alexander Hamilton might have been right to think the United States "an empire in many ways the most interesting in the world"; but I shall only explore at certain moments when empire and (for lack of a better term) the identity of the United States in the world were raised, either expressly by contemporaries or by the actual historical situation. I begin with a delineation of the formation of the peculiar republican empire in the late 1780s, though I use Thomas Jefferson rather than Hamilton as a representative figure because his break with existing political models is sharper and coincides better with what actually happened in the following century.[8] I then periodize the crucial shifts in the nature of the body politic during nineteenth and early twentieth century, against which backdrop I examine what some have seen as the imperial expansion of the Cold War. I end with a consideration of the recent epoch when the United States, for a moment, decided that it would assume a very conventional form of imperial rule for the benefit of everyone. Since the matter under inquiry is political form, I shall deal only briefly with the religious dimensions. Having discussed them at some length elsewhere, I am fully aware how preponderant they are; but here they must chiefly be taken as givens.[9]

When Jefferson approvingly referred to the United States as an empire, he did not have the models of Britain or Rome favorably in mind. After all, this was arguably the first postcolonial nation, the result of imperial rule dissolved. For Jefferson, in fact, the United States was to be the sort of empire that the British should have been or perhaps indeed was thought to have been before despotism and tyranny presumably destroyed the rights of Englishmen who happened to live across the Atlantic. Empires for him (as far as anything determinate can be said of this voluble but mercurial character) rule over an extended territory that is not a single sovereignty, something large, powerful, and of world-historical importance. The crucial and unprecedented aspect of the United States as an empire was that it was to be free and devoid of any dominant, imperial center. This was not only an "empire of liberty," as he called it, but also an "empire for liberty."[10] Less often noted, his second formulation indicated a space that was intrinsically free and singularly designated to serve the higher purpose of freedom itself. Jefferson's innovation, contrary to all orthodoxy, was to make imperial expansion take place in the name of self-determination—the very essence of liberty as it was understood. Hence there was no contradiction when he spoke of the natural suitability of the United States for "extensive empire & self-government."[11] The two aspects went hand in hand. In fact, the latter presupposed the former. Jefferson himself had played an instrumental role in rendering this concept possible through the Northwest Ordinance of 1787, which allowed the addition of new "states" into the original Union on an equal basis. The Ordinance defined the "territories" initially under federal governance as inherently destined to become states, the requirement being that each at a certain stage would reenact the kind of founding compact that was said to characterize the original membership in the federation. Each territory, filling up gradually through immigration from existing member states, would thus "prove" itself before gaining entry; but the concept of full and equal statehood was inscribed in the whole procedure from the beginning. Though the biological metaphor is not exactly right, one might call this "empire by cellular self-replication," a sort of serial process of constantly renewed sameness. Such a settlement which endlessly reproduces the original moment and principle of liberty in an agrarian setting is surely colonization in the strongest meaning of the word; but it is not a conventional empire (even if understood only as command and rule over something extensive).[12]

The moment when empire meets self-determination is a dialectical and quite radical break. It is worth noting that Jefferson, in typical anthropomorphic fashion, conceived of these new exemplars of "self-government" as analogues of eighteenth-century bourgeois subjects. To be a state and thus a member is to be a person in the sense of someone who is fully rational and autonomous. The concomitant idea of self-determination thus should not be taken lightly. To be a full subject-self, to be sovereign in a way, is precisely to be able to act without any external determinations. Yet at the same time any such new autonomous subject-self would naturally find it rational to join that which is already a compact of similarly free entities.[13]

This political union–republic, interestingly, is not at all a "nation" in the emergent European sense. For Herder, and later on Mazzini, the state presupposes a rooted people, a sequence of generations born in a particular territory, a homeland if you will, and a particular "culture," something grown over a long time, to go with it. From the liberal perspective of the nineteenth century it was then possible to imagine that a fully free and developed "nation" of this kind would naturally want to see the development of other such free nations and live in harmony with them, the world becoming a series of autonomous polities filled with specific "peoples," each with a unique character and a unique contribution to make to the glory of the world. This scenario, of course, failed to materialize. In the "Empire of and for Liberty," one is confronted with something quite different: a perpetually growing space for the demonstration of the higher historical purposes of humankind as such, all in the name of self-determination and autonomy. It is a timeless, physically indeterminate space of movement and colonization. A "homeland," however, it is not.

Spatially, then, this union is theoretically under perpetual construction both inside and outside its borders. As an expanding political form of no particular nationality, it has no intrinsic limit. The territorial growth of such a political entity would by definition extend the sphere of liberty. Moreover, expansion had the potential to cancel the historical cycle according to which, typically, rising republics eventually become corrupt and die. To maintain the original spirit of liberty, then, expanding the federation was, pari passu, a good thing and in accordance with the direction of rational history. There were admittedly actual limits to the United States as a federation: Jefferson happened to think Cuba the southern end because expansion beyond that island would require a big navy, something which in turn would undermine the republican nature of the original body politic. He was uncertain about other directions, but generally his vision was expansive. And if the existing union would face natural limits at some point, one could always imagine the creation of—essentially similar—unions adjacent to the original. Temporally, such spatial replication freezes time in a qualitative sense and removes the historical spectre of decline. For there can be no new and better stage in history beyond the perfect union-republic. The "idea" can only grow or self-destruct.

As embodied universality, in fact, such a "nation" could tolerate no qualitative deviations. Mixtures and "blots," as Jefferson put it, must not be allowed. Heterogeneity, qualitative heterogeneity, from rational freedom could have no legitimacy and had to be eliminated. The unfortunate Amerindians, certainly an anomalous presence, found out in no uncertain terms what this meant. Replication of the same was not an empty formula. For Jefferson, arguably, the more sinister danger always lurked within: dark forces that could lead the empire of liberty into corruption, regression and ultimately death.[14]

The structural answer to this historical problem of past, present, and future was thus dual: eternal vigilance against enemies within and constant expansion without. The initial formulation of the Monroe Doctrine might so be read as a statement about historical irreversability: the western hemisphere is declared to have entered a new stage and the United States takes it upon itself (in theory) to see to it that the decolonized states would not become colonies once again, or at least colonies of Europe. For the first time, a sphere of influence is thus invested with an explicit political principle.

In the course of the first half of the nineteenth century, the Union expanded transcontinentally in this manner. Even the war of conquest against Mexico in 1846 that cut that country in half was carried out in the name of the expansion of the principle of liberty, a justification that had been fused powerfully by then with the protestant vision of providential election in the form of physical "destiny." Thus the deterritorialized, timeless name of liberty was invested with physical meaning in actual geography. The dialectical result, however, was intensifying conflict. How could expansion of the free and self-determining also be the expansion of slavery? Could anyone be free if some were always unfree? Who possessed a self capable of being free? Was African descent actually compatible with having a self in the first place? How could one be free if slavery of those naturally condemned to it were not there to demonstrate the opposite of freedom? Was it not, moreover, the very mark of a free state to be able to withdraw from a compact freely entered? Regionalization of identity along these conflictual notions of liberty had to be adjudicated by means of the bloodiest war in the Western world during the century between 1815 and 1914. The victorious North, having thus fought on the symptomatic basis that one could not live half-slave and half-free, proceeded to impose its own concept of universal liberty, indeed to make the United States into a single body without blots.[15]

This newly integrated body politic, consequently, could no longer be imagined in quite the old Jeffersonian manner. Still the embodiment of universal purposes, it nevertheless came to be seen as somehow complete, at least for the foreseeable future, in the territorial sense. Available objects for acquisition had become racially and politically suspect. The exception, Canada, showed no signs of wanting to follow the rational course of entry into the Empire of and for Liberty. Yet the full-grown body was only full in its contours. Within, of course, it was filling up at astonishing speed through the twin processes of immigration and industrialization. But cellular replication of the self was over (only to be reinvented in modified and unexpected form in the early Union of Soviet Socialist Republics, but that is another story).

From now on, any additions would have to be conceived otherwise. The "humanitarian" effort to liberate Cuba by means of war with Spain in 1898 could thus not initially be grasped in terms of any inclusion of the island in the Union, as Jefferson and others had envisaged a century earlier. Liberating Cuba in fact turned out to mean a U.S. protectorate over the Cubans, while the other acquisitions in the Treaty of Paris, from the Philippines to Puerto Rico, were classed as imperial possessions pure and simple. And so, in many instances, they remain. Guam, as the courts decided in 1985, is "an instrumentality" of the United States Congress, an instrumentality, one might add, extensively resurfaced with tarmac for the purpose of projecting massive air power.[16] Even Castro's Cuba has had to accept de facto the continued colonial presence of a U.S. military base.

The Empire for Liberty thus became an empire of a conventional kind. This was duly recognized at the time and hotly debated, if only momentarily. The name, it should be underlined, was primarily invoked by anti-imperialists, indicative of a certain discomfort with the idea across the political divide. Was the very idea of the United States as embodied liberty in fact compatible with empire, especially in an epoch when imperialism, a movement and system, was so directly associated with the dominant European state order? A comforting answer along liberal and Christian lines was indeed available in the language of responsibility and obligation, parents and children. It was easy, then, to classify the newly acquired "subjects" as immature, childlike entities in need of proper uplifting and tutelage. The master signifier under which this project was carried out was of course "civilization"; but just as in Jefferson's days, the perennial and decisive question was who might count as a "full" and "sovereign" person, the foundation of any given "sovereign" liberal nation. At some future and unspecified date, then, these wards would become capable of governing themselves. The catch was law and order, the establishment of which might initially require large-scale exertion of military violence, or, to use another term, pacification. An obvious model for the whole concept and process was available near to hand in the treatment of the Amerindian population at home.

It was partly here too that the solution was found to a second, more specific problem, for which the Consitution offered no answer. Could the Union, whose reunited body had demonstrated its restored health and vigour in the war, add territory that was not meant to become a state, a real part of it? Not for the first time in American history, it was left to the courts to decide a politically difficult issue. Justice White, in the Insular Cases of 1901, came to invent accordingly the important distinction between "incorporated" and "unincorporated" territories, the latter to be designated for such purposes as Congress might find fit to determine, a view essentially confirmed, then, in the decisions of 1985. The former edict verified, in effect, that the body might now grow again but in a new fashion. Two separate but not necessarily incompatible concepts were at work. One the one hand, there was the ancient idea (first codified by Aristotle and given juridical form by the Romans) of instrumentality: tools of the sovereign self, be they things, human beings, or animals, to be used for whatever purposeful activity the master so might choose. On the other hand, there was the curious idea of a body with appendages which are part of the body at the same time as they are not. The conceptual precedent, again, lay in the gradual subjugation of the Amerindians: a population that was both inside and outside the United States, subjects but not members of it. Even the pure externality of the instrumentalist perspective was ultimately compatible with the dominant liberal language of benevolence and uplifting of the retrograde or less fortunate. The central point, however, is that the United States now had a clear framework for keeping territory in subjugation in perpetuity and, accordingly, that people in these territories were not destined to become members of the Union of freedom or indeed necessarily ever free at all.[17]

Contrary to erstwhile hopes and predictions, the chief importance of these appendages turned out to be military rather than commercial, Panama perhaps offering the partial exception. The moment of classical imperialism itself passed relatively quickly. After establishing the Caribbean basin as a de facto protectorate and an area of naval domination with rights of intervention, the United States assumed a more traditional posture of benevolent peace and rationality vis-à-vis the outside, often coupled with control, formal or informal, of the financial infrastructure, a "normality" punctured by sundry military interventions of the disciplining kind. There was no more direct territorial acquisition, the unprofitability of which had become obvious. After 1914 and the implosion of the entire world of "civilization," it was in any case impossible to speak fervently in favor of "empire." From now on, the term passes into the realm of the negative, though the liberal idea of tutelage would survive vigorously in the euphemistic form of "mandates" from the Versailles treaties to the UN system after 1945.

"Empire," then, went through two distinct phases as a political category and project. The initial "Empire for Liberty" was seen as a space of no determinate, stable boundaries, as a perpetual, open-ended colonizing process of republican reenactment in adjacent domains. This came to a crushing halt in the Civil War, which generated in a kind of internal republican reenactment on the basis of a northern concept of liberty. The United States became a homeland, albeit a peculiar one. Eventually this consolidated body entered a second phase, which one might call the Empire of Civilization. The new colonial outside was grasped either as lastingly inferior (on racial grounds) or as subject (in the very distant future) to uplifting. The European Other, meanwhile, was deemed to be mired in various sclerotic states of declining civilization. This view was confirmed when Europe collapsed in conflagration, only to be saved to no little degree by the rising center of Western civilization across the Atlantic. In the first phase, "empire" signifies rule over extended territory with connotations of glory and world-historical significance, while in the second it becomes a sign of civilization and the obligation to engage in progressive control and direction of the uncivilized, a task that also entailed infusing them with the inherent virtues of commerce. This conceptual shift does not, however, take place on a continuous line: "empire" forms no coherent semantic or political field that can evolve over the entire historical period. In the antebellum period, the term is a convenient shorthand at times for the extraordinary process of border expansion. Its descriptive value then lies largely in its counterintuitive or even ironic qualities. The United States as empire is thus distinct because it is not imperial rule. This empire is homogeneous. In fact, it has no other object than the growth of the very principle of independence, the natural and proper system for the diverse desires of those capable of being free. What is outside the empire is either to be rendered identical with, and then included in, the homogeneity, or else only contingently and occasionally meaningful. In the second phase, by contrast, "empire" is reintroduced in ways that are conventional within Western standards at the turn of the century, i.e., as *mission civilisatrice*. The object of the operation is now centered on subjugation and subjects. This is a bit troublesome, but not for too long.

Empire itself soon faded from the political horizon, the constitutent issue of identity less so. Whereas the United States was of course absolutely different from the rest of the world in the first phase, the civilization moment made it an integral part, although putatively the most advanced and enlightened, of the "civilized world." As always, the notion of sameness and integration fit awkwardly within the political culture of the United States. It was only possible around 1900 because the development was quite distant and unimportant for the country as a whole. This was also why the potential contradictions and anomalies of the imperial edifice could be contained. None of it mattered very much. Though, to reiterate, "the civilizational empire" is still with us and an overpowering fact for those on the receiving end, Samuel Flagg

Bemis was right in saying that its historical moment proper was brief and its ideological character suspect. It is another matter that the idealist vision of the United States he used as a measure of normality was a remarkably rosy one, if not a total fantasy. Up-lifting and tutelage in any case has now gone on for more than a century, a fact that seems to trouble hardly anyone at all in the United States. With the partial exception of Puerto Rico, none of these insular possessions has had any "organic" impact on the body politic. Cuba, interestingly, began to have such an effect only at the moment when it broke militantly with the mould. Latterly, it has become absurdly important every four years because of the pivotal electoral votes of the state of Florida. Otherwise the lack of imperial concern is an expression of a rule so obvious that it is often ignored, insofar as it is even visible: the United States means more for and to the outside than the outside means for and to the United States.

Civilizational empire was succeeded by Woodrow Wilson's collective security, a project that could be (and indeed was) accused of un-American qualities on account of its "multilateralism"; but it actually preserved American exceptionalism in that the United States was conceived as a unique, mosaic lawgiver to the world. A failure but a grand one, Wilson's gambit also featured a vision of republican reenactment but now in the universal name of popular sovereignty understood as homeland. Collectively, these were to be assembled in a global compact of theoretical equality (though the firm leadership of the elect, in particular the United States and its political embodiment, Wilson himself, was presupposed throughout). Elevating self-determination to a universal principle, however, was entirely compatible with a revised version of *mission civilisitrice:* "mandates" for the benevolent development of colonial areas. "Empire," in any case, had become a bad word and the United States throughout made every attempt to call its relatively limited moves something else.[18]

World War II posed the Wilsonian question anew; but there was in fact nothing much Wilsonian about Rooseveltian grand strategy and nothing much Wilsonian about the Cold War aftermath either. FDR himself was convinced that the historical time of European empires had passed, though as a good and orderly Progressive he was also as enamored with the idea of policing the unruly as he was with the idea of maintaining mandates. He can indeed be described as a second Bemisian aberration, for in his thinking, profoundly Progressive as it was, he presupposed no basic separation between the United States and the rest of the world, only a connecting line.[19]

The nature of the Cold War is pertinent here to the extent that it served to recast and partly displace the issue of empire. A handy way of tracing this event is to begin with the incisive and always useful James Burnham, an intellectual of considerable political influence in the 1940s. Though "empire" had become politically incorrect as self-description, Burnham used it unabashedly in 1947 in calling for a global American presence in the fight against Communism. He wanted the United States, as he put it, to become "world-dominating," by which he meant that it should be able everywhere to decide "the crucial issues upon which political survival depends." Keenly aware, however, that empire was now a suspect term, Burnham proposed to call his strategy something more pleasant-sounding, namely, "the policy of democratic world order." This approach, in all its essentials, was arguably the one adopted. In 1950, the foundational Cold War analysis of the Truman administration, NSC 68, took a position that was quite close to Burnham's, but without of course any reference to a U.S. empire.[20]

The imperial referent tended to be reserved instead for the Soviet side and, in a very minor key, the older European empires in various degrees of decline. If the official line was not quite "anti-imperialism" (a term tainted by its featured place in Moscow's political lexicon), it was nonetheless against empire. To be against empire, then, meant chiefly to be against the Soviet Union. Though the language was that of liberty and freedom, it did not follow that one was against friendly empires (much less that one cared to remember one's own). Because they could be placed within the comforting historical narrative of gradual emancipation, empires of Cold War allies were not only acceptable but in some cases actually to be supported with heaps of aid. This was not an embarrassing contradiction. It followed from the Cold War matrix: everything that was not totalitarianism was freedom or potential freedom (freedom-in-the-making). In consonance with the ideology of pacification and policing during the imperial period proper, it was easy to see that a stage of "authoritarianism" might well be necessary if the long-term interest of freedom were to be served in the zone of instability, which was indeed a very large zone of "the free world."[21]

What was most analytically problematic for the contemporaries in 1947 was in fact not the Soviet empire but the rather more amorphous world of freedom, potential or real, and how one was to related to it. Two quite diverging concepts crystallized as to what this really entailed and the kind of world such leadership should or could create. By 1950 one of the two had emerged entirely victorious. As these positions, in their baldest articulation, have a certain contemporary relevance, they deserve a word.

The first and losing perspective was represented by Burnham's central target within the Truman administration, the still powerful Kennan (but, let it be said, few others). Its essentials can be stated briefly. Kennan accentuated "particularity." The United States, on this view, was only one nation-state among many others, though for historically specific and unexpected reasons it happened to be in a position where it was called upon to lead. To do so successfully, however, was to recognize the limited significance of the United States as an example for the world and the limited applicability of its particular norms for others. Imagining oneself as the embodiment of universal right was an error likely to cause serious policy mistakes, none more egregious than assuming the Wilsonian role of lawgiving (and, later on, the policy of militarization). The realistic object of policy, on the contrary, should be to build up the few traditional power centers in the world that could serve the equally traditional purpose of counterbalancing the Soviet Union. This, in turn, would initially necessitate a strong effort to make certain that these balancing centers would not in fact be open to Soviet penetration. Close allies such as Britain, meanwhile, were not newfound client states but equals fallen temporarily on hard times. "Empire" in Kennan's scheme was not a problem: it was a historical fact and as such beyond good and evil. Colonial powers civilizationally close to the United States should be supported against destabilizing nationalist opposition, though Kennan, as a meticulous reader of Gibbon, was also aware of the long-term difficulties in holding faraway provinces in subjugation. Some imperial cases were at any rate hopeless and better abandoned.[22]

The other view—let us call it "universalist"—was most forcefully expressed in NSC 68. Following Burnham, the analysis criticized (in muted form) containment for its allegedly passive qualities and, as mentioned, advocated a massively expanded U.S. role in the world. Unlike the panoramic "review" of the world Kennan had offered in PPS 23 of 1948, NSC 68 was almost exclusively concerned with the United States and its monumental struggle against the Soviet Union. Other "free" nations are mentioned in passing, mainly as supporting cast. They have no independent function. Moreover, the document places the struggle (to the point of obsession) within the global polarity of "slavery" and "freedom."[23] To secure the space of freedom against the formidable world-conquering empire in the East then requires a commensurate exertion of effort, a sort of continuation of the successful mobilization of World War II against similar kinds of world conquerors: a total gathering of forces to fight the totalitarians. This, then, is a struggle to death, a world war which happens for purely contingent reasons to take a cold form. To "lead" the embattled sphere of freedom in such circumstances is a call for command—imperium in the strictest sense of the word. Closer inspection thus reveals a second, internal distinction between the land of the free itself and the rest of "the free world." The latter is conceived not at all as a domain of autonomous, self-determining subjects but as clients in need of assistance (as indeed many of them successfully liked to portray themselves); or, alternatively, as troops to be called up, forces to be marshalled. This was entirely logical. If one declares (i) "freedom" to be the natural state of humankind, (ii) the perverse empire of slavery as the fundamental subversion of that state, and (iii) the United States as the (messianic) protector of the survival of true humankind as well as its the true embodiment, it follows that there can be no equals to that power even in the world of putative freedom. Amidst the larger dichotomous divide and the drawing of battle lines, it was impossible to accept as legitimate any desire on the part of "free" auxiliaries to choose anything but subservience. Choosing wrong was to turn away from right, as defined by a supreme power invested with the authority to correct waywardness. Having no equals, then, meant full assumption of the obligation to lead, protect and conquer, the right to command.

The vision of a final struggle between freedom and slavery was a good domestic strategy for the permanent mobilization of the United States abroad, but it had shortcomings as global prescription since, elsewhere, the Cold War was not always similarly conceived and the sundry interests of the free world could not be controlled according to the principle of command. There was accordingly an inherent discrepancy between the theoretical claim to command in a global war, the supreme right to decide, and the actual conflicts, indeed the actual structure of the world. In one respect certainly the thrust outwards resulted in something rather like Burnham's ideal. For the creation of military alliances and base installations across the globe put the United States in the position of potential commander over immense areas. As conquering the citadels of evil proved impossible, what followed was in fact a version of nine-teenth-century imperial pacification and policing, where, typically, no war was ever declared but put forth as corrections of a disorderly, dis-eased, and abnormal state. Yet even if there were in fact regions of utter domination (e.g., Latin America), the totality was not an integrated im-perial system proper but a complex, overlapping series of power net-works with no single governing center or logic. Economic circuits followed quite different rules, ideology yet others. Thus international capitalism was reconstructed under U.S. auspices but remained only partly under its adjudication. Immensely powerful economically and militarily, the United States could in fact afford to take a relatively gen-erous view of the economic aspect as long as the military system re-mained intact. Witness the lenient and open attitude toward Japanese capital in the 1950s. Meanwhile, a diffused sort of ideological power, chiefly in the form of commodified mass culture, proved hugely suc-cessful, even withstanding the moment of profound U.S. delegitimation when the great effort to combat the Empire of Slavery bogged down on the uncongenial terrain of Vietnam and the truth of the thrust was re-vealed as its opposite. The enormous disparity between the United States and everybody else in the 1950s, then, was thus the condition of possibility for the differentiated system which combined, to put it sim-ply, a militarist structure of domination with a managed, liberalizing international economy and a diffused ideological culture of mass con-sumption.[24]

These complexities and the absence of any formal empire generate, as indicated earlier, the urge to rewrite empire as metaphor. The alter-native "hegemony" is thus sometimes preferred because it allows for differentiated power and also for consent on the part of auxiliaries and subjects. It is a more "accurate" description of how the structure looked. Consent tends, however, to eclipse the coercive component to the point of total obscurity. In less able hands, hegemony thus becomes a mere euphemism for Cicero's old idea that the imperium was really a patricinium, a form of benevolence or guardianship for the benefit of everyone involved, an idea which James Harrington in seventeenth-century England would resurrect in an expansionist republican frame. Often, then, hegemony turns out merely to mean anointed leadership without the connotations of dominance encapsulated in the original Greek concept.[25] And ultimately the universal claims of the United States in the struggle to death featured the right to decide on pain of immense violence.

Reiterating and revising Burnham's suggestive proposition, one might say that the United States was at very least claiming the negative right to decide how the crucial issues could *not* be decided. This, in turn, was but a permutation of the nineteenth-century invention represented by the Monroe Doctrine, as it developed from 1823 down to the Roosevelt Corollary of 1904: declaring an irreversible, territorialized political principle as well as the basic right to eradicate any threats to it. Leading the free world, then, was doubtless an imperial gesture, a declaration of sovereignty over sovereigns. It was not itself, however, an expression of any logic of empire. In other words, one cannot derive the will to supremacy from any imperial function. The effect was imperial but the sources of U.S. conduct lie elsewhere.

And so Jefferson's Empire for Liberty, contrary to his every wish, ended up a belligerent power with massive military forces and corrupting interests everywhere. Of the eventual setbacks and gradual loss of clarity here, I will say little. Even in the West, at one point, "imperialism" gained credence as a designation for the foreign policy of the United States. The end of the Cold War proper in 1963—the end, that is, of the struggle to death after it had very nearly produced that death in global conflagration—combined with the continung disaster in Vietnam, was also the end of the imperial gesture as a universal claim to sovereignty.

Henceforth, the United States would make its moves on the grounds of more conventional interests, namely, the particular interests of a Great Power. The destruction of Salvador Allende in 1973 and the interventions in southern Africa may stand as examples. Once again, however, particularism proved an unstable foundation, its limitations exposed with the greatest clarity by the succeeding popularity of Ronald Reagan's pastiche of a crusade in the early 1980s.

Reagan's reinvention of the Cold War, replete with massive transgressions in the name of final battles, was of course predicated on the persistence of something that could be construed as an Evil Empire. The subsequent implosion of the Soviet counterpoint in 1989–91 thus served radically to confuse things. The absence of ideological polarity robbed the situation of any clear strategic meaning. Confusion, however, now mattered little. That neither of the two approaches the United States adopted toward the world in the 1990s had any extensive grounding in the political culture was of no great consequence. There was first George Bush the Elder's ill-fated "New World Order," a very short moment of limited geopolitical realism in the name of international multilateralism and legality. It was followed by Bill Clinton's "more and better globalization." Centered on the U.S. economy, Clinton's policy was coherent and, for a while, hugely successful. When perpetual capitalist expansion ceased to be perpetual, the policy had run its course. Behind it, politically, was nothing. What followed instead after the spectacular terror of September 11 was a new line with very deep roots indeed.

What ensued was in fact a full-fledged version of the always-latent notion of the United States as a world empire; and the moment has now come, in conclusion, to return to this suggestive notion of Otto Hintze's, not as self-description but as a way of thinking about the sources of the United States' conduct. The material underpinnings for the thrust to global supremacy were of course already present in the

1990s: massive military superiority, economic and political hegemony on a global scale. No matter how "indispensable" the United States was officially supposed to be, there seemed to the unreconstructed activists to be something humdrum and petty-minded about ever-increasing doses of free trade. The alternative, a vigorous and invigorating form of imperial rule for the benefit of universal (American) values, centering initially on the Middle East and the surrounding regions but with the rather more ambitious aim ultimately to effect regime change in the People's Republic of China, the one potential future threat, was of course facilitated enormously by the monumental event of September 11; but it is important to recollect that this vision was already well worked out by neoconservatives during the sordid, disappointingly successful days of Bill Clinton. It was a potent combination of secular and religious (or more precisely, Protestant, as some of the most vocal opposition to it originated in some Catholic circles) messianism: the notion that the United States has a historically or theologically grounded right and duty to remake or save the world according to its own universally valid, timeless principles. Just like Rome or for that matter the regime of the Celestial Mandate in imperial China, the United States can never have an equal in the world. Even regimes that are linguistically, culturally, and politically similar can never be conceived as identical. The outside, in short, exists de facto but cannot be recognized as qualitatively equivalent. The difference here between Rome and China on the one hand and the United States on the other is that nonrecognition for the former means that the outside, however much of a nuisance in reality, is essentially meaningless, a conceptual nullity; whereas for the latter, it is something that is by definition always problematic in the sense that it must either be actively rejected or actively reworked.

The vast ambition, in any event, of the geostrategic rulers around George Bush the Younger to achieve global domination, the unapologetic revision of the Burnham model of empire from a negative right to disallow disagreeable decisions by minions wherever one might see fit to a positive right to change regimes in the biblical "likeness" of the United States—this ambition is already running afoul of its its own systemic preconditions. For not only is the moment of such integrated empires long gone, so is the very possibility of projecting an integrated form of universal power in the name of any particular power. The differentiated and highly vulnerable structure of twenty-first-century capitalism permits no such thing, as the United States is now discovering. Violent disruption on an unimaginable scale by small, mercurial forces is now an always-present threat. Meanwhile, the circuits of inexorably expanding capital require only the predictability of law and order, not the kind of violent disorder and illegalities brought about by the will to empire.

Notes

2. *Imperial Language* by Marilyn B. Young

1. Rebekah Scott, "Cheney in Region for a Day of Small-game hunting," *Pittsburgh Post-Gazette,* December 9, 2003.
2. According to the American Heritage Dictionary of the English Language, " 'gook' is a disparaging term for a person of East Asian birth or descent," whose origin is probably an alteration of "goo-goo," the disparaging term for a "native inhabitant of the Philippines."
3. Peter Maass, "Professor Nagl's War," *New York Times Magazine,* January 11, 2004, 30.
4. Dexter Filkins, "Tough New Tactics by US Tighten Grip on Iraq Towns," *New York Times,* December 7, 2003, A1.
5. Ibid.
6. Anthony Shadid, "U.S. Hunt for Baath Members Humiliates, Angers Villagers," *Washington Post,* June 15, 2003, A14.
7. Maass, 38.
8. Ibid.
9. Quoted in Marilyn B. Young, *The Vietnam Wars, 1945–1990* (New York: Harper-Collins, 1991), 344–45, n. 13.
10. Maass, 30.
11. There are three civilians under contract with the Defense Department among the 1,300 soldiers Reilly commands, but all are engaged in intelligence operations and do not serve as interpreters. Raymond Bonner, "For G.I.s in Isolated Town, Unknown Enemy is Elusive," *New York Times,* October 31, 2003, A12.
12. Ibid.

13. Maass, 24.

14. Ibid.

15. Edward Wong, "G.I.'s Fire on Family in Car, Killing 2, Witnesses Say," *New York Times,* January 13, 2004, A14.

16. On January 20, 2004, in southern Afghanistan, a helicopter attacked a house in a village, killing eleven people, four of them children. ("11 Civilians Reported Killed in a U.S. Raid in Afghanistan, *New York Times,* January 20, 2004, A8.) Six children were killed when a wall fell during an assault on a complex in eastern Paktia; the next day, nine children were found dead after an attack on a mountain village in Ghazni.

17. Dexter Filkins, " 'Liberty or Death' Is a Grim Option for the Local Councils in Iraq's Young Democracy," *New York Times,* February 15, 2004, 16. Asked about local insurgents, a member of the Falluja Town Council was stopped from responding by one of his colleagues: "Shut up, I know what I am going to tell him." Then, not realizing the reporter had understood his intervention, he went on to claim that only foreigners were responsible for the attacks, not Iraqis.

18. There is a growing literature on the subject, which by and large ignores earlier discussions of counterinsurgency during and after the Vietnam War. In 1962, President John F. Kennedy explained that the world faced "another type of war, new in its intensity, ancient in its origins—war by guerrillas, subversives, insurgents, assassins; war by ambush instead of combat; by infiltration instead of aggression, seeking victory by eroding and exhausting the enemy instead of engaging him. . . ." In addition to the army's special-forces group (the "Green Berets"), the Kennedy administration established the Special Group Counterinsurgency. One version of why the United States lost the Vietnam War insists that the switch from counterinsurgency to "big unit" warfare was responsible.

19. Maass, 30.

20. Joel Brinkley, "General Sees More Attacks as Elections Near," *New York Times,* December 8, 2003, A14.

21. Young, 271.

22. Walden Bello, "The Economics of Empire," *New Labor Forum,* Fall 2003, http://www.qc.edu/newlaborform (accessed January 4, 2004).

23. Max Boot, *The Savage Wars of Peace: Small Wars and the Rise of American Power* (New York: Basic Books, 2002), xx.

24. Kaplan, 3. He claims this to be the definiting quality of an imperial military and cites Bryon Farwell's *Mr. Kipling's Army* as evidence.

25. Ibid., 6.

26. Ibid., 7.

27. Michael Mann, *Incoherent Empire* (London: Verso, 2003), 27.

28. Kaplan, 8. Colonialism, he says, is cosmopolitanism.

29. David Brooks, "A Burden Too Heavy to Put Down," *New York Times,* November 4, 2003, A25. The soldiers at Abu Ghraib prison—and their superiors—seem to have mustered the necessary courage.

30. Jim Lobe, "Bush Lies Uncovered," *Alternet Mobile Edition,* February 23, 2004, http://www.alternet.org/mobile/index.html (accessed February 26, 2004).

31. Chalmers Johnson summarizes the argument of his book in "America's Empire of Bases," TomDispatch.com, January 15, 2004, http://www.nationinstitute.org/tomdispatch (accessed January 17, 2004).

32. Kaplan, 12.

33. Ibid., 17.

34. Ibid., 23–24.

35. Ibid., 18.

36. Robert Kagan, "Power and Weakness," *Policy Review,* no. 113 (June/July 2002). There is a sense in which Kagan is right. The United States and Europe do live in different worlds. These are defined not, as Kagan would have it, by European military weakness and American military strength but rather by a sharp difference in values and in the way people live. As Tony Judt pointed out in a recent essay, rates of poverty are consistently and considerably higher in the U.S. than in Europe, as are infant mortality rates and income disparities. European economies are more productive, the economic security and health of its population greater by far. There is little to attract Europeans to the American model which, Judt concludes, "is unique and not for export." See Judt, "Its Own Worst Enemy," *New York Review of Books,* August 15, 2002.

37. Robert Kagan, "A Tougher War for the U.S. Is One of Legitimacy," *New York Times,* January 24, 2004, www.nytimes.com (accessed January 25, 2004). Later in the essay Kagan worries that Europeans do not share America's sense of the global threat of terrorism and weapons of mass destruction; nor will they "accord the United States legitimacy when it seeks to address those threats by itself. . . ." What, then, is to be done? The dilemma is tragic: "To address today's global threats, Americans will need the legitimacy that Europe can provide. But Europeans may well fail to provide it." The only hope, for Kagan, is that in due course Europe will come to its senses.

38. J.M. Coetzee, *Waiting for the Barbarians* (New York: Penguin Books, 1980), 133.

3. *The Drums of War* by John Prados

1. Eric Schmitt and James Dao, "Iraq is Focal Point as Bush Meets with Joint Chiefs," *New York Times,* January 11, 2001, A18.

2. Jane Perlez, "Capitol Hawks Seek Tougher Line on Iraq," *New York Times,* March 7, 2001, A8.

3. Jim Hoagland, "Policy Wars Over Iraq," *Washington Post,* April 8, 2001, B7.

4. Bob Woodward, *Bush at War* (New York: Simon & Schuster, 2002). Note that Woodward was given access to materials that were specifically denied to congressional committees investigating the antecedents of September 11.

5. Ibid., 48–49.

6. Ibid., 78–101, esp. pp. 91, 99.

7. Peter Beaumont, Ed Vulliamy, and Paul Beaver, "Bush Orders Backing for Rebels to Topple Saddam," *The Observer,* December 1, 2001.

8. Nicolas Lemann, "How It Came to War," *The New Yorker,* March 31, 2003, quoted, p. 37.

9. Judiciary Watch, Press Release, August 17, 2002.

10. Julian Borger and Ewen MacAskill, "U.S. Targets Saddam," *The Guardian,* February 14, 2002.

11. Ibid.

12. Woodward, *Bush at War,* quoted, 321.

13. Borger and MacAskill, "U.S. Targets Saddam."

14. Suzanne Daley, "French Minister Calls U.S. Policy Simplistic," *New York Times,* February 7, 2002, A14.

15. Dana Milbank, "Taking Iraq Policy for a Circular Spin," *Washington Post,* December 3, 2002, A23.

16. Somini Sengupta, "Security Council Tries to Ease Tensions Between the United States and Iraq," *New York Times,* May 23, 2002, A14.

17. Woodward, *Bush at War,* 106.

18. Mike Allen, "Bush Resumes Case Against Iraq," *Washington Post,* April 18, 2002, quoted, A13.

19. The following account of the military planning for Iraq is assembled primarily from press articles that reflected leaks regarding the matter. The most important among the stories are listed below. See Eric Schmitt, "US Plan for Iraq Said to Include Attack on 3 Sides," *New York Times,* July 5, 2002 (Secretary Rumsfeld ordered an investigation into the leak which led to this story); Patrick E. Tyler, "The Warpath: Pressures Build on

Iraq," *New York Times,* July 5, 2002; Schmitt, "US Considers Wary Jordan as Base for an Attack on Iraq," *New York Times,* July 10, 2002; Vernon Loeb and Karl Vick, "US Official Confident of Turkey's Support," *Washington Post,* December 5, 2002; Thomas E. Ricks, "Timing, Tactics on Iraq War Disputed," *Washington Post,* August 1, 2002; Schmitt and James Dao, "Airpower Alone Can't Defeat Iraq," *New York Times,* July 31, 2002; Thom Shanker, "Bush Hears Options Including Baghdad Strike," *New York Times,* August 7, 2002; and Woodward, "A Struggle for the President's Heart and Mind," *Washington Post,* November 17, 2002.

20. Greg Miller and John Hendren, "Hussein Said to Plan for Urban Battle vs US," *Los Angeles Times,* August 8, 2002, quoted, A18.

21. Bush claims regarding the Iraqi threat are dissected in detail by the author in *Hoodwinked: How George Bush Sold Americans a War with Iraq* (New York: New Press, 2004).

22. Robert S. McNamara with Brian VanDeMark, *In Retrospect: The Tragedy and Lessons of Vietnam* (New York: Times Books, 1995), 37.

23. *The Senator Mike Gravel Edition: The Pentagon Papers: The Defense Department History of United States Decisionmaking on Vietnam* (hereafter cited as "Pentagon Papers"), (Boston: The Beacon Press, 1971), 2: 23–120.

24. Leslie H. Gelb and Richard K. Betts, *The Irony of Vietnam: The System Worked* (Washington, DC: The Brookings Institution, 1979). Gelb and Betts describe presidents as choosing "Option B" in between the politically or militarily undesirable "A" and "C" options.

25. David Halberstam, *The Best and the Brightest* (New York: Random House, 1972).

26. Memorandum, McGeorge Bundy–Lyndon B. Johnson, June 30, 1965 (declassified July 17, 1980). Lyndon B. Johnson Library: LBJ Papers, National Security File: Memos to the President, box 4.

27. I made this point originally in *Keepers of the Keys: A History of the National Security Council from Truman to Bush* (New York: William Morrow, 1991), 228.

28. McNamara and VanDeMark, *In Retrospect,* 332.

29. Ibid., 321–23.

4. *American Hegemony and European Autonomy, 1989–2003: One Framework for Understanding the War in Iraq* by Thomas McCormick

1. Immanuel Wallerstein, "U.S. Weakness and the Struggle for Hegemony," *Monthly Review,* July–August 2003, http://www.monthlyreview.org/0703wallerstein.htm. Also see Wallerstein, *The Decline of American Power* (New York: New Press, 2003).

2. The analysis in this paper grows from a revision-in-progress for a new edition of my *America's Half-Century: U.S. Foreign Policy in the Cold War and After* (Baltimore: Johns Hopkins University Press, 1995); and from my essay, "American Hegemony and the Rhythms of Modern History, 1914–2000," in *Looking Back at the 20th Century: The Role of Hegemonic State and the Transformation of the Modern World System,* ed. Shigeru Akita and Takeshi Matsuda (Osaka, Japan: Osaka University of Foreign Studies Press, 2000).

3. Charles Kindleberger, *The World in Depression, 1919–1939* (Berkeley: University of California Press, 1986), 11.

4. William K. Tabb, "The Two Wings of the Eagle," *Monthly Review,* July–August 2003, http://www.monthlyreview.org/0703tabb.htm.

5. Mary Kaldor, *The Imaginary War: Understanding the East–West Conflict* (Oxford: Blackwell, 1990).

6. See Kevin H. O'Rourke and Jeffrey G. Williamson, *Globalization and History: The Evolution of a Nineteenth-Century Atlantic Economy* (Cambridge, MA: MIT Press, 2000).

7. "Europe Gets a Defense Giant," *The Economist,* October 14, 1999.

8. Walter LaFeber, *America, Russia, and the Cold War, 1945–2000,* 9th ed. (Boston: McGraw-Hill, 2002), 384.

9. Thomas Friedman, "The Strategic Bombing Was Smart After All," *Pittsburgh Post-Gazette,* January 20, 1999, A15.

10. Robert Kagan, *Of Paradise and Power: America and Europe in the New World Order* (New York: Knopf, 2003).

11. Josef Jaffe, *Financial Times,* January 28, 2003, 15.

12. Philip Stephens, *Financial Times,* May 23, 2003, 13.

13. Quoted in *Financial Times,* August 12, 2003, 11. The *FT* reported that in a public opinion poll in Eastern Europe, two-thirds had a favorable view of the EU's role but only one-third thought so of the United States. Moreover, more than two-thirds favored a common foreign policy and defense policy in the EU, not a divided one.

14. *Financial Times,* August 8, 2002, 10.

15. Quoted in Mauren Dowd, *New York Times,* March 3, 2003, A29; quoted in *Financial Times,* April 14, 2003, 13.

16. *New York Times,* April 2, 2003, A11.

17. *Financial Times,* April 7, 2003, 4. *LeMonde* reported that neoconservatives had originally favored breaking OPEC to get oil at $15 a barrel and revive a slack global economy. But a Pentagon task force headed by Douglas Feith concluded that the scheme was too impractical to work (Yahya Sadowski, *Le Monde,* April 2003).

18. Phillip Stephens, *Financial Times,* May 13, 2002, 12.

19. *New York Times,* May 21, 2002, W1.

20. Fernand Braudel, *Afterthoughts on Material Civilization and Capitalism* (Baltimore: Johns Hopkins University Press, 1977), 86.

21. See Karl Polanyi, *The Great Transformation* (Boston: Beacon Press, 1957).

22. See James O'Connor, *The Fiscal Crisis of the State* (New York: St. Martin's Press, 1973), the classic analysis of America's first fiscal crisis and its impact on foreign policy. The idea was revived in the 1980s by Paul Kennedy, *The Rise and Fall of the Great Powers* (New York: Random House, 1987) but has enjoyed renewed currency during the past six months. For example, see Niall Ferguson and Lawrence Kotlinifff, "The Fiscal Overstretch that Will Undermine an Empire," *Financial Times,* March 15, 2003, 15.

5. *Anti-Americanism and Anti-Europeanism* by Mary Nolan

1. Dan Diner, *Feindbild Amerika: über die Beständigkeit eines Ressentiments* (Munich: Propyläen, 2002), 8.

2. Stanley Hoffmann, "The High and the Mighty: Bush's National Security Strategy and the New American Hubris," *American Prospect* 13, no. 24, January 13, 2003; Tony Judt, "Its Own Worst Enemy," *New York Review of Books,* August 15, 2002; and Claus Leggewie, *Amerikas Welt: Die USA in unseren Köpfen* (Hamburg: Hoffmann und Campe, 2000).

3. Pew Research Center, "What the World Thinks in 2002" (italics in original), Dec. 4, 2002, http://people-press.org/reports/display.php3? report ID-165.

4. William Wallace, "Living with the Hegemon: European Dilemmas," in *Critical Views of September 11: Analyses from Around the World,* ed. Eric Hershberg and Kevin W. Moore (New York: The New Press, 2002), 101.

5. The National Security Strategy of the United States, www.whitehouse.gov/nsc, 5.

6. Ibid.; Anatol Lieven, "The Push for War," *London Review of Books* 24, no. 19 (October 3, 2002); and Hoffmann, "The High and Mighty."

7. "US Sneers at 'Chocolate Makers,'" News24, September 2, 2003, http://www.news24.com/News24/World/News/0,,2-10-1462_1410833,00.html

8. "Amerikakritik ist ein Freundschaftsdienst," interview with Günter Grass, *Spiegel Online,* October 10, 2001, http://www.spiegel.de. See also, Alfred Grosser, "Les hors-la-loi," *Le Monde,* April 26, 2003, 8.

9. Lieven, "The Push for War."

10. Paul Berman, *Terror and Liberalism* (New York: W.W. Norton, 2002).

11. Jonah Goldberg, "Chirac Envy," *The National Review Online,* February 19, 2003, http://www.nationalreview.com/goldberg/goldberg021903.asp; and Molly Ivins, "Cheese-eating Surrender Monkeys, eh?" *Star-Telegram.com,* Feb. 20, 2003, http://www.dfw.com/mld/startelegram/news/columnists/mollyivins/5222243.htm. For a sampling of popular Francophobia, type "Cheeseeating surrender monkeys" into your search engine.

12. Alex Fak, "A History of French-Hating," *The American Enterprise,* September 2003, 11.

13. Interview on the *Charlie Rose Show,* September 24, 2003, http://www.charlierose.com/archives/archive.shtm.

14. http://www.house.gov/ryan/hottopicarchive/PresJointRessigning101602.html.

15. Robert Kagan, "Power and Weakness," *Policy Review* 113 (June–July 2002). See also his book on the same theme, *Of Paradise and Power: America and Europe in the New World Order* (New York: Knopf, 2003). For a discussion of the Nietzschean character of the arguments of Kagan and other neoconservatives, see Steven Lukes, "The New Supermen," *Open Democracy,* September 11, 2002, http://www.opendemocracy.net/debates/article-2-50-181.jsp.

16. Francis Fukuyama, *The End of History and the Last Man* (New York: Free Press, 1992).

17. Volker Berghahn, *America and the Intellectual Cold Wars in Europe* (Princeton: Princeton University Press, 2001).

18. Christina Hoff Sommers, "Men—It's in Their Nature," *The American Enterprise,* September 2003, 5.

19. Ibid.

20. William Safire, "Bad Herr Dye," *New York Times,* January 23, 2003.

21. *New York Post,* January 24, 2003; and Thomas Friedman, "Our War With France," *New York Times,* September 18, 2003.

22. Timothy Garton Ash, "Anti-Europeanism in America," *New York Review of Books,* February 13, 2003.

23. Petra Goedde, *GIs and Germans: Culture, Gender and Foreign Relations, 1945–1949* (New Haven: Yale University Press, 2003).

24. Charles A. Kupchan, *The End of the American Era: U.S. Foreign Policy and the Geopolitics of the Twenty-first Century* (New York: Knopf, 2002); and Andrew Moravesik, "Striking a Transatlantic Bargain," *Foreign Affairs,* July/August 2002, 74–89.

25. The Pew Research Center, "Views of a Changing World 2003," Jun. 3, 2003 http://people-press.org/reports/display.php3?report-ID-185, 23.

26. The Pew Research Center, 2002, 2–3.

27. The Pew Research Center, "America's Image Further Erodes, Europeans Want Weaker Ties," March 18, 2003, http: people-press.org/reports/display.php3?report ID-175.

28. *Candidate Countries Eurobarometer 2003,* 37–38. http://europa.qou.si/javno-mnenje/eurobarometer-2003.pdf.

29. "What the World Thinks of America," poll taken May–June 2003, http://news.bbc.co .uk/1/shared/spl/hi/programmes/wtwta/poll/html/default.stm.

30. Lieven, "The Push for War."

31. See endnote 11.

32. David Ellwood, "Comparative Anti-Americanism in Western Europe," in *Transactions, Transgressions, Transformations: American Culture in Western Europe and Japan,* ed. Heide Fehrenbach and Uta G. Poiger (New York and Oxford: Berghahn, 2000), 31.

33. Ibid., 32–33. The missile controversy has been most thoroughly, albeit one-sidedly studied by Jeffrey Herf, *War by Other Means: Soviet Power, West German Resistance, and the Battle of the Euromissiles* (New York: Free Press, 1991).

34. Sanford J. Ungar, "The Roots of Estrangement," in *Estrangement: America and the World* (New York and Oxford: Oxford University Press, 1985), 14–18.

35. In late 1990 and early 1991 these debates were analyzed at length in both *Der Spiegel,* which opposed sending troops, and the *Frankfurter Allgemeine,* which favored so doing.

36. The Pew Research Center, "Among Wealthy Nations . . . U.S. Stands Alone in its Embrace of Religion," December 19, 2002, http://people-press.org/reports/display.php3?reportID-167.

37. Ibid., 99.

38. Joseph Nye, *The Paradox of American Power: Why the World's Only Superpower Can't Go It Alone* (New York and Oxford: Oxford University Press, 2002); Clyde Prestowitz, *Rogue Nation: American Unilateralism and the Failure of Good Intentions* (New York: Basic, 2003); and the Joint Declaration: Renewing the Transatlantic Partnership, signed by Madeleine Albright, Zbigniew Brzezinski, and Warren Christopher among others. See also endnote 24.

6. *Iraq Is Not Arabic for Nicaragua: Central America and the Rise of the New Right* by Greg Grandin

1. In *Vital Interests: The Soviet Issue in U.S. Central American Policy,* ed. Bruce D. Larkin (Boulder: L. Rienner Publishers, 1988).

2. Walter LaFeber, *Inevitable Revolutions: The United States in Central America* (New York: Norton, 1994), 280.

3. Ibid., 273

4. See, in addition to LaFeber, *Inevitable Revolutions,* John Coatsworth, *Central America and the United States* (New York: Twayne Publishers, 1994).

5. Comisión para el Esclarecimiento Histórico, *Guatemala: Memoria del silencio* (Guatemala: United Nations Operating Projects Services, 12 volumes, 1999).

6. NSA, Department of State, "US-Guatemalan Relations–Arms Sales," Nov. 26, 1982.

7. "Reagan Denounces Threats to Peace in Latin America," *New York Times,* Dec. 5, 1982.

8. See the 1986 speech reprinted in Larkin, *Vital Interests.*

9. Walter LaFeber, "Thomas C. Mann and the Devolution of Latin American Policy: From the Good Neighbor to Military Interventions" in *Behind the Throne: Servants of Power to Imperial Presidents, 1898–1968,* ed. Walter LaFeber and Thomas McCormick (Madison: University of Wisconsin Press, 1993).

10. David Ronfeldt, "The Future Conflict Environment," in Larkin, *Vital Interests.*

11. See the documents Department of State, Office of Public Diplomacy for Latin America and the Caribbean, "Public Diplomacy Action Plan: Support for the White House Education Campaign," March 12, 1985, and Department of State, Office of Public Diplomacy for Latin America and the Caribbean, "Duties of TDY [Psychological Operations] Military Personnel," May 30, 1985.

12. "U.S. Security in Latin America," in Larkin, *Vital Interests,* 71.

13. Social and economic figures come mostly from the CIA's World Factbook, found online at http://www.cia.gov/cia/publications/factbook/geos/gt.html.

14. David Gonzalez, "Central America's Cities Grow Bigger, and Poorer," *New York Times,* March 17, 2002.

15. Gonzalez, "Malnourished to Get Help in Guatemala," *New York Times,* March 20, 2002.

16. Department of State, "Terror and Counter-Terror," March 29, 1968.

7. *Improving on the Civilizing Mission?: Assumptions of United States Exceptionalism in the Colonization of the Philippines* by Michael Adas

1. Taft to J.G. Schmidlapp, Jun. 15, 1900, *William Howard Taft Papers,* Series 3, Reel 30, Manuscript Division, Library of Congress, Washington, DC.

2. There were, of course, good reasons for these concerns. But they had more to do with an absence of European or American immunities to radically different disease environ-

ments than to innate racial characteristics or the heat, humidity, and miasmatic conditions that were usually the focus of discourses on the ill-health of Anglo-Saxons and other "white races" in the tropics. See especially the work of Philip Curtin, including *The Image of Africa* (Madison: University of Wisconsin Press, 1964), chapter 3; *Death by Migration: Europe's Encounter with the Tropical World in the Nineteenth Century* (New York and Cambridge: Cambridge University Press, 1989); and *Disease and Empire* (Cambridge and New York: Cambridge University Press, 1998). Also highly informative on European explanations for their high mortality rates and ill-health in the tropics is David Arnold, *Colonizing the Body: State Medicine and Epidemic Disease in Nineteenth-Century India* (Berkeley: University of California Press, 1993), especially chapters 1 and 2.

3. London, 1898.

4. "America in the Far East: II.—The Anglo-Saxon in the Tropics," *The Outlook* 60, no. 15 (December 1898), 903–4.

5. Of the extensive literature on American diplomatic duplicity and military operations, Leon Wolff's *Little Brown Brother* (Garden City, NY: Doubleday, 1961) and the more recent *"Benevolent Assimilation": The American Conquest of the Philippines, 1899–1903* (New Haven: Yale University Press, 1982) by Stuart Miller remain the most revealing. The most detailed treatment of the costs in terms of disease and famine of the violent occupation of the islands can be found in Ken DeBevoise, *Agents of Apocalypse: Epidemic Disease in the Colonial Philippines* (Princeton: Princeton University Press, 1995). On Kipling's poem as a response to America's colonial takeover, see Wolff, ibid., pp. 189–90.

6. On Root, see Philip C. Jessup, *Elihu Root* (New York: Dodd, Mead & Company, 1938), 1:300; and Wright, "The Situation in the Philippines," *The Outlook,* September 12, 1903, 111.

7. Charles B. Elliott, *The Philippines to the End of the Military Régime* (Indianapolis: The Bobbs-Merrill Company, 1917), 59–60; Carl Crow, *America and the Philippines* (Garden City, NY: Doubleday, 1914), 241; Francis Burton Harrison, *The Corner-Stone of Philippine Independence* (New York: The Century Co., 1922), 331, 338–39; and Leonard Wood, "A Word about the Philippines," in the *Report of the Thirty-Third Annual Lake Mohonk Conference on the Indian and Other Dependent Peoples,* October 20–22, 1916, 153.

8. The phrase was used by Norbert Lyons, the associate editor of the American-owned *Manila Daily Bulletin,* to characterize the first decade and a half of United States colonization in the islands. See, "Some Observations on Race Contact," in the *Lake Mohonk Conference Report,* 148.

9. Wright, "Situation in the Philippines," 111.

10. Elliott, *Philippines to the End of the Military Régime,* 80–83; Harrison, *Corner-Stone of Philippine Independence,* 54–59; and Lyons, "Some Observations on Race Contact," 148–49.

11. Harrison, *Corner-Stone of Philippine Independence,* 325.

12. Ibid., 326, 329–30, 338–39.

13. *Report of the Special Mission to the Philippines* (Manila, 1921), 12.

14. April 10, 1917, Box 34, *David Prescott Barrows Papers,* Bancroft Library, University of California at Berkeley.

15. Wright, "Situation in the Philippines," 111.

16. "Some Results of Our Government in the Philippines," in Mrs. Campbell Dauncey, *The Philippines: An Account of Their People, Progress, and Condition* (Boston and Tokyo: J.B. Millet Company, 1910), 35.

17. Harrison, *Corner-Stone of Philippine Independence,* 320.

18. *De Laatste Eeuw van Indië: Ontwikkeling en ondergang van een koloniaal project* (Amsterdam: Bert Bakker, 1994), 83–85.

19. From his instructions to the second Philippine Commission, reprinted in W. Cameron Forbes, *The Philippine Islands* (Boston and New York: Houghton Mifflin, 1928), 442.

20. *Report of the Taft Philippine Commission* in *Reports of the War Department for the Fiscal Year Ended June 30, 1900* (Washington, DC, 1901), 1:122–224.

21. For samples of American contempt for their Spanish predecessors, see Wright, "Situation in Philippines," 114–15; Jacob G. Shurman, *Philippine Affairs* (New York: C. Scribner, 1902), 62–127; and L. Donald Warren, *Isles of Opportunity* (Washington, DC: Review and Herald Publishing Association, 1928), 63–64.

22. Harrison, *Corner-Stone of Philippine Independence,* 337–39.

23. For sample expressions of American pride in the scientific nature of their colonial initiatives drawn from widely disparate projects and departments, see Shurman, *Philippine Affairs,* 67 (legislation relating to economics and finances); an anonymous article on "Versatility of the American Army," *Army and Navy Journal,* September 7, 1912, 6 (psychology and policies towards the "pagan" and primitive peoples of "the southern islands"); and David Barrows to the General Superintendent Department of Public Instruction, October 5, 1901, 1 and Barrows to Dean C. Worcester, April 7, 1902, 2 (approaches to education and his ethnological studies of the Filipino peoples) in *Barrows Papers,* Box 1, Bancroft Library.

24. Elliott, *Philippines to the End of the Military Regime,* 54–59, quoted portion, 59.

25. Harrison provided perhaps the most important exception in this regard, but see also Crow, *America and the Philippines,* 241–42.

26. Daniel Headrick's *The Tentacles of Progress* (New York: Oxford University Press, 1988) provides a useful overview of these processes. For important historical accounts with reference to specific colonial sites, see (for British India), the essays in *Technology and the Raj,* ed. Roy MacLeod and Deepak Kumar (New Delhi: Sage Publications, 1995); Arnold, *Colonizing the Body;* and E.M. Whitcombe, *Agrarian Conditions in Northern India* (Berkeley: University of California Press, 1972); (for the Netherlands Indies) Doom, *Laatste Eeuw,* especially chapters four to seven; and H.W. van den Doel, *De Stille Macht: Het Europese binnenlands bestuur op Java en Madoera, 1808–1942* (Amsterdam: Bert Bakker, 1994), chapter 5; and (for French Indochina) Frédéric Hulot, *L'Indochine—Le Yunnan: Le chemins de fer de la France d'Outre-mer* (Saint-Laurent-du-Var, 1990), vol. 1; Pham Cao Duong, *Vietnamese Peasants under French Domination* (Berkeley: Center for South and Southeast Asia Studies, 1985), especially pp. 9–23, 136–51; and Anne Marcovich, "French Colonial Medicine and Colonial Rule: Algeria and Indochina," in *Disease, Medicine, and Empire,* ed. Roy McLeod and Milton Lewis (London: Routledge, 1988), 103–17.

27. "Our Duty to the Philippines," *The Independent* 51, December 28, 1899, 3466–67.

28. Elliott, *The Philippines to the End of the Commission* (Indianapolis: The Bobbs-Merrill Company, 1917); 271. For sample expressions of these sentiments by Elliot's administrative predecessors, see James F. Smith's 1908 "Message of the Governor-General to the Philippine Commission and the Philippine Assembly," in the Harrison Papers, Container 42, especially pp. 1–7; W. Cameron Forbes, the Secretary of Commerce and Police, "Extracts from Letter of the Secretary of Commerce and Police," in Forbes, *The Philippine Islands,* 1:408–9; 2:455–58.

29. Elliott, *Philippines to the End of the Commission,* 277–78.

30. From a rather large literature on the history of the engineering profession in the United States in this period, perhaps the most insightful and broadly conceived remain Edward Layton's *Revolt of the Engineers: Social Responsibility and the American Engineering Profession* (Cleveland: Press of Case Western Reserve University, 1971); and David Noble, *America by Design: Science, Technology, and the Rise of Corporate Capitalism* (New York: Knopf, 1977).

31. On these trends in the academic disciplines, see Dorothy Ross, *The Origins of American Social Science* (Cambridge: Cambridge University Press, 1991); and the increasing confidence that social science theories could be applied to human societies, John M. Jordan,

Machine-Age Ideology: Social Engineering and American Liberalism, 1911–1939 (Chapel Hill: University of North Carolina Press, 1994).

32. Wim van den Doel drew my attention to this key difference and thereby set in motion the line of argument that follows.

33. One of the few serious explorations to date of the significance of these measures in American colonization and Filipino responses to them can be found in Vicente L. Rafael's essay "White Love: Surveillance and Nationalist Resistance in the U.S. Colonization of the Philippines," in *Cultures of United States Imperialism,* ed. Amy Kaplan and Donald E. Pease (Durham: Duke University Press, 1993), 185–218.

34. And, as George W. Stocking Jr. and Henrika Kuklick have shown, in the Pacific Islands more generally as well as in sub-Saharan Africa, where development was also seen to stop at the savage level of existence. See, George W. Stocking, *Victorian Anthropology* (New York: Free Press, 1987), chapter 7; and Kuklick, *The Savage Within: The Social History of British Anthropology, 1885–1945* (Cambridge: Cambridge University Press, 1991), especially chapter 4.

35. Rodney J. Sullivan, *Exemplar of Americanism: The Philippine Career of Dean C. Worcester* (Ann Arbor: Center for South and Southeast Asian Studies, 1991).

36. Barrows to Dean C. Worcester, April 7, 1902, *Barrows Papers,* Box 1.

37. Robert W. Rydell, *All the World's a Fair* (Chicago: University of Chicago Press, 1984), chapter 6.

38. On these divergent strategies, see the studies in *Compadre Colonialism: Studies in the Philippines under American Rule,* ed. Norman G. Owen (Ann Arbor: Center for South and Southeast Asian Studies, 1971); and Peter W. Stanley, *A Nation in the Making: The Philippines and the United States, 1899–1921* (Cambridge, Mass.: Harvard University Press, 1974); compared, for examples, to Van den Doel, *Stille Macht,* chapter 6; Richard G. Fox, *Lions of the Punjab: Culture in the Making* (Berkeley: University of California Press, 1985), chapter 8; and Michael Adas, "The Reconstruction of Tradition and the Defense of the Colonial Order," in *Articulating Hidden Histories,* ed. Jane Schneider and Rayna Rapp (Berkeley: University of California Press, 1995), 291–307.

39. Elliott, *Philippines to the End of the Military Régime,* 54–55.

40. Ibid., 58–60.

41. Wright, "Situation in the Philippines," 111; Taft to Captain Charles T. Barker, July 13, 1901, *Taft Papers,* Series 3, Reel 33; Elliott, *Philippines to the End of the Commission,* iii; Nicholas Roosevelt, *The Philippines: A Treasure and a Problem* (New York: J.H. Sears & Company, 1926), 15; and Paul Thomas Gilbert quoted passage, *The Great White Tribe in Filipinia* (Cincinnati: Jennings and Pye, 1903), 302–3.

42. The late-nineteenth century French debates over assimilation and shift to association are discussed at length in Hubert Deschamps, *Les méthodes et les doctrines de la France du XVIe siècle à nos jours* (Paris: Armand Colin, 1953); and Raymond Betts, *Assimilation and Association in French Colonial Theory, 1890–1914* (New York: Columbia University Press, 1961).

43. Van Doom, *Laatste Eeuw,* chapter 6; David W. Del Testa, *"Paint the Trains Red": Labor, Nationalism and the Railroads in French Colonial Indochina, 1898–1945,* Ph.D. dissertation, U. of California at Davis, 2001, chapter 1; Eric Stokes, *The English Utilitarians and India* (Oxford: Clarendon Press, 1959), and Michael Adas, *Machines as the Measure of Men* (Ithaca: Cornell University Press, 1989), chapters 3 and 5.

44. Here I am abbreviating the concept of the peasantry developed by Eric Wolf in his seminal study of *Peasants* (Englewood Cliffs, N.J.: Prentice-Hall, 1966), chapter 1.

45. Eduardo Lachica, *Huk: Philippine Agrarian Society in Revolt* (Manila: Solidaridad, 1971), chapters 2 and 3; Philippines, Bureau of Agriculture, *A Half-Century of Philippine Agriculture* (Manila, 1952); and Norman G. Owen, *Prosperity Without Progress: Manila Hemp and Material Life in the Colonial Philippines* (Berkeley: University of California Press, 1984).

46. The fullest study of this prolonged agrarian crisis remains F.A. Shannon, *The Farmer's Last Frontier* (New York: Farrar & Rhinehart, 1945).

47. J.S. Furnivall, *Colonial Policy and Practice: A Comparative Study of Burma and the Netherlands Indies* (Cambridge: Cambridge University Press, 1948).

48. For samples of official stress on the central importance of market mechanisms in the "development" of the Philippines, see William Howard Taft, *Present Day Problems* (New York: Dodd Mead, 1908), 26–27; Elliott, *Philippines to the End of the Commission,* 300ff; Forbes, *Philippine Islands,* 8.

49. See, for example, *Report of the (3rd) Philippine Commission,* 1903, part 1, 59–60.

50. Glenn Anthony May, *Social Engineering in the Philippines* (Westport, CT: Greenwood Press, 1980), especially chapter 3.

51. See, for example, Para Villanueva de Kalaw, "The Filipino Woman in the Past and Present," *The Philippine Review* 2, no. 12 (December 1917).

52. Reynaldo Clemena Ileto, *Payson and Revolution* (Manila: Ateneo de Manila University Press, 1979); David Sturtevant, *Popular Uprisings in the Philippines, 1840–1940* (Ithaca: Connell University Press, 1976); Lachica, *Huk;* and Benedict J. Kerkvliet, *The Huk Rebellion* (Berkeley: University of California Press, 1977).

53. Health problems, his own and those of family members, became a recurring concern in Taft's voluminous correspondence with officials and friends back in the United States.

54. Though he implicitly argues for a much broader impact than his small sample of doctors and patients warrants, this underside of the American colonial venture has been explored in interesting ways by Warrick Anderson in "The Trespass Speaks: White Masculinity and Colonial Breakdown," *American Historical Review* 102, no. 5 (1997): 1343–70. See also, De Bevoise, *Agents of Apocalypse.*

55. *Report (3rd) of the Philippine Commission,* 1903, pp. 31–32; and Crow, *America and the Philippines,* 58–60.

9. *Japan and the United States in Re-Imperial Times* by Carol Gluck

1. Walter LaFeber, "The Bush Doctrine," *Diplomatic History* 26, no. 4 (Fall 2002).

2. Michael Hirsh, "Bush and the World," *Foreign Affairs,* September/October 2002.

3. Michael H. Hunt, "In the Wake of September 11: The Clash of What?," *Journal of American History* 89, no. 2 (September 2002).

4. Eric Heginbotham and Richard J. Samuels, "Japan's Dual Hedge," *Foreign Affairs,* September/October 2002.

5. Wada Haruki, "Kita no Peresutoroika wa seikō suru ka" [Can the North's Perestroika Succeed?], *Sekai,* November 2002.

6. Kang Sangjung, "Hokutō Ajia anteika kujō ni michitta daiipō" [The First Agonizing Step Towards Stabilizing Northeast Asia], *Ronza,* November 2002.

10. *Onward, Liberal Soldiers?:*
The Crusading Logic of Bush's Grand Strategy and What Is Wrong with It by Edward Rhodes

The author wishes to acknowledge past and ongoing research support from Rutgers College and Rutgers University Research Council.

1. George W. Bush, "Remarks by the President at 2002 Graduation Exercise of the United States Military Academy, West Point, New York," available at http://www.whitehouse.gov/news/releases/2002/06/20020601-3.html.

2. "The National Security Strategy of the United States of America, September 2002," available at http://www.whitehouse.gov/nsc/nss.html.

3. "National Security Strategy," i.

4. Bush, "West Point," 2.

5. For one excellent account of the Wilsonian character of the Bush administration's for-

eign policy, see Fareed Zakaria, "Our Way," *The New Yorker,* October 14 and 21, 2002, 72–81.

6. Bush, "West Point," 4.
7. "National Security Strategy," ii.
8. Ibid., iii.
9. Bush, "West Point," 2.
10. Ibid., 4.
11. Ibid., 4.
12. "National Security Strategy," 29, 30.
13. Ibid., 6.
14. Ibid., 15.
15. Ibid., 15. Earlier, the "National Security Strategy" noted that "We must be prepared to stop rogue states and their terrorist clients before they are able to *threaten* or use weapons of mass destruction against the United States and our allies and friends" (14, italics added).
16. Ibid., 6.
17. Ibid., 29.
18. Ibid., 29.
19. Bush, "West Point," 4, 5. Bush goes on to acknowledge that "America cannot impose this vision." He does, however, argue that American power broadly understood should be used to move the world toward it: "We can support and reward governments that make the right choices for their own people. In our development aid, in our diplomatic efforts, in our international broadcasting, and in our educational assistance, the United States will promote moderation and tolerance and human rights." He also implies that American power—including America's military tools—should be used to create the conditions around the world that are associated with creating a peaceful, liberal, all-embracing world order. "We will," he bluntly states, "defend the peace that makes all progress possible." Bush, "West Point," 5.
20. "National Security Strategy," 1.
21. Ibid.
22. Ibid.
23. Ibid.
24. Ibid., i.
25. Ibid., 3 (italics added).
26. Ibid., iii.

27. Ibid., i, ii.

28. Condoleezza Rice's January 2000 *Foreign Affairs* article was, and continues to be, widely viewed as the Bush campaign's foreign-policy platform. Dr. Rice, of course, now serves as National Security Advisor in the Bush administration. See Rice, "Promoting the National Interest," *Foreign Affairs* 79 no. 1 (January/February 2000), 45–62.

29. Bush, "West Point," 3. It is worth noting that even during the Cold War the same concerns were, from time to time, raised—that totalitarian dictators did not worry for the fate of "their" nation so long as their own power or their ideology was unharmed (and that, therefore, the United States needed to target leadership cadres or the sinews of political power) and that "crazy" leaders (e.g., the Chinese) could not be kept in check. Such claims thus deserve careful scrutiny.

30. My thinking on these points has been deeply influenced by a reading of the works of one of the most influential and most extraordinary, and now most completely forgotten, shapers of American foreign policy, Charles Evans Hughes, secretary of state from 1921 to 1925. For an exploration of Hughes's appreciation of liberalism's necessarily organic nature, see Edward Rhodes, "Charles Evans Hughes Reconsidered, or: Liberal Isolationism in the New Millennium," in *The Real and the Ideal: Essays on International Relations in Honor of Richard H. Ullman,* ed. Anthony Lake and David Ochmanek (Lanham, MD: Rowman and Littlefield, 2001), 153–202.

31. "National Security Strategy," 1 (italics added).

32. Ibid., 1. The president is explicit about what these values are: "freedom, democracy, and free enterprise" involve the right "to be able to speak freely; choose who will govern them; worship as they please; educate their children—male and female; own property; and enjoy the benefits of their labor."

33. Ibid., ii.

34. Charles Evans Hughes, *The Pathway of Peace* (New York: Harper and Brothers, 1925).

11. *A Most Interesting Empire* by Anders Stephanson

1. For an overview, see Arnold Leibowitz, *Defining Status: A Comprehensive Analysis of United States Territorial Relations* (Dordrecht, Boston: Martinus Nijhoff, 1989). Denmark is arguably territorially a larger empire, but its chief possession, Greenland, is de facto under the geopolitical suzerainty of the United States.

2. Depending on time and place, this war has been known under a variety of names. The designation in the United States, "the Spanish-American War," hides symptomatically

the Cuban participation. The Spanish-Cuban-American War, as it is known in Cuba, is better but elides in turn the independent Phillippine aspect.

3. In the 1960s and early '70s, there was of course an explosion of interest in imperialism in general and the United States in particular. This came to a predictable end with the end of the involvement in Southeast Asia. In the mid-1980s, there began a rejuvenation of an older, sociological kind of academic inquiry, roughly descendant from Max Weber's comparative concerns. A central work here was Michael Mann's *The Sources of Social Power, Vol. I: From the Beginning to 1760 AD* (Cambridge: Cambridge University Press, 1986). Simultaneously, there appeared in the case-study method of mainstream U.S. social science Michael Doyle's significant *Empire* (Ithaca: Cornell University Press, 1986). Yet it was the entirely new phase in geopolitics after 1990 with its apparent "unipolarity" (an oxymoron) that turned "empire" into a field, if not a master signifier. Michael Hardt and Toni Negri's controversial and much debated *Empire* appeared from Harvard University Press in 2000. The separate strain through cultural studies to post-colonial studies originated to no small degree in Edward Said's *Orientalism* (1979); but the independent and sophisticated current in India now known as subaltern studies was already in existence and became influential as well. A good collection on empire from a comparative perspective is *After Empire,* edited by Karen Barkey and Mark von Hagen (Boulder, CO: Westview Press, 1997). Since September 11, there has been a veritable onslaught of argument about "the American Empire." Some conservatives, interestingly, have been highly critical. See e.g., Andrew J. Bacevich, *American Empire: The Realities and Consequences of U.S. Diplomacy* (Cambridge: Harvard University Press, 2002).

4. The allusions here are to William Appleman Williams, *Empire as a Way of Life* (New York: Oxford University Press, 1980) and Geir Lundestad, *American "Empire" and Other Studies of American Foreign Policy in a Comparative Perspective* (Oxford: Oxford University Press, 1990), though the original idea was put forth in his article "Empire by Invitation" in *SHAFR Newsletter,* September 15, 1984.

5. One important, earlier presence here was S.N. Eisenstadt. See his *The Political Systems of Empires* (New York: Free Press, 1963). "Empire" in historical sociology has otherwise been one of several forms of state, less an object of inquiry in itself.

6. Lenin's theorization became Soviet orthodoxy of the most entrenched sort, the frame indeed within which all international politics was ultimately conceived. That the "highest stage" went on and on never occasioned any basic rethinking until the days of Gorbachev. Hardt and Negri are partly a response to this impasse, an original attempt to rethink the problem by finding empire in the very form of decentered, globalized cap-

italism. Heavily theoretical though their work is, one still wonders in the end why this form is necessarily to be called "empire." Perhaps it is meant as Brechtian estrangement effect. For another kind of reflection in the Marxist tradition see David Harvey, *The New Imperialism* (Oxford: Oxford University Press, 2003).

7. Otto Hintze, *The Historical Essays of Otto Hintze* (New York: Oxford University Press, 1975). The German term *Weltreich* is semantically not directly related to the Latin imperium but it makes sense: "By 'world empire' I mean those states of ancient times and of non-European civilization which established a universal authority in an area they regarded as the known and inhabited world, and which recognized no other states as equal" (468n).

8. Hamilton's formulation comes from *The Federalist* no. 1. Almost all references to the United States as empire in *The Federalist* are to be found in his contributions. Empire in itself is neither good nor bad. It is used as a designation for rule involving many states and enormous size. See also John Robertson's interesting "Empire and Union: Two Concepts of the Early Modern European Political Order," in *A Union for Empire: Political Thought and the British Union of 1707,* ed. John Robertson (Cambridge: Cambridge University Press, 1995).

9. Anders Stephanson, *Manifest Destiny: American Expansion and the Empire of Right* (New York: Hill & Wang, 1995). I develop the specifically messianic aspect further in "Law and Messianic Counterwar from FDR to George W. Bush," in *Americanism,* ed. Michael Kazin and Adam Rothman (forthcoming).

10. In the immense literature on Jefferson, see Robert W. Tucker and David C. Hendrickson, *Empire of Liberty: The Statecraft of Thomas Jefferson* (New York: Oxford University Press, 1990); Peter S. Onuf, *Statehood and Union: A History of the Northwest Ordinance* (Bloomington: Indiana University Press, 1987); John Lauritz Larson, "Jefferson's Union and the Problem of Internal Improvements," in *Jeffersonian Legacies,* ed. Peter Onuf (Charlottesville: University Press of Virginia, 1993). Hamilton, it should be added, would not have disagreed with Jefferson, but his concern was chiefly how to achieve control and cohesion while avoiding despotism, less the idea of promoting any world-historical principle of liberty as such. I leave aside the ticklish issue of whether Jefferson as president in fact turned out to be a Hamiltonian.

11. See his letter to Madison, April 27, 1809. *The Papers of James Madison* (Presidential Series, vol 1), ed. Robert Rutland et al. (Charlottesville: University Press of Virginia, 1984).

12. The metaphor becomes paradoxical when the voluntarist component of the founding

moment is taken properly into account: what is "reproduced" is not a biological code or essence but the act of proving one's ability to determine oneself freely, an act defined precisely by the absence of any outside or prior determination. My metaphor in any case turned out to be unoriginal. Robert Bartlett uses a similar one in describing the medieval Germanic colonization of eastern Europe: "What they were doing was reproducing units similar to those in their homelands. The towns, churches and estates they established simply replicated the social framework they knew from back home. The net result of this colonialism was not the creation of 'colonies,' in the sense of dependencies, but the spread of a kind of cellular multiplication, of the cultural and social forms found in the Latin Christian core." Robert Bartlett, *The Making of Europe: Conquest, Colonization and Cultural Change, 950–1350* (Princeton: Princeton University Press, 1993), 306. The process seems in turn rather similar to the successive waves of Greek colonization in the Mediterranean after the eighth century B.C. One basic difference with the United States, of course, is that Washington was a functioning federal center, albeit a weak one, in the nineteenth century.

13. Again, then, there is a dialectic: free choice becomes its opposite, a foregone conclusion. Among the numerous works on autonomy and freedom I have used are Quentin Skinner, *Liberty Before Liberalism* (Cambridge: Cambridge University Press, 1998); Fred D'Agostino, "Two Conceptions of Autonomy," *Economy and Society* 27, no. 1 (1998); and David Brion Davis, *The Problem of Slavery in the Age of Revolution, 1770–1823* (Ithaca: Cornell University Press, 1975). Autonomy as a criterion or precondition of selfhood (the capacity to determine rationally and freely without any outside influence) goes back of course to classical Greek thought.

14. As Jefferson writes to Madison in 1801: "it is impossible not to look forward to distant times, when our rapid multiplication will expand itself beyond those limits, and cover the whole north, if not the southern continent with a people speaking the same language, governed in similar forms, and by similar laws; nor can we contemplate with satisfaction either blot or mixture on that surface." Quoted in Tucker and Hendrickson, *Empire of Liberty,* 160–61. Saint-Just, in a different register, expressed the same imperative more unequivocally in the French Revolution: "No liberty for the enemies of liberty!"

15. I am drawing here on my *Manifest Destiny* (New York: Hill and Wang, 1995).

16. On this development, see Leibowitz, *Defining Status,* passim. On Puerto Rico, see *Foreign in a Domestic Sense: Puerto Rico, American Expansion, and the Constitution,* edited by C.D. Burnett and B. Marshall (Durham: Duke University Press, 2001).

17. Ibid. See in particular also the pathbreaking work of Efrén Rivera Ramos, *The Legal Construction of Identity: The Judicial and Social Legacy of American Colonialism in Puerto Rico* (Washington: American Psychological Association, 2001) and idem, "The Legal Construction of American Colonialism: The Insular Cases, 1902–1922," *Revista Juridica de la Universidad de Puerto Rico* 65 (1996): 227–328.

18. After World War II, sensitivity in this regard made even the word "possession" excessively blunt. See Peter C. Stuart, *Isles of Empire: The United States and Its Overseas Possessions* (Lanham, MD: University Press of America, 1999), introduction.

19. For more on FDR as an aberration, see Stephanson, "Law and Messianic Counterwar."

20. James Burnham, *The Struggle for the World* (New York: John Day, 1947), 53–55, 182–83, 221.

21. On the authoritarian/totalitarian distinction and the logic of supporting the former see David Schmitz, *Thank God They're on Our Side: The United States and Right-wing Dictatorships, 1921–1965* (Chapel Hill: University of North Carolina Press, 1999).

22. There is now a very substantial historiography on Kennan in this epoch. My own perspective, of which this paragraph is a condensation, may be found in *Kennan and the Art of Foreign Policy* (Cambridge, MA: Harvard University Press, 1989).

23. On NSC 68, see Stephanson, "Liberty or Death: the Cold War as US Ideology," in *Reviewing the Cold War: Approaches, Interpretations, Theory,* ed. O.A. Westad (London: Frank Cass, 2000).

24. Here I am following Mann's concept of a differentiated and contingently combined set of power structures: economic, military, ideological, and political. He has used it to good effect recently in his incisive study of the United States, *Incoherent Empire* (London: Verso, 2003); but I note that he is still using "empire" as though the idea was not in need of problematization as such. The imperial aspect, so prominent in his first volume of *Social Power,* disappeared strangely enough in *The Sources of Social Power: Volume II, The Rise of Classes and Nation-States, 1760–1914* (Cambridge: Cambridge University Press, 1994).

25. Hegemony does have the advantage of allowing one to think the East–West division as a thousand-year line of demarcation down the Elbe and the kind of differences in modes of rule and dominance it has generated. Yet one should then recall that if Gramsci saw the absence of civil society and inverse dominance of the state in the East, he underestimated the coercive power within the West. Given the emphasis on the consensual dimension of hegemony here, it is interesting that U.S. officials in the 1950s used the term to describe the evil Soviet empire: it appears for instance in NSC 68 and

in the Solarium exercise of the early Eisenhower administration. On guardianship and patricinium, see Robert M. Kallet-Marx, *Hegemony to Empire: The Development of the Roman Imperium in the East from 148 to 62 B.C.* (Berkeley: University of California Press, 1995); James Harrington, *The Commonwealth of Oceana: A System of Politics,* ed. J. Pocock (Cambridge: Cambridge University Press, 1992), 221–23; and Nicholas Greenwood Onuf, *The Republican Legacy in International Thought* (Cambridge: Cambridge University Press, 1998), 128–31. I have learned much from David Armitage on this topic, specifically from his "The Origins of Anti-Imperialist in Early-Modern Britain" (unpublished paper).

Contributors

Michael Adas is the Abraham E. Voorhees Professor of History at Rutgers University. His publications include *Machines as the Measure of Men: Science, Technology and Ideologies of Western Dominance,* which won the 1991 Dexter Prize. His new book, *Dominance by Design: Technological Imperatives and America's Civilizing Mission,* will appear in 2005.

John W. Dower is the Ford International Professor of History at MIT. His publications include *War Without Mercy: Race and Power in the Pacific War* and *Embracing Defeat: Japan in the Wake of World War II,* which won several prizes, including the National Book Award for Nonfiction, the Pulitzer Prize for General Nonfiction, the Bancroft Prize in American History, and the John King Fairbank Prize in Asian History.

Lloyd C. Gardner is the Charles and Mary Beard Professor of History at Rutgers University. He is the author of many books on U.S. foreign policy, including *Pay Any Price: Lyndon B. Johnson and the Wars for Vietnam.*

Carol Gluck is the George Sansom Professor of History at Columbia University. Among her books are *Japan's Modern Myths: Ideology in the Late Meiji Period* and *Asia in Western and World History.*

Greg Grandin teaches Latin American history at New York University. His books include *The Blood of Guatemala: A History of Race and Nation,* which won the Latin American Studies Association's award for the best book in the humanities and social sciences, and *The Last Colonial Massacre: Latin America in the Cold War.*

Charles S. Maier is the Leverett Saltonstall Professor of History at Harvard. He is the author of several books, including *Dissolution: The Crisis of Communism and the End of East Germany, In Search of Stability: Explorations in Historical Political Economy,* and *Recasting Bourgeois Europe.* He has also edited several collaborative volumes, including *The Marshall Plan and Germany* and *Changing Boundaries of the Political.*

Thomas McCormick is Professor Emeritus at the University of Wisconsin. His publications include *China Market: America's Quest for Informal Empire, 1893–1902* and *America's Half-Century: United States Foreign Policy in the Cold War and Beyond.*

Mary Nolan is Professor of History at New York University. She is the author of *Visions of Modernity: American Business and the Modernization of Germany* and the co-editor of *Crimes of War: Guilt and Denial in the Twentieth Century.*

John Prados is a Senior Researcher at the National Security Archive. His many books include *Presidents' Secret Wars* and *Lost Crusader: The Secret Wars of CIA Director William Colby.*

Edward Rhodes is Dean of Social and Behavior Sciences at Rutgers University. He is the author of *Power and MADness: The Logic of Nuclear Coercion* and co-editor of *Presence, Presentation, and Persuasion.*

Anders Stephanson, the James P. Shenton Associate Professor of the Columbia Core, specializes in twentieth-century American foreign relations as well as history and theory. His published works include *Kennan
and the Art of Foreign Policy* and *Manifest Destiny*. He is currently working
on a new book on the Cold War and its historiography.

Marilyn B. Young is Professor of History at New York University. Her
books include *The Vietnam Wars, 1945–1990*.

Index

Abrams, Elliot, 135, 139
Acheson, Dean, 10, 11, 13, 24
Adams, Brooks, 160
Afghanistan:
   in Arc of Crisis, 102
   Cold War and, 208–9
   nation-building in, 186, 199, 203, 240
   Soviet invasion of, 15, 20, 82, 128, 209
   U.S. attacks in, 38, 79, 94, 106, 108, 113,
      117, 205, 233, 247
   and war on terrorism, 12, 18, 22, 58, 61,
      207–9, 210, 221
Africa:
   free trade agreements with, 105, 106
   U.S. interventions in, 273
   U.S. lack of interest in, 209
Age of Reason, 27
Albright, Madeleine, 93
Allende Gossens, Salvador, 45, 273
al-Qaeda, 12, 18, 24, 55–56, 208, 213, 222,
   247
Amartya Sen, 213
American Farm Bureau, 29, 31
American Revolution, 27, 40–41
Amerindians, 169–70, 260, 263
Anglo-Iranian Oil Corporation, 13
Annan, Kofi, 58
anti-Americanism:
   anti-Semitism and, 124
   antiwar protestors and, 124
   Atlantic bond threatened by, 249
   Bush as object of, 123, 124, 125
   in context, 127–31
   environmentalism in, 130

evolution of, 127–28
future of, 131–32
opinion polls on, 125–27
people separate from government in, 124,
   125–26
principles and paths of, 118–19, 123–24,
   130
use of term, 114
and world order, 123–25
Anti-Ballistic Missile Treaty, 118
anti-Europeanism:
   in context, 129–30
   future of, 131–32
   masculinity in, 122–23, 130
   opinion polls and, 127
   principles and paths of, 118, 119, 124, 130
   use of term, 114
   and world order, 121–23, 127
anti-Semitism, 124
Arafat, Yasser, 102
Arbenz Guzmán, Jacobo, 150–51
Aristotle, 263
Asia:
   Central, former SSRs in, 102
   civilization in, 160
   financial crisis of, 78, 87, 89
   free trade agreements with, 105
   Great East Asia War, 201, 211; see also
      World War II
   Japan as imperial power in, 171, 179–80,
      183–84, 188, 190, 191–93, 201, 202, 205
   outsourcing jobs to, 88
   regeneration of societies in, 159
   unstable nations in, 82, 88

Balkan crisis, 83, 84, 85, 90, 92–93, 96, 130
Ball, George, 68–69
Barrows, David, 160, 170
Baseworld, 43–44
Bay of Pigs, 61
Bemis, Samuel Flagg, 265–66, 267
Bentinck, William, 175
Berger, Sandy, 93
Berlin, Soviet forces in (1953), xvii
Bertolucci, Bernardo, 192
Besant, Annie, 159
bin Laden, Osama, 20, 26, 208, 210
Blair, Tony, 28, 59, 93, 94, 98, 102, 131, 198
Blitzer, Wolf, 9
Blix, Hans, 3, 5
Bonaparte, Napoleon, 32–33
Boot, Max, 41
Borton, Hugh, 204
Braudel, Fernand, 109
Bremer, L. Paul III, 99, 104
Brinkley, Joel, 39
British empire, xi, xii, 5, 40, 44–45, 156–58, 174–75, 177, 257
Brooks, David, 42–43
Brzezinski, Zbigniew, 15, 102
Bundy, McGeorge, 67–69
Burke, Edmund, xi
Burnham, James, 267, 268–69, 272, 274
Bush, George H. W.:
    administration of, 47, 78
    assassination attempt and, 53
    Carlyle Group and, 29–30
    the economy and, 20
    end of Cold War and, 83
    Gulf Crisis and, 16–18, 19, 52, 57, 83, 84, 206, 208
    New World Order of, 273
Bush, George W.:
    administration of, see Bush administration
    authority to wage war, 63–64
    election of (2000), 96, 219, 237
    Europe and, 132
    farm subsidies and, 29, 31
    militarization of, 59, 94–107
    moralism of, 234, 235–38
    political critique of, 123–24, 125
    presidential transition of, 54–55
    speeches of, 7–8, 12, 22, 25, 30–31, 46–47, 50, 56, 57, 60–61, 63, 143, 227–31, 233–34, 237–38, 242, 250, 251

    treaties put aside by, 21, 118, 207, 219
    utopian ambitions of, 229–30
    "We are America," 22, 28, 31
Bush administration:
    antiwar protests and, 64
    Axis of Evil and, 23, 24, 25, 57, 60, 208, 219
    domestic dissent contained by, 144–45
    energy policy of, 47
    evasion of accountability in, 51, 57, 70, 150
    factions within, 95
    and global U.S. empire, 233, 241–42
    Iraq war and, 24, 26, 50–52, 57–65, 70–71, 150
    Joint Chiefs and, 54, 61, 62, 64
    liberalism and, 239–50
    military budget of, 49
    on military power, xii
    nation-building and, 98
    neoconservatives in, 55, 57, 61, 80, 117
    preemptive action promised by, xi, 60–61, 79, 94–95, 103, 106, 108, 110, 117, 189, 218, 231–32
    Principals Committee in, 57
    righteous empire of, 25–31, 117, 130, 234, 235–38, 241, 248, 250–52
    September 11 attacks and, 55–56, 57, 79, 208, 210, 222
    war plans of, 61–65, 117
    WMD spectre used by, 3–4, 7, 60, 63–64
Bush at War (Woodward), 56
Bush Doctrine, xi, 79, 94–95, 103, 106, 108, 216, 218
Byrd, Robert, 25–26

Carlucci, Frank, 29
Carlyle Group, 29–31
Carter, Jimmy, 14, 15, 137, 138, 139, 141
Carter Doctrine, 103
Casey, William, 139
Castro, Fidel, 137, 138, 141, 262
CEDAW (Convention to End All Discrimination Against Women), 118–19
Central America, see Latin America
Cheney, Dick, 32, 130
    as neoconservative, 57, 96
    and stabilization in Iran, xviii
    and war on Iraq, 56–59, 70, 219
Chile, 45, 137, 149, 273

China:
Celestial Mandate in, 274
civilization in, 160
disintegration of society in, 159
economic emergence of, 82
Japanese aggression on, 183, 190, 191, 193, 205
"last emperor" of, 192–93
Manchuria/Manchukuo in, 183, 190, 191, 192–95
outsourcing jobs to, 88
revolution in (1949), 11
Sino-American agreement, 86–87
Sino-Soviet split in, 11
in WTO, 87
Chirac, Jacques, 132
CIA:
disclosure of operatives of, 27
in Iran, 13–14
in Iraq, 56, 57, 58, 61, 64, 150
in Latin America, 142, 143, 146, 150–51
Vietnam War and, 142
Cicero, 272
Civil War, U.S., 264
Clinton, Bill:
Balkan crisis and, 85, 206
centrism of, 20
counterproliferation and, 59–60
global economy and, 78, 79, 83, 273–74
Iraq policy of, 22, 54, 83, 93–94, 109
militarization and, 79, 90–94, 107–8, 208
Coetzee, J.M., xvi, xvii, 48–49
Cohen, Eliot, 40
Cold War:
agent theory in, 6–7, 11, 12
anti-Communism in, 115, 206, 229, 250, 267
balance of power in, 81, 116, 129, 217, 232, 237–38, 269
brinksmanship in, 217
compromises in, 45
Domino Theory in, 14
empire in, 267–71
end of, 16, 20, 59, 75, 77, 78, 81, 83, 91, 92, 107, 116, 129, 208, 218, 272
first battle of, 13
freedom vs. slavery in, 269–71
good vs. evil in, 141
Japan and, 199, 202, 203, 205
Korean War and, 10, 202, 208
Latin America and, 139, 141, 143, 149, 271

NATO in, 91, 92
NSC-68 and, 90, 267–69
power networks in, 269, 271
proxy wars in, 208
Sino-Soviet split in, 11
universalism in, 269
use of force in, xvii, 13
U.S. mission in, 5, 104, 206, 270–71
Vietnam War and, 7, 11, 38, 139, 208, 271, 272
zone of instability in, 268
Colombia, 45, 136, 145, 147
Committee of Santa Fe, 138, 141
Contra War, 135, 140, 141, 144, 145, 149–50
Crow, Carl, 156
Cuba:
communism in, 137, 138, 141
Florida and, 266
Guantánamo Bay prison in, 253, 262
influence in Latin America, 137, 139
Jeffersonian expansion to, 259–60
nation-building in, 149
in Spanish-American War, 261–62
U.S. intervention in (1961), xvii, 25, 103, 136
Cuban Missile Crisis, 81, 217
Czechoslovakia, Soviets in (1968), xvii

Dayton Accords (1995), 85, 92
Diner, Dan, 114
Dominican Republic, 136, 137
Doorn, J.A. van, 161–62
Downing, Wayne, 61
Dulles, John Foster, 11, 14

Egypt, revolution in (1952), 5
Eisenhower, Dwight D., 30, 65
Eisenhower administration, 13, 14, 148
Eisenhower Doctrine, 11, 103
Elliott, Charles, 156, 157, 158, 164–67, 172, 173
Elphinstone, Mountstuart, 175
empire:
alliance vs., xii–xiii
amnesia of, 201
barbarians entering, xiv, 26–27, 275
of Baseworld, 43–44
by cellular self-replication, 258
civilizational, 264–66
Cold War and, 267–71

empire (*cont.*)
  consensual, xii, 271–72
  destruction of, 40
  efforts to create, 246–47
  expansionism of, xii, xvii–xviii, 259–65
  frontiers of, xiv–xix
  functions of, xiii
  imperialism as implementation of, 40
  imperialism vs., 32–33, 46
  incorporated vs. unincorporated territories of, 263
  language of, 32–49
  liberal, 40, 148
  of and for liberty, 257–58, 259–60, 262, 264, 272
  as metaphor, 271
  overseas colonial realms of, xiii, xviii
  responsibilities of, xii
  of righteousness, 25–31
  right-wing radicalism of, 191–92
  self-determination of, 258–59
  stratification within, xiv–xv
  unique qualities of, xii–xiii
  unreason of, 48
  use of term, 253–57, 264–65, 267
  violence in exercise of, xix, 275
  world order and, *see* world order
Enders, Thomas, 140
Europe:
  Americanization of, 116
  anti-Americanism in, 113–32, 249
  balance of power in, xvii, 80, 111
  Central and Eastern, 120
  Cold War and, *see* Cold War
  colonial rule by, xiii, 68, 120, 156, 157–59, 161–62, 164–65, 168, 171, 172, 174–75, 178, 179, 193
  diplomacy and consensus-building in, 96
  economic slowdown in, 77, 90
  Iraqi oil and, 94
  NATO and, 77, 79–80, 81, 83, 85, 90–92, 95, 108, 113, 129
  "New" vs. "Old," 80, 97–98, 108
  postwar reconstruction of, 119–21
  Rhenish economic model in, 131
  U.S. missiles in, 128
  U.S. social compact with, 77–79, 104, 107, 109
  U.S. unilateral action and, 28, 45, 47, 58, 79, 97–99, 103

European Aeronautical and Space Company (EADS), 91
European Union:
  Balkan crisis and, 85, 92–93, 96
  coalitions sought in, 79, 104
  creation of, 78, 82–83
  currency of, 78, 82
  division within, 97–98, 111
  free trade agreements of, 82–83, 88, 101, 106
  frontiers and, xiv
  Gulf Crisis (1991) and, 129–30
  indirect war on, 75, 80, 83–87, 101–2
  marginalization of, 117–18, 123
  Middle East peace and, 102
  migration from Third World to, 88–89
  military force for, 106, 118, 131
  miracle of, 111, 115
  nation-building and, 101–2
  nuclear threat to, 106
  social policy in, 131
  transformationists and, 99–102
  U.S. militarization and, 93–107
  U.S. vs., *see* anti-Europeanism

Ferguson, Niall, 41
Fox Quesada, Vincente, 88
France, *see* Europe; European Union
Franks, Tommy, 61–62, 122
Friedman, Thomas, 41, 94, 122
frontiers:
  dimming of, 27–28
  importance of, xiv–xv
  use of force in, xvii–xix
  zones of "chaos" and, xviii
Fukuyama, Francis, 121
Fulbright, J. William, 101

G8 summit, 207, 218
Galbraith, John Kenneth, 67, 68
Garner, Jay, 44
Germany:
  in European Union, 97; *see also* European Union
  Gulf Crisis (1991) and, 129–30
  postwar occupation of, 182, 202–3
  postwar reconstruction of, 7, 8, 103, 240–41
  reunification of, 120, 129
  U.S. special relationship with, 96, 97, 123
Gilbert, Paul, 173

Gilpatric, Roswell, 66
Glaspie, April, 16–17
globalization:
    backlash to, 82, 88, 89, 107
    diminishing returns of, 104–5, 110
    of drug trade, 147
    economic multilateralism and, 80, 82, 109,
        273
    free-trade ideology of, 76, 78, 83, 86, 87
    nation-states in, 209–10
    neoconservatives and, 99
    of terrorism, 209–10
Gorbachev, Mikhail, 16
Grass, Günter, 118
Great Britain:
    decline in hegemony of, 110–11
    and Iraq policy, 4, 13, 59, 84, 98
    and neoconservative region-building, 102
    U.S. special relationship with, 77, 96, 97
Grenada, 137, 141
Griffis, William, 154, 155–56
Group of 21, 29
Guatemala:
    coffee exports of, 146–47
    democracy in, 145, 148–49, 240
    leftist government in, 137, 138
    military atrocities in, 139–40, 141, 147,
        149, 150–51
    nation-building in, 149
    social issues in, 146, 147
    unimportance of, 139
    U.S. intervention in (1954), xvii, 136, 139
Gulf Crisis (1990–91):
    Bush I and, 16–18, 19, 52, 57, 83, 84, 206,
        208
    civilian deaths in, 210
    as good war, 129, 208
    oil and, 5, 78, 82, 84
    postwar issues in, 53, 129–30

Haig, Alexander M., Jr., 139
Haiti, 136, 146, 240
Halberstam, David, 67, 206
Hamilton, Alexander, 256, 257
Harrington, James, 272
Harrison, Francis, 156–59, 161, 164, 165, 171,
    178
hegemony:
    consent of subjects in, 271–72
    decentering beyond, 111–12, 131

decline of, 110
habits of, 205–8, 217
meanings of term, 76, 109, 271–72
military, 230–33
responsibilities of, 87, 105, 110, 118
stabilizing role of, 109, 112
"stakeholder," 80
Higgins, H.C., 163
Hintze, Otto, 256, 273
Hirohito, Emperor of Japan, 187–88, 202,
    204–5
Hiroshima, 189, 196
Hitler, Adolf, 17–18
Hoffmann, Stanley, 114
Honduras, 136, 146, 147, 240
Hopkins, Harry, 6
Hughes, Charles Evans, 251
Hungary, Soviets in (1956), xvii
Huntington, Samuel, 213
Hussein, Saddam:
    al-Qaeda and, 222
    as hands-on dictator, 187
    loyalists to, 38, 150
    overthrow of, xviii, 3, 18, 20–21, 22, 35, 54,
        55, 56, 57–58, 61, 94, 219
    September 11 attacks and, 12, 22, 117
    unpredictability of, 84
    U.S. demonizing of, 17–18, 21, 23, 51, 70,
        208
    U.S. support for, 5, 10, 15–17
    WMDs and, 3–4, 7, 17, 21, 23, 52–53, 58,
        60, 63, 93
    see also Iraq

imperialism:
    classical, 264
    language of, 32–42, 46–49, 262
    liberalism and, 242, 246–50, 263
    movement and system of, 262
India, 98, 156, 160, 170, 171, 174–75, 179
Indian peoples of Americas, 169–70, 260,
    263
Indonesia, Japanese aggression on, 183
Insular Cases (1901), 263
International Atomic Energy Agency (IAEA),
    101
International Court of Justice, 145
International Criminal Court, 119, 207,
    211
International Monetary Fund (IMF), 111

Iran:
    in Axis of Evil, 23, 24, 25, 57, 60, 102, 107
    CIA in, 13–14
    destabilization of, 100, 101
    EU free trade agreement with, 101
    illiteracy and poverty in, 146
    nuclear program of, 101, 106
    oil in, 13
    revolution in, 10, 13–14, 103, 217–18
    shah in, 5, 10, 13–15, 103, 138–39, 141
    Soviet troops in, 13
    stabilization in, xviii, 84
    U.S. hostages in, 14, 15
    U.S. intervention in (1953), xvii, 127
    war with Iraq, 5, 7, 16, 19
Iran-Contra Scandal, 144
Iraq:
    American Embassy in, 4
    antiwar protestors and, 124
    in Axis of Evil, 23, 24, 57, 60, 102, 221
    behavior-modification phase in, 39
    coalition for war in, 40, 44, 104
    comparisons of Latin America and, 137,
        144, 146, 149–52
    comparisons of Vietnam and, 9, 51–52,
        65–71, 110, 136, 150
    decisions leading to war in, 52–58
    democracy in, 47
    disarmament of, 3, 5, 64
    economic reforms for, 99–100
    face of evil in, 42–43
    factionalism in, 187
    handover of power in, 4, 9, 28
    inadequate planning for war in, 189
    Kuwait invaded by, 16–18, 19, 52, 82, 129,
        208
    legitimacy as issue in, 184, 186
    nationalism in, 70
    nation-building in, 4, 7–9, 50, 64, 70, 98,
        99–100, 149, 152, 186
    no-fly zones over, 53, 55, 78, 84
    nuclear threat in, 189, 248
    occupation of, 3–12, 19–20, 33–39, 44,
        64–65, 70, 102, 113, 150
    oil in, 5, 8, 18, 51, 53, 57, 80, 94, 104, 189
    ongoing insurgency in, 38–39, 50
    Operation Desert Fox in, 90, 93, 108, 109
    permanent U.S. protectorate in, 103–4
    post-Gulf War period (1991–1998) in,
        83–84

    regime change in, 20, 22, 23, 54, 55, 100,
        219, 222, 247, 248
    sanctions against, 19, 52, 53–54, 55, 78, 94
    shock and awe in, 22, 27, 70
    structuring for engagement in, 57–65
    transformationists and, 80, 99–102
    as U.S. ally in Cold War, 15–16
    U.S. attacks on, 6, 19, 22–24, 26, 27, 39, 51,
        52–65, 84, 94, 106, 108, 117, 218–19,
        221, 247
    U.S. containment policy in, 84, 93
    U.S. covert operations in, 53, 56, 61
    U.S. demonizing of, 62
    U.S. mission in, 5–9, 19, 23–24, 43, 44, 50,
        104–7
    war on terrorism and, 4, 7, 12, 24, 28–29,
        30, 38, 43, 50–51, 56, 57–65, 219
    war with Iran, 5, 7, 16, 19
    weapons inspections in, 52–53, 58, 63, 64,
        84, 93
    World War II as model for, 119
Islamic militancy, 82
Israel:
    creation of, 18
    Iraq and, 15, 21
    nuclear monopoly of, 100, 101
    occupied territories and, 35, 150
    Palestine and, 100, 101–2
    suicide bombing in, 18
    U.S. special relationship with, 103

Jackson, Henry, 99
Japan:
    and accidents of history, 216–23
    anachronisms in, 198–200
    autonomy of, 215–16
    bilateral syndrome in, 201, 204, 220
    Cold War and, 199, 202, 203, 205
    constitution of, 186, 205
    Control Faction in, 194–95
    demilitarization in, 183, 186, 188
    "double hedge" of, 220
    economic problems of, 78, 89
    economic prosperity of, 202, 203, 271
    educational system revamped in, 186,
        188
    Great Depression in, 194
    Gulf Crisis (1991) and, 129
    habits of history in, 205–11
    human resources in, 187–89

as imperial power, 171, 179–80, 183–84, 188, 190, 191–93, 201, 202, 205
labor laws in, 185–86
land reform in, 185
League of Nations and, 192
national socialism in, 196
natural resources lacking in, 188–89
North Korea and, 220–21
oil imports of, 103
opportunity to start anew, 184–87
Pearl Harbor attacked by, 183, 188, 193, 201
postwar reconstruction of, 7, 8, 103, 201, 204, 240–41
propaganda of, 192–93
road to war, 190–92
terrorism in, 195
total war waged by, 190, 194–97, 202
tunnel vision in, 200–205, 215
U.S. occupation of, 182–97, 201, 202–4
U.S. post-September 11 relations with, 198–223
U.S. reformist idealism in, 184–87
U.S. terror-bombing of, 189, 196
in World War II, 183–84, 190–91
zaibatsu in, 195–96
Japanese Americans, internment of, 212
Jefferson, Thomas, 10–11, 245, 257–62, 272
Johnson, Chalmers, 43–44
Johnson, Lyndon B., 18, 65, 67–68, 69
Jordan, 61, 62
Judt, Tony, 114

Kagan, Robert, 47–48, 121, 135
Kaldor, Mary, 81
Kalischer, Peter, 36
Kaplan, Robert D., 27, 40, 41–42, 44–46
Kennan, George, 268–69
Kennedy, Edward M., 4
Kennedy, John F., xii, 61, 65–69, 101, 141–42, 217
Kennedy, Paul, xii
Khalid, Rashid, 32
Khomeini, Ayatollah Ruhollah, 14, 15
Kidd, Benjamin, 154, 155
Kindleberger, Charles, 76
Kipling, Rudyard, 155, 156
Kirkpatrick, Jeane, 137, 138–39, 140–41, 145, 151
Kissinger, Henry A., 6, 138, 209
Korea, 202, 205

Korean War, xvii, 10, 33, 202, 203, 208, 211, 250
Krauthammer, Charles, 17
Kristol, William, 101, 136
Kupchan, Charles, 131
Kuwait:
    Iraqi invasion of, 16–18, 19, 52, 82, 129, 208
    oil in, 5
    as staging center, 61
Kyoto Treaty, 21, 118, 207

language, 32–49
    of anti-imperialism, 267
    of imperialism, 32–42, 46–49, 262
    of militarism, 41–45
Laos, 66
Latin America, 135–52
    Bush administration on, 144–45
    CIA in, 142, 143, 146, 150–51
    Committee of Santa Fe and, 138, 141
    crime in, 147
    current issues in, 145–49
    democracies in, 145, 148–49, 152
    "democratic realism" applied to, 142
    extremists and civil war in, 150–51
    free trade agreements with, 105, 145
    leftist governments in, 137, 139, 141
    Marxist Christianity in, 144
    nation-building in, 149–50, 152
    New Right and, 135, 137, 138–40
    "public diplomacy" and, 142–43, 144
    and the spectre of Vietnam, 137, 138–39, 141, 142, 143, 151
    U.S. interventions in, xvii, 25, 103, 128, 136–38, 140–41, 240, 264, 273
League of Nations, 192
Lebanon, U.S. intervention in, 103
Leggewie, Claus, 114
Lemann, Nicolas, 56
Leser, Eric, 30
Lewinsky, Monica, 93
liberalism:
    alternate conception of, 244
    development of, 240–41
    freedom to choose, 242–43, 247–48
    imperialism and, 242, 246–50, 263
    international community as fruit of, 241–42
    international institutions of, 248
    misunderstanding of, 241

liberalism (*cont.*)
    never-ending struggle for, 246
    philosophy of, 239, 247, 253
    real war of, 242–46
    threats to, 244–46, 248–49
Lieven, Anatol, 118, 127
Lincoln, Abraham, 141
Luce, Henry, 161, 206
Lundestad, Geir, 116

Maass, Peter, 33–35, 38
Maastricht Treaty (1992), 78, 82
MacArthur, Douglas, 201, 204
Mahan, Alfred Thayer, 160
Major, John, 29
Manchuria, Japanese takeover of
        (Manchukuo), 183, 190, 191, 192–95
Manifest Destiny, 193, 206
Mann, Michael, 42, 48
Mann, Thomas, 142
Marshall Plan, xix, 120
Maude, F.S., 33
McKinley, William, 162
McNamara, Robert, 66–70
Metcalf, Charles, 175
Mexican War (1848), 51, 260–61
Mexico, 86, 88, 136
Middle East:
    Arab-Israel issues in, 18
    Arc of Crisis in, 102–4, 107, 108
    civilization in, 160
    counterinsurgency theory applied in, 180
    development gap in, 146
    enemies in, 24
    Gulf War in, *see* Gulf Crisis
    nation-building in, 149, 152
    oil in, 5–6, 8, 13, 51, 53, 80, 82, 84, 103,
        107, 108
    peace process in, 12, 102
    PNAC aims in, 21, 54, 137
    power transferred from Europe to U.S. in,
        19–20
    Six-Day War in, 18
    transformationist region-building in, 80,
        100–102, 149
    U.S. military presence in, 6, 19–20, 84, 103
Mill, John Stuart, 187
Mongolia, military in, 44
Monroe Doctrine, 193, 260, 272
Montagu-Chelmsford reform (1918), 159

Morgan, J.P., 136
Mossadegh, Mohammed, 13, 14
Mubarak, Hosni, 24

Nagasaki, 189, 196
Nagl, John, 34–35, 36–37, 39
National Security Council (NSC):
    Iraq and, 56, 57, 61, 62, 65
    Latin America and, 144
    Vietnam and, 66–67
Negroponte, John, 135
neoconservatives:
    agenda of, 95–96, 117, 141
    anti-Europeanism of, 121, 131
    in Bush administration, 55, 57, 61, 80, 117
    and invasion of Iraq, 61, 71
    messianism of, 274
    and Middle East policy, 19, 21–23, 99–102,
        137, 146, 149, 150–52
    New Right and, 135
    of PNAC, 20–21, 54, 137
    precursors of, 138, 151
    revolutionary agenda of, 100
    and September 11 attacks, 96, 274
    as transformationists, 80, 99–102
Neruda, Pablo, 136
Netherlands Indies, 156, 159, 164, 170, 174,
        177, 279
New Deal, 10, 185
New Right:
    Committee of Santa Fe and, 138
    Latin America and, 135, 137, 138–40
Ngo Dinh Diem, 67, 69
Nicaragua, 135–46, 148, 149–50
Nidal, Abu, 15
Nieva, Gregorio, 160
Nixon, Richard M., 138, 140
Nixon Doctrine, 103
North, habits of, 207–9, 215
North, Oliver, 144
North American Free Trade Agreement
        (NAFTA), 86, 88
North Atlantic Treaty Organization (NATO):
    Article V of, 79, 95, 113
    Balkan crisis and, 85, 92
    coalitions sought in, 79
    in Cold War, 91, 92
    establishment of, xix
    expansion of, 79, 80, 90–92, 95, 108
    France's departure from, 77

uncertain future of, 129
U.S. dominance of, 77, 83, 92, 107–9
U.S. retreat from, 110
North Korea:
in Axis of Evil, 23, 25, 57, 60, 102, 107, 221
Japan and, 220–21
nuclear program of, 82, 106, 221, 248
Northwest Ordinance (1787), 258
NSC-68, 90, 267–69
Nuclear Test-Ban Treaty, 118
Nye, Joseph, 131, 222

OPEC:
curbs on, 100, 103
U.S. influence in, 104
Oslo peace process, 96

Pahlavi, Shah Mohammed Reza, 5, 10, 13–15, 103, 138–39, 141
Paine, Thomas, 25
Palestine, 15, 71, 100, 101–2
Panama, 136, 264
Panama Canal, 138
Paraguay, constitution of, 45
Paris Peace Conference (1919), xvii
PATRIOT Act, 25, 28, 144–45
Patten, Christopher, 58
Perle, Richard, 55, 101, 137
Persian Gulf, see Middle East
Philippines, 153–81
agrarian initiatives in, 176–78
autonomy of, 47
Baguio area of, 157, 164, 180–81
Benguet region of, 163
citizens treated as children, 162, 262
civilizing mission in, 154–55, 158, 169, 180, 262
counterinsurgency theory in, 180
engineering imperialism in, 165–68
expatriate settlers' roles in, 179–80
goal to remake in U.S. image, 157, 162, 165, 173–77
Huk Rebellion in, 180
infrastructural improvement in, 156, 162, 165–69, 174, 177
insurrection in, 51
Japanese massacres in, 183
Japanese occupation of, 180, 193
model of, 46–47, 159–60
natural resources of, 166

preparation for self-government in, 157, 159, 161–63, 165–68, 170–75, 178–80
"primitive society" of, 162, 169–70
resistance to U.S. rule in, 155, 168, 170
scientific nature of U.S. activity in, 163–65, 168
social engineering in, 161, 165, 168–71, 179
as Spanish colony, 164, 166, 169, 170–71, 178
in U.S. colonial empire, 154–56, 157–59, 160–81, 249, 262
U.S. intervention in, 25, 33, 44, 47, 176
U.S. occupation of, 47, 154–56, 157
women's roles in, 179
Pierce, Franklin, 136
Poindexter, John, 139
populists, xv
Powell, Colin L., 4, 8–9, 12, 22, 54, 55, 62, 84, 93
Powell Doctrine, 93
PPS 23 (1948), 268, 269
Preble, Christopher, 19
Prestowitz, Clyde, 131
Project for a New American Century (PNAC), 20–21, 54, 137
Puerto Rico, 136, 253, 262, 266
Putin, Vladimir, 58
Pu Yi, 192

Reagan, Ronald, 11, 15–16
Evil Empire of, 12, 16, 208, 273
Latin America and, 135–36, 137, 139–40, 141, 143, 144, 145, 149, 273
Reagan administration, 138, 140, 144, 145
Reagan Doctrine, 90, 103
Realists, 246
Reid, Whitelaw, 46
Reilly, Greg, 37
revolution, agent theory of, 5, 6–7, 11, 12
Rice, Condoleeza, 217, 219
Ríos Montt, José Efraín, 140, 149
Roman empire, xi, xiv, xvi, 26–27, 40, 42, 254, 256, 257, 263, 274
Roosevelt, Franklin D., 6, 185, 267
Roosevelt, Kermit, 14
Roosevelt, Nicholas, 173
Roosevelt, Theodore, 136, 160, 272
Root, Elihu, 156
Rostow, Walter, 66, 67

Rove, Karl, 96
Rumsfeld, Donald H., 27, 57, 60, 130
    and attack on Iraq, 12, 33, 56, 61, 62,
        64–65, 219
    Iran-Iraq war and, 16
    as neoconservative, 96, 99
    on occupation of Iraq, 8, 150
    September 11 attacks and, 12, 22, 56
    on war on terrorism, 12, 56, 58, 61–62
Rusk, Dean, 11, 66, 67–68
Russia:
    Middle East peace and, 102
    natural resources of, 104
    see also Soviet Union
Rwanda, 206

Safire, William, 122
El Salvador, 136–43, 145–48, 149
Sanchez, Ricardo, 26, 39
Sandinistas, 135, 137–38, 139, 140, 141, 143,
    145, 146, 149–50
Sandino, Augusto, 136
Sanger, David E., 47
Sansom, George, 204
Sanzō, Nosaka, 204
Sassaman, Nathan, 35
Saud, King Abdul Aziz Bin Abdul Rahman
    Al-, 5
Saudi Arabia:
    Islamic militants in, 100
    oil in, 5, 6
    terrorists from, 6, 19
    U.S. aid to, 6
    U.S. military in, 6, 19–20, 103
    as U.S. "partner," 6, 14, 19, 20
Schmidlapp, J.G., 153
Schroeder, Gerhard, 120, 132
Schumpeter, Joseph, 101
September 11 attacks:
    Bush administration and, 55–56, 57, 79,
        208, 210, 222
    Bush Doctrine and, xi, 79, 108, 218
    political effects of, xix, 79, 81–82, 96, 115,
        207–8, 221–22, 254, 255, 274–75
    Saddam and, 12, 22, 117
    security-related effects of, 56, 108, 113,
        207, 210, 218, 273–75
    terrorists and, 6, 12, 20, 24, 55–56, 208,
        209–10, 219, 222
Sheehan, Neil, 39

Shigeru, Nanbara, 204
Shinseki, Eric, 64
Shurman, Jacob, 165–66
Smith, Jacob, 46
Somalia, 85, 93, 209
Somoza, Anastasio, 139, 140, 141
South America see Latin America
Soviet Union:
    in Afghanistan, 15, 20, 82, 128, 209
    anti-imperialism in, 267–68
    in Cold War, see Cold War
    collapse of, 78, 81, 82, 85, 115, 117, 207,
        218, 253, 254, 273
    détente and, 77
    as Evil Empire, 12, 16, 208, 273
    Sino-Soviet split in, 11
    use of force by, xvii
Spanish-American War (1898), 51, 253,
    261–62
Stephens, Philip, 98, 104
Straw, Jack, 102
Sudan, 209
Syria, 24, 25, 100, 101, 102, 146

Taft, William Howard, 153–54, 155–56, 158,
    160–61, 164, 173, 180–81
Taylor, Maxwell, 66
Taylor-Rostow Report (1961), 66, 68
Third World:
    autonomy of, 12
    Cold War and, 81, 208
    frontiers of, 27–28
    and Group of 21, 29
    migration from, 88–89
Tojo Hideki, 194, 196
transformationists, 80, 99–102
Truman, Harry, 102–3
Truman administration, 267–69
Truman Doctrine, 5, 103
Turkey, 61, 62, 64, 98, 103
Twain, Mark, 168

Ungar, Sanford, 128
Unilateralism, 182
United Defense Industries, 29–30
United Nations:
    establishment of, xix, 264
    and Gulf Crisis, 52
    and Latin America, 140, 145, 146
    and Middle East development, 146

and Middle East peace, 102
relevance of, 45, 118, 131, 210, 220
roles of, 111
and sanctions against Iraq, 53–54, 55, 94
and U.S. unilateral actions, 21, 58, 59, 63,
    97, 98, 108, 118
weapons inspectors from, 53, 58, 63, 64, 84,
    93, 117
United States:
anti-colonial credentials of, 40–41, 255,
    259–60
anti-Europeanism in, 113–32
arrogance in, 219–22, 234, 238–39
ascendancy of, xix, 160, 269
citizens in, 221–23
in Cold War, *see* Cold War
counterproliferation and, 59–60
"democratic realism" for, 142
economic prowess of, xvi, xvii, 75–76, 86–87
economic slowdown in, 77–78, 79, 89
as empire, xi–xiii, xix, 24–25, 27, 41, 44,
    47–49, 155, 203–4, 211, 253–75
exceptionalism in, 216–17, 234–35, 266
expansionism of, 259–65
free trade agreements with, 40, 105, 274
global mission of, 5–9, 270–71
habits of the nation, 209–10
hegemony of, xiii, 75–78, 80, 81–83, 87, 95,
    106, 107, 109–12, 118, 207, 230, 270
immigrants in, 214, 261
isolation of, 10, 42–44, 128–29, 217, 222,
    237, 253
militarization of, 79, 90–109, 110
military power of, xii, xvi, xvii, xix, 47–49,
    60–61, 75–76, 80, 81, 92, 106, 107, 118,
    121, 207, 228, 230–33
multiculturalism in, 212–13
National Security Strategy of, 60–61, 113,
    117–19, 218, 220, 222, 227, 230–33, 235,
    236, 242
protectionism in, 105, 110, 270–71
proxy armies for, 137, 150
as self-appointed world model, 24–25, 70,
    76, 99, 101, 141, 142, 241–42, 274–75
as sole superpower, xiii, xvi, 75–76, 81, 117,
    205, 207, 217, 218, 220, 221, 253
suffocation of consensus in, 221–22
unilateral actions of, 21, 26, 27, 48, 50,
    58–64, 70, 79, 97, 98, 105, 108, 118,
    216–17, 218, 222

Vaky, Viron, 151
Vann, John Paul, 39
Vietnam, coffee exports of, 146–47
Vietnam Syndrome, 16
Vietnam War:
antimilitarism vs., 142, 144
Cold War and, 7, 11, 38, 139, 208, 271, 272
comparisons of Iraq and, 9, 51–52, 65–71,
    110, 136, 150
counterinsurgency in, 39, 180
impact on subsequent foreign policy, 137,
    138–39, 141, 142, 143, 144, 151, 211, 250
as new kind of war, 143
Six-Day War and, 18
U.S. intervention and, xvii, 33, 36, 39, 43,
    101, 127, 137
War Crimes Hearings in, 215

Waiting for the Barbarians (Coetzee), xvi
Walker, William, 136
Wallace, William, 116
Walzer, Michael, 48
war on terrorism:
in Afghanistan, 12, 18, 22, 58, 61, 207–9,
    210, 221
counterproliferation and, 59–60, 189
domestic dissent contained in, 144–45
European containment of, 95
funding of, 7
habits of critique in, 210–11
habits of history and, 206–11, 219
in Iraq, 4, 7, 12, 24, 28–29, 30, 38, 43,
    50–51, 56, 57–65, 219
moral duty in, 237, 238–39
prevention of new sufferings in, 211–16
September 11 and, 81–82, 108, 208
Washington Consensus, 87
Weinberger, Caspar, 139
White, Edward D., 263
Wilhelm, Tom, 44
Wilson, Woodrow, 23, 24, 141–42, 217, 235,
    241, 243, 249, 266
Wolfowitz, Paul:
and attack on Iraq, 12, 22–23, 56, 62,
    219
on "democratic realism," 142
and Latin America, 137, 138, 141, 142
and military in Middle East, 19–20
as neoconservative, 19, 55
Wood, Leonard, 156

Woodward, Bob, 22, 55–56, 58, 60
Woolsey, James, 23–24
Worcester, Dean C., 169–70
World Economic Forum, 213
world order:
  ad hoc support of, 81
  anti-American vs. anti-European views of,
    121–25, 127
  balance of power and, xvii, 116–17
  collective security in, 266
  common ground in, 213–15
  counterproliferation and, 59–60
  cycles of, 109–10
  democratic, 267
  environmental degradation vs., 88–89,
    130
  frontiers and, xv–xix
  global economy and, 76, 77–78, 88–90
  interdependence in, 207
  international commerce and, xviii, 271
  international institutions for, 111
  international law and, 45, 47, 118, 119, 121,
    210, 243, 247, 269
  liberal philosophy of, 239–40
  multilateralism in, 131, 207, 266
  nationalism and, 70, 117
  national self-determination in, xvii,
    234–35
  unilateral action and, 26, 27, 60–61, 70, 98,
    105, 118, 230
  universal principles in, 46
  visible hand in, 110
World Social Forum, 213
World Trade Organization (WTO):
  Cancún meeting of, 29, 31, 105
  China as member of, 87
  deadlock in, 111
  establishment of, xix
  protests against, 88
World War I, 229, 256, 264
World War II:
  democracy at war in, 229, 264, 266
  as Great East Asia War, 201, 211
  Holocaust in, 18
  Middle East and, 5–6
  Pearl Harbor attack in, 183, 188, 193, 201,
    209
  postwar social compact, 77–79, 104, 107,
    109
  reconstruction after, 7, 119–21, 249
  and total war, 190, 194–97, 202
  war deaths in, 183
World War IV, 23
Wright, Luke, 156, 157, 161, 164, 173

Zoellick, Robert, 40, 105